Why C? Why the Instant Guic

Since the proliferation of computer languages nearly a quar there's only one that's still moving from strength to strengt flexibility and power, the C language remains the ultimate gateway to the programming world. As modern implementations of C continue to develop and push back programming frontiers, every programmer who isn't C-worthy needs a quick route into original C in order to keep up. Whether you're bandy-legged in BASIC, cock-a-hoop in COBOL or sitting pretty in PASCAL, this book should interest you.

As with all our Instant series, our aim is to produce a thorough yet fast-paced guide to a popular and developing language. All the language's major topics, concepts and constructs, including key programming elements such as structures, arrays and pointers are dealt with in detail in the first half of this book. In the second half we focus on particularly powerful and involved concepts, such as input/output, the pre-processor and system specifics, at a level that'll leave you feeling confident in the C environment. Finally, we round off with a complete tutorial showing you how to write a proper C application which will illustrate how many C elements integrate into a whole. We hope that Instant C will act as your critical C reference guide, becoming your key to a unique and exciting programming world.

What is Wrox Press?

Wrox Press is a computer book publisher which promotes a brand new concept - clear, jargon-free programming and database titles that fulfill your real demands. We publish for everyone, from the novice through to the experienced programmer. To ensure our books meet your needs, we carry out continuous research on all our titles. Through our dialog with you we can craft the book you really need.

We welcome suggestions and take all of them to heart - your input is paramount in creating the next great Wrox title. Use the reply card inside this book or mail us at:

feedback@wrox.demon.co.uk
or
Compuserve 100063, 2152

Wrox Press Ltd.	**Tel:** **(312) 465 3559**
2710 W. Touhy	**Fax:** **(312) 465 4063**
Chicago	
IL 60645	
USA	

Instant C

Ivor Horton

Wrox Press Ltd.®

Instant C

© 1995 Ivor Horton

Published by Wrox Press Ltd. Unit 16, 20 James Road, Tyseley, Birmingham, B11 2BA
Printed in the USA
Library of Congress Catalog no. 95-060735
ISBN 1-874416-24-9

Trademark Acknowledgements

Wrox has endeavored to provide trademark information about all the companies and products mentioned in this book by the appropriate use of capitals. However, Wrox cannot guarantee the accuracy of this information. Use of a term in this book shouldn't be regarded as affecting the validity of any trademark or service mark.

Credits

Author
Ivor Horton

Technical Editor
Julian Templeman

Series Editor
Adrian M. Sill

Managing Editor
John Franklin

Technical Reviewers
Darren Gill
Julian Dobson
John Franklin

Beta Testers
Bruce Thompson
Graham Butler

Operations Manager
Gina Mance

Production Manager
Deb Somers

Design\Layout
Eddie Fisher
Greg Powell
Neil Gallagher
Graham Butler

Indexer
Simon Gilks

Proof Readers
Emma Duncombe
Mel Orgee

Cover Design
Third Wave

For more information on Third Wave, contact Ross Alderson on 44-121 236 6616
Cover photo supplied by The Image Bank

About the Author

Ivor Horton has been in the computer industry for 30 years. He has applied and taught most programming languages in a wide variety of contexts. He has design and implementation experience of a wide variety of systems involving mainframes, on-line control systems and PCs. He has extensive knowledge of engineering and scientific applications and systems, particularly in the context of Computer Aided Design and Computer Aided Manufacturing.

INSTANT

Summary of Contents

INSTANT

Table of Contents

Table of Contents

Table of Contents

Table of Contents

Table of Contents

Table of Contents

Table of Contents

Table of Contents

Table of Contents

Table of Contents

Table of Contents

Instant

Introduction

Welcome to the latest Instant Guide from Wrox Press, Instant C. This book has been designed as a guide to learning one of the most popular programming languages ever created. Introducing everything you need to know in order to become a capable and knowledgeable programmer of the C language, this book will enable you to understand the concepts involved and the essential techniques. Because we at Wrox Press believe that our readers are intelligent creatures, we won't waste time by patronizing you with over-simplistic examples. We will be introducing new practical advice and a fresh approach to many exciting techniques from some of the industry's finest developers.

What Can C Do for Me?

Most people, even those with little computer experience, will have come across the C programming language. For decades, C has enjoyed a dominance rivaled by very few other languages, and market status that still demands a great deal of respect today. In fact, many new pretenders to the throne of global domination that C achieved actually use C as a subset of their whole system, effectively making it an obligatory language to learn.

Who Should Use This Book?

Instant C contains the information necessary to transform the reader from a person with knowledge of a different computer language, to one who is a competent C programmer with the ability to write efficient, well-structured and clear code. The types of people likely to benefit from this book are:

- The programmer who wants to move up to the industry standard usually from BASIC, Pascal or COBOL.
- The C programmer who needs a quick revision on the C programming language.
- The amateur C programmer who requires a no-nonsense reference guide.
- Everybody who requires a concise and informative guide to all the aspects of the C programming language.

What You Should Know

To get the most out of this book, you should have some basic programming knowledge; you don't need to have spent five years of your life learning assembler, but you should understand the basic concepts that are common to most programming languages. Since we are going to take this tour at quite a fast pace, we won't be dwelling on basic programming techniques that you already know, and we won't be discussing specific features of systems that you may or may not have. What you will be learning is how to program in C, and how to write programs that *you* want to write.

If you have no programming experience at all, don't worry, because we start from the very beginning. We won't be shirking our responsibilities to you, because we are covering *everything* you need to know, but be prepared - we're not going to dally with every last detail of the language.

As all programming languages require a basic grasp of mathematics, we will assume that you understand some of the principles behind the major concepts. Don't worry, we won't be using calculus and umpteen different theorems, but you simply can't avoid brushing against the subject when you're dealing with programming.

Conventions Used

To help you to find your way around this book easily, we have used various styles to highlight different references. Each style has been chosen to give you a clear understanding of the information that we have supplied.

Dialog

All code and programs are highlighted with a gray background, so that you can locate them easily. For example:

```
/* EX2-02.C Using char variables */

#include <stdio.h>                              /* For input and output */

int main()
{
   char First = 0x41;
   char Second = 'B';
   char Third = Second + 1;

   printf("\nUsing character variables is as easy as %c%c%c,
                                    First, Second, Third);

   return 0;
}
```

When we need to show the whole program, we sometimes repeat parts of our code. We have shaded lines, which are new additions to the program, and those lines which are repeated, are left unshaded. This will enable you to immediately see where new code has been added:

```
struct Phone
{
   char *pName;                         /* Pointer to a name */
   char *pNumber;                       /* Pointer to telephone number */
   struct Phone *pLeft;              /* Pointer to Phone object<current */
   struct Phone *pRight;             /* Pointer to Phone object>=current */
};
```

Fonts and Styles

Throughout Instant C we will consistently use the following styles and fonts for a variety of textual distinctions:

- When code or a command is mentioned in the middle of a sentence, we write it in `this_style`, so as to emphasize its origin. Filenames, such as `FILENAME.C,` however, are always written in that style.

- Important words are introduced in **this style**. These are significant words that we are meeting for the first time. Subsequently they will appear as normal text.

- Actual keys that you press will be displayed in *this style*, for example, press the *Return* key. Note that *Ctrl-K* depicts the depression of a *Control* key with the *K* key.

- Output text that appears on your screen, such as field names, menu items or headings appear in this style.

- When we introduce the syntax of code, we will use the following bracket styles:

[	]	Optional.
<	>	Obligatory.

- If a word needs to be emphasized, then we will italicize it, *like this*.

We have attempted to break the text up, by using appropriate and consistent headings and with the judicious bulleting of lists.

> When an important piece of information needs to be *really* emphasized, then we will place it in a stand-alone box like this.

C Variance

C is such a popular language that it forms a highly competitive market, which, while organizations such as ANSI (see Chapter 1) strive to develop standards, spawns a host of different modes and environments where conventions differ. When using C, you must bear in mind that different systems, variants and versions *will* produce different responses and output.

Tell Us What You Think

One last thing: we've tried to make this book as enjoyable and accurate as possible. We are here to serve the programming community, so if you have any queries, suggestions or comments about this book, let us know. We are always delighted to hear from you.

You can help us ensure that our future books are even better, by simply returning the reply card at the back of the book or by contacting us direct at Wrox. For a quick response, you can also use the following e-mail addresses:

feedback@wrox.demon.co.uk
Compuserve: 100063,2152

Please return the reply card at the back of the book and tell us what you think of the book, the style of presentation and the content. We are always ready to listen to comments and complaints (although we do prefer unadulterated adoration!).

Getting Started

Thank you for buying Instant C. We hope you enjoy it and become a proficient programmer of C in as short a time and as smoothly as possible. All our efforts have been aimed at bringing you maximum satisfaction, and if you want to learn C, then we're convinced that this book will fulfill all your immediate requirements. Anyway, you've bought this book to learn C, and we shall not hold you from it any longer. Dip in and enjoy!

Chapter

Programming in C

This chapter is just a toe in the water. We'll start by looking at the general characteristics of C, and why it's still the language of choice for so many development environments. We'll also get a feel for how the strategy of developing a C program proceeds. In this chapter you'll learn:

- What the primary advantages of C are.
- How a C program is structured.
- What a simple C program looks like.
- What libraries are and how they're used.
- How C programs are processed in some typical development systems.
- What differences arise with C programs in different computer environments.

The Characteristics of C

If you were only allowed one programming language, you would most likely choose C, as it has so many advantages over all the others available. So just what are these advantages?

Prevalence

C was originally developed in the UNIX environment by Dennis Ritchie in the 1970s. Since then, because it has proved to be such an effective programming language, it has become available in the majority of computing environments.

> **If you know how to program in C, then you can write programs on almost any type of computer.**

You will find C compilers on personal computers, UNIX workstations, minicomputers, as well as mainframe computers and many embedded microprocessors in control applications. This prevalence has also had a large effect on the cost of C compilers, with many excellent versions dropping their cover price dramatically.

Portability

Program portability is the ability to transfer a program in source form from the original development environment to different computers, and to successfully generate a working version with little or no effort. With an ANSI standard defined for the language, you have the potential to write code that can be easily moved from one machine to another.

> **In 1983, the American National Standard's Institute (ANSI) commissioned a committee to standardize the C language. Finally ratified in 1990, ANSI C standardizes existing practice, includes enhanced features and formalizes library support routines.**

The value of this in large commercial application developments is hard to overstate.

Flexibility

Most of the UNIX operating system was written in C, as was Microsoft Windows, and it remains a preferred language for systems programming. C provides you with the ability to write low-level code (efficient, but difficult to learn), whilst retaining all the advantages of a high-level language (less efficient, but easy to learn). For this reason, many commercial applications are written in C.

Easy to Learn

Because C is so compact, you will find it very easy to learn, so you can become a competent programmer very quickly. Of course, writing good quality code needs time and experience, as with all programming languages, but the volume of existing code that you can use as a model and the range of commercial tools to help you is of enormous assistance.

Efficient

As C is a compact language with a simple structure, it's easy to generate efficient machine code directly from it. The pre-written support libraries, which are implicitly used, are professionally written and optimized. There are also specialized high performance libraries available. Many people program in BASIC because it's easy to use, but it has the disadvantage that it's usually executed via an interpreter. If you contrast the performance of an application written in C with that of an equivalent BASIC program, then you'll find that the C program can execute much faster.

Variance

To maintain its position at the top of the programming tree, C has given birth to several new versions. New languages such as C++ are taking the C language as a subset, whilst making additional use of new programming methods and styles.

> **C++ development systems will also compile C, so if you want to use C on a PC, and you think that you might want to use C++ some time in the future, then purchasing C++ might be a cost-effective option.**

Let's make a start by looking at how a C program hangs together, and get a grasp of some of the basic terminology.

The Structure of a C Program

For the moment we are just going to get the basic concepts straight, without getting into specific details. All of the examples of C programming that appear here are just to illustrate the principles involved, and we will be looking at what they do in much more depth in the following chapters.

Let's see what a complete C program looks like. Here's a simple one consisting of the function **main()** plus one additional function **Response()**:

We will now discuss these main aspects of a typical C program.

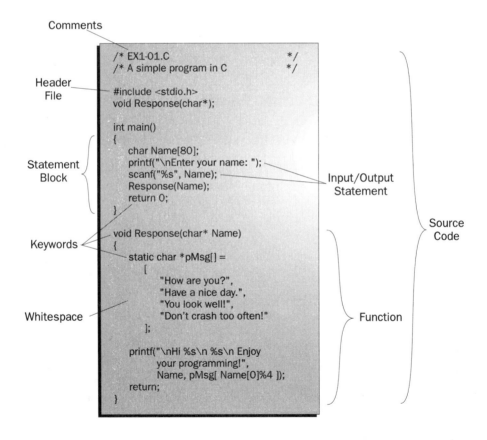

```
/* EX1-01.C                        */
/* A simple program in C           */

#include <stdio.h>
void Response(char*);

int main()
{
    char Name[80];
    printf("\nEnter your name: ");
    scanf("%s", Name);
    Response(Name);
    return 0;
}

void Response(char* Name)
{
    static char *pMsg[] =
        [
            "How are you?",
            "Have a nice day.",
            "You look well!",
            "Don't crash too often!"
        ];

    printf("\nHi %s\n %s\n Enjoy
        your programming!",
            Name, pMsg[ Name[0]%4 ]);
    return;
}
```

Comments

Header File

Statement Block

Keywords

Whitespace

Input/Output Statement

Source Code

Function

Statements

The basic unit of C programming is a **statement**, and the collection of statements that make up a program are referred to as the **source code**. A statement in C always ends with a semi-colon. An example of a statement is:

```
OurWeight = MyWeight + YourWeight;
```

The effect of this statement is to add together the values of two things called `MyWeight` and `YourWeight`, and to store the result in something called `OurWeight`. Statements are generally executed in sequence in a program, unless a statement specifically changes the sequence of execution.

Whitespace

The example statement mentioned above has several spaces embedded, to make it more readable. It wouldn't matter if they were omitted and written as '`OurWeight=MyWeight+YourWeight`', because the C compiler can separate out the component parts, or 'tokens', which make up the statement.

These filler characters are called **whitespace** characters and also include space, newline, carriage return, tab and form feed. You can put in as many as you like and even space a statement out over more than one line. The exception is within a quoted string, which we'll discuss later.

You must use whitespace where there could be ambiguity; for instance, if the statement '`int number = 0;`' was written as '`intnumber = 0;`', then the compiler believes that you're referring to a variable called `intnumber`. We could quite happily write '`int number=0;`', because the equals sign and the zero are correctly interpreted by the compiler, even without whitespace.

Blocks

Statements can be grouped together in a block by placing them between braces. An example of a statement block is:

```
{
    int MyWeight = 180;
    int YourWeight = 300;
    OurWeight = MyWeight + YourWeight;
}
```

This block of code specifies two things called **MyWeight** and **YourWeight** as having values of 180 and 300 respectively, and then adds them together putting the result in something called **OurWeight**. Note how the statements are indented within the block. This is a visual cue to the extent of the block. Indenting statements isn't mandatory practice and it isn't part of the language definition - the compiler will compile correct code regardless of how it's laid out. However, indenting statements properly to make a program more readable is good programming style, so you should get into the habit of indenting statements appropriately from the start.

Wherever you can write a statement within a C program, you can also have a block of statements, so blocks can be nested within one another. We'll come back to the subject of containing statements within a block in Chapter 2.

Functions

A program in C consists of one or more **functions**. A function is a self-contained block of program code, which performs a specific set of actions or calculations and has a name by which it is referenced. It can have values passed to it, and it can return a value. A simple function might look something like this:

```
int treble( int value )
{
    return 3*value;
}
```

This particular function calculates three times the value that is passed to it. The first line of the function definition specifies the name of the function, what kind of data is passed to it and what sort of value it returns. The computation that the function performs appears in the statement that sits between the braces. There will usually be several statements between the braces. The program statements making up the function are called the **function body** and are always enclosed between braces. In the previous example, the body of the function consisted of only one statement. We'll see more about how functions are defined in Chapter 5.

Function Execution

A function is executed by calling it in a program statement using the function name. We could use the function called **treble()** that calculated and returned three times the value passed to it, by using the statement:

```
Result = treble( 5 );
```

The value 5 between the parentheses, called the **argument**, is passed to the function **treble()**, and the value that is returned from the function is stored in something called **Result**. When a function is being referred to in the text within this book, it will always be written with parentheses after the function name - as in **treble()**. This is to distinguish a reference to a function from references to other things that have names, which we will discuss later.

Any given function can be called many times from different points in a program.

The Function main()

A C program always contains a function called **main()**, and execution starts with its first statement. Let's consider the execution of a hypothetical program:

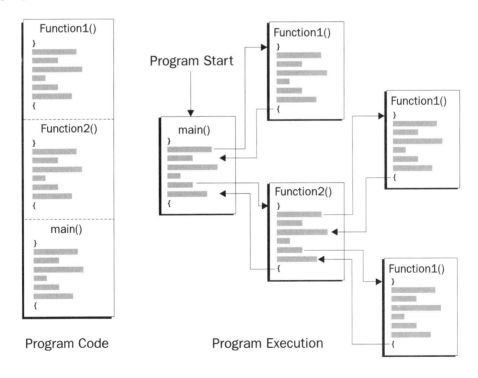

Program Code   Program Execution

The Functional Structure of a Program

On the left, the illustration shows a representation of the code for a program containing three functions. On the right, the diagram shows the sequence in which the functions making up the program might be executed. The arrows indicate how the sequence of execution of the statements in the program passes from one function to another, and then back again when execution of a particular function is completed.

As with all C programs, execution starts at the beginning of the function `main()`. The function `main()` first calls `Function1()` and then `Function2()`. `Function1()` is also called twice from within `Function2()`, so it's actually used a total of three times within the program. At the end of program execution, control passes back to where it started from - the operating system.

A practical application written in C will typically consist of a large number of small functions, each with a well-defined purpose. Functions other than `main()` may be called in any sequence from anywhere in the program, as many times as required. As we shall see when we get to discuss writing our own functions, a function can even call itself.

Source Code

With a small C program, the complete program text (the **source code**) can be contained in a single file. However, with large C programs, storing the complete program, which may run to thousands of lines of code, can become quite unmanageable. Therefore, the source code for a complete C program can be evenly distributed across several separate program files in order to manage it efficiently.

Comments

Comments are included in a program to explain how it works. They aren't part of the program and are ignored by the compiler, they're just there to help the programmer read it more easily. The text of a comment is bounded by /* and */. For example, the first line of a program could be:

```
/* EXAMPLE.C A Simple Program Example */
```

The comment above only covers part of a single line, but they can span several lines, for example:

```
/*
    EXAMPLE.C
    A Brilliant Program Example
*/
```

If you want to highlight some particular comment lines, you can always add characters to embellish them with a frame:

```
/*******************************
 *   EXAMPLE.C                  *
 *                              *
 *   A Brilliantly Simple       *
 *     Program Example          *
 *                              *
 *******************************/
```

Good Practice

As a rule, you should always comprehensively comment your programs. They should always be sufficient for another programmer to understand the purpose and workings of any particular piece of code. You should also comment any unfamiliar terminology, new concepts and additional information. Throughout this book we will be adopting the standard Wrox policy of thorough, easy-to-follow commenting. This will enable you to understand every step of every program at the appropriate point.

Like many programmers, you'll find that putting comments in a program is an awful chore, unless you get into the habit of putting them in early on in your programming career. However, it's worth steeling yourself to make the effort. If you don't pick up the habit now, then the first time that you have to fix a program without adequate comments will be an educational experience.

Keywords

There are several words with very specific meanings which form part of the C language. These are called **keywords**. Examples of keywords are **long**, which defines something as having integer values, or **sizeof,** which is an operator. Keywords are reserved words, which means that you can't use them for any other purpose - if you do, the compiler will get confused. We'll identify each particular keyword as we work through the language. Appendix C contains a list of all the keywords in C.

15

Input and Output

There is no input and output of any kind within the C language. These operations are provided solely by standard functions that are external to the compiler. Nonetheless, they are standard. You will find the same set of input and output facilities available with any ANSI-standard or ANSI-compliant compiler. The support for standard input is via the process of reading from a file called **stdin**. This usually corresponds to the keyboard, but it can be redirected from other files or pipes by an operating system command. Two standard output files are supported, called **stdout** and **stderr**, both of which are connected by default to the screen. Normal screen output uses **stdout**, while **stderr** is used for error messages. Note that while **stdout** may be redirected elsewhere, **stderr** is fixed.

Some compilers provide input/output functions in addition to those defined as standard, but naturally there's no guarantee that these will be available in other C development contexts. We'll stick to the standard functions in this book.

By itself, input and output is a rather tedious topic. There's a lot to it and grinding through all the detail at a single sitting is about as interesting as watching paint dry. It's also quite hard to take it all in, in one go. For this reason, although there is a specific chapter on file operations in this book, there is no specific chapter on keyboard input, or output to the screen. Instead we will develop our understanding of this piecemeal, as we introduce aspects of these operations in a useful context through examples in this book. Appendix A provides a complete rundown on formatting input/output.

Libraries

A **library** is a store for functions and is a very important aid to implementing C programs. They provide a means of vastly enriching the basic capabilities of the language, and offer support for an enormous range of applications. There is a set of standard libraries defined for C, and provided with every ANSI C system in a set of **library files**. These include basic input/output facilities, file operations, mathematical functions and many others. If you stick to the standard set, then you can rest assured that the same facilities will be available on any ANSI-standard compliant system, and that your program should run with minimal change, provided you have written it with portability in mind.

To use a particular standard library, it's necessary to incorporate a file called an **include file**, or a **header file**, into your source program file. These contain information necessary to enable your program to use the standard library functions, as well as definitions of standard symbols of various kinds. We'll be discussing the standard libraries as we learn the language, and Chapter 7 covers the use of libraries as a specific topic.

Whatever C compiler you're using, you're certain to have some additional libraries supplied with it, beyond those within the standard set. Once you're comfortable with the C language, a little time spent investigating what these libraries contain will pay substantial dividends. In most cases you'll find capabilities that will save you a considerable amount of time when you're writing your own application. A vast range of other C libraries are also widely available from any popular and reliable source.

Compiling and Executing a C Program

You will create your first C program using some kind of editor. The original program in C is usually referred to as **source code** and is saved in a **source file**. The process of converting your C program into a form that can be executed on your computer involves three further steps: **pre-processing,** which executes commands that alter the source file, **compiling** the source code, which converts the C language statements to machine code and **linking** the output from the compilation process, which adds library functions and knits it all together. The pre-processing phase is normally integrated with the compile operation, although with C in the UNIX environment, it is usually possible to obtain the output from the pre-processing phase before it is compiled. The overall process of generating an executable program is shown here:

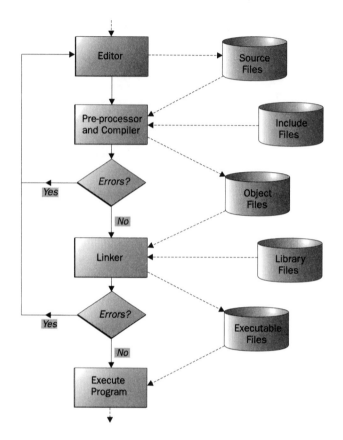

Of course, if errors are produced at any particular stage, then the final output file from processing the program isn't produced. In almost every case, an error necessitates going back and fixing the source code using your editor. Getting through to having something you can execute doesn't mean that you have a working program, there may still be errors in the logic of the program. These errors can't be detected by the compiler or the linker and are usually the hardest to locate and understand.

Let's now take a look at the main steps in producing an executable C program.

Editing

This is the process of creating or modifying your source code. The result of this process is a text file containing the source code for your program. By convention, your C source file has the extension **.c**, so you should use recognizable labels like **MYPROG.C**, **TRYOUT.C** or some other descriptive name. Most compilers will expect the source file to have a name with the extension **.C**.

Text Editors

Many modern compilers feature an 'integrated development environment', which includes an editor, specifically designed for editing programs. If yours doesn't, then you can use a text editor, such as **vi** or **emacs** under UNIX, or EDIT under MS-DOS. Using word processors, like Word or WordPerfect though, isn't usually a good idea, because the additional formatting information which they include in the file will cause the compiler to choke. You can save the file without the formatting tokens, but it's much easier to use a simple text editor.

Editing Environments

Many commercial C compilers have their own specific editor that provides assistance in managing your programs and helping to minimize errors. Indeed, products from both Microsoft and Borland provide a complete environment for writing, managing, developing and testing your programs. Here's a typical commercial editing environment:

This provides a full screen editing environment where you can make additions or modifications to your program simply by positioning the cursor where you want to make a change, and typing it in. The editor also provides syntax highlighting, with different language elements displayed in different colors. This gives you visual cues to where you have made errors in entering a program.

Compilation

This is the main process of translating your original C program into a machine language that the computer can directly execute. Before the compilation process starts, all the pre-processor commands are executed. These instructions generally modify your source file in various ways - usually by adding the contents of a file, modifying statements within the program, or by selectively including or excluding portions of your source file depending on initial conditions. We'll look into how pre-processor commands are used in Chapter 9.

Error Generation

The compiler will detect several different kinds of errors during the translation process, and most of these will prevent the machine language module, usually called an object module or object file, from being generated. Various messages are generated by the compiler to tell you what sort of error has been detected. For example, the TC++ for Windows environment will show you something like this:

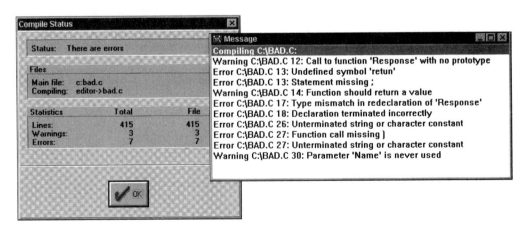

Cascading Errors

Initially, a common cause of confusion is that just one error can result in a whole stream of invective from your compiler, referring to a large number of different errors. Here's an example of this, using the Borland command-line compiler to compile the **EX1-01.C** program:

```
Borland C++ 4.5 Copyright (c) 1987, 1994 Borland International
ex1-01.c:
Error ex1-01.c 25: { expected in function Response
Error ex1-01.c 29: Declaration syntax error in function Response
Error ex1-01.c 29: Declaration missing ; in function Response
Warning ex1-01.c 29: 'pMsg' is assigned a value that is never used in function
Response
Warning ex1-01.c 29: Parameter 'Name' is never used in function Response
Error ex1-01.c 31: ) expected
Error ex1-01.c 33: Declaration terminated incorrectly
Error ex1-01.c 34: Unexpected }
*** 6 errors in Compile ***
```

This erroneous program has the opening brace missing, but everything else is okay. This is detected by the compiler and noted in the first error message, but then we get five other error messages and two warnings, all derived from the same error. This is often called a **cascading error**, or an **error cascade**.

It's not a deficiency in the compiler, but an erroneous statement is outside the rules, so there's always the possibility that various other things could be wrong. Also, an error in one statement can easily make another incorrect, as it may leave things undefined that subsequent statements assume exist.

Error Revision

The above error is very obvious, but it isn't always so. The basic approach that is adopted most often is, after considering the messages carefully, to fix those errors that you know you can, and have another go at compiling. Always correct errors in order, so that cascading errors are hopefully all removed in one step. All errors at this and later stages usually necessitate going back to the editor and re-editing the source code. Of course, if only one source file is in error, then you only need to go back, edit that file and recompile it again. When you finally succeed in compiling your program, you'll have the object files ready to be input into the next phase but this in itself doesn't guarantee that your program is error-free - errors in the logic of the program can't be picked up by the compiler.

Environment Help

Compiling in the development environment supplied with a compiler can provide a little additional help in finding errors. Running the same example through the Borland Turbo compiler development environment produces the output shown here:

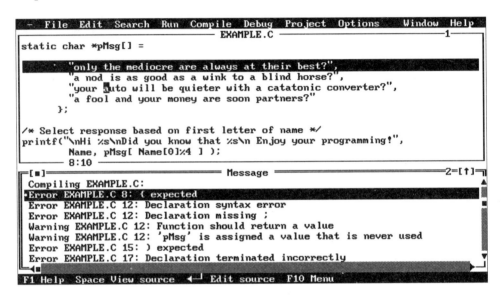

Here, the line of code where the error was recognized is highlighted, which in many cases is the line you need to fix. With an interactive development environment it becomes very easy to step through each of the errors in sequence, correcting them as you go, but you always need to remember the possibility of a cascading error.

Linking

Linking your program is the process of integrating everything into a single executable file, bringing in library functions where necessary. Under UNIX, this is performed by the loader; under MS-DOS, a proprietary linker is usually supplied with the compiler.

A frequent cause of linking errors when you've just installed a compiler system is that your environment isn't correctly set up, or that you haven't specified where the libraries are to be found. If the linker (or loader) is unable to find the library functions it needs, then it can't create an executable version of your program. The error messages that you're likely to encounter depend on the environment in which you are working, although they usually give a clear indication of what is missing. You'll need to turn to your documentation to make sure that all the setup options are in place and correct.

Execution

Once an executable file has been produced (it should have a `.EXE` extension), it can be run. This is usually achieved by selecting the Run option from the relevant menu in your editing environment. If you don't have an interactive editing system, then you can simply execute it as you would any other application - directly from the command-line prompt or program selection utility in a Windows environment.

Operating System Effects

The environment of your operating system may affect how you implement your programs. The UNIX environment, for example, provides mechanisms where one program can initiate another, and where one program can communicate with another. While this may affect the overall approach you might take to implementing an application, it won't affect the C language implementation, and therefore won't affect the programming techniques that you'll use.

UNIX also differs from DOS in the way that it calls a program for execution: more information is passed to the function `main()`, than in DOS. We'll look at this in Chapter 5. There are also a whole range of system functions for communicating with the operating system, and these vary considerably between environments.

Throughout this book we'll be sticking to ANSI-standard C and trying to avoid getting embroiled in system specific aspects of all the particular environments where you may be using C.

Summary

With ANSI-standard implementations of C now generally available, C is an excellent choice of programming language for just about any environment. Of course, for UNIX workstations and IBM compatible PCs, it's still the most widely used computer programming language available. It has the merit of combining power with simplicity, and ease of use with ubiquity. If you've used any other general purpose programming language, then you should find C easy to learn and much more effective, and if you haven't written a program before, then your choice of a language to start out with is excellent.

In this chapter we have seen that:

- A C program is defined in terms of **statements**. These may include **keywords**, which are **reserved words** that can't be used for any other purpose.

- Statements may include **whitespace**, which consists of blanks, tabs, comments or newline characters. Whitespace is used to space out statements for readability and is ignored by the compiler (except within a character string constant).

- A C program consists of one or more **functions**. A function is a self-contained block of code, which performs a particular calculation and is executed by stating its name. There's always a function called **main()** in any C program, and execution starts at the beginning of it.

- The **source code** for a C program is contained in one or more **source files**. A program can be spread across as many source files as you find convenient.

- C programs use functions provided by **standard libraries**. To use the functions in a standard library, you must include the appropriate **header file** in your source file. The header file, also referred to as an **include file**, provides standard definitions relating to library functions necessary for the compiler to process your program correctly.

The translation of a C program into a form which can be executed involves two steps: **compiling**, which produces a set of machine code files for the program from the source files and **linking**, which adds functions from libraries and assembles the object modules into a single executable program module.

Now that we have a feel for the generalities, it's time to get down to specifics. We start programming in C in the next chapter.

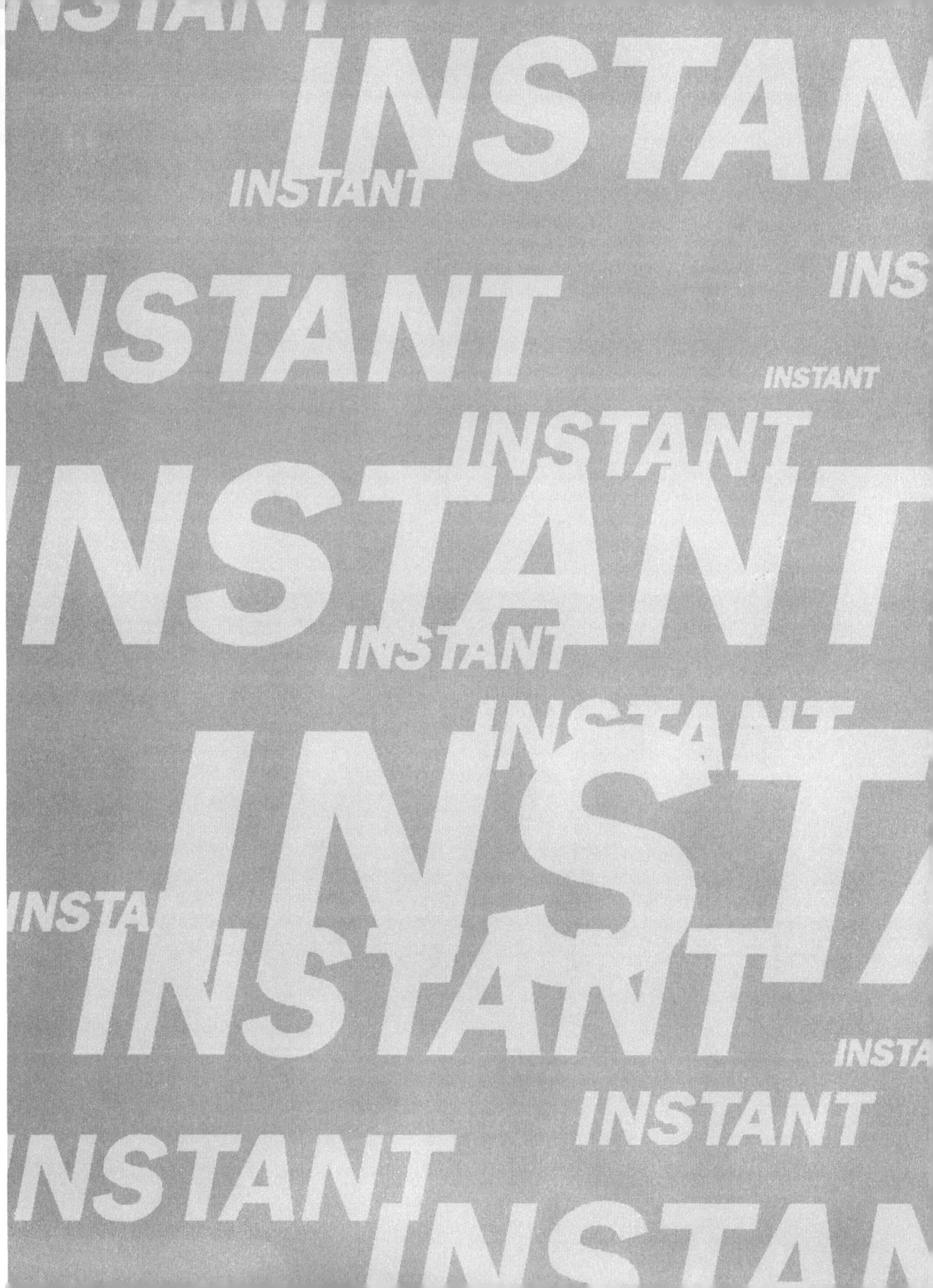
INSTANT
INSTANT
INSTANT
INSTANT
INSTANT
INSTANT

Chapter

Variables, Data Types, and Computation

You're now going to learn about the fundamentals of computing in C - how to read data into a program, how to calculate things with it, and how to show some results. By the end of this chapter you will understand:

What variables are in C.

What kinds of data you can handle in C.

How to define and name variables, and how to specify constants of various kinds.

How to perform arithmetic calculations and what operators we can use.

What bitwise operations are, and how they work.

The rules governing the sequence of calculations in C.

How operations between values of different types are carried out, and how a value of one type can be converted into another.

What is meant by variable scope.

Variables

A **variable** is a named bit of memory in your computer, where you can store some piece of data. It's called a variable because the data can be changed as the program progresses. Variables can store various kinds of data, but each individual variable can only hold one particular type of data, specified when you first define it.

Let's now look at the rules for naming C variables and some of the different types of data that we can store.

Naming Conventions

The name we give to a variable is called an **identifier**, or rather more conveniently, a **variable name**. It's a very flexible system whereby identifiers consist of a string of letters, digits and the underscore character, but must begin with a letter. Some examples of valid variable names are:

Cost	debit	pShape	Value_	MAXIMUM	DimeStore

A variable name cannot include any other characters and mustn't start with a digit, so `8_Ball`, `2big`, and `6_pack` aren't allowed. Neither is `Hash!` or `Jim-Bob`. This last example (using a dash or a hyphen) is a very common mistake; `Jim_Bob` would be quite acceptable though. Of course, `Jim Bob` wouldn't be allowed because whitespace characters aren't valid characters in variable names. Note that the variable names `democrat` and `Democrat` are not names for the same variable, since upper and lower case letters are treated as distinct characters.

Since an underscore character counts as a letter, you can define variables with names starting with an underscore character such as `_This` and `_That`, or even `__Those` (with two underscores). This is best avoided however, since there are pre-defined variables within the standard libraries that also take these forms, so you could quite conceivably clash with them, accidentally causing serious problems.

Apart from variables, there are quite a few other things in C that have names, and they can all have identifiers of up to 31 characters in length.

Their names have the same definition constraints as variable names, so the name of anything in C is governed by this one set of rules.

ANSI Identifiers

In ANSI standard C, at least 31 characters must be significant for identifiers. This means that all ANSI standard C compilers will process and differentiate variable names with up to 31 characters. Some compilers will support identifiers with names over 31 characters, but ignore excess characters, and others will even differentiate names with more that 31 characters regardless. For most purposes 31 characters in a name is more than adequate, and if you regard this as a hard limit then you can be sure that your variable names will be acceptable in any compiler that is ANSI-standard compliant.

Hungarian Notation

You can call your variables by whatever names you like within the definition rules, but a systematic approach to naming them can help you to avoid some common errors.

One approach that was used in the code for Microsoft Windows, is **Hungarian Notation**. This uses a prefix of one or more characters to each variable name, providing an indication of what kind of data the variable contains. A few of the more common prefixes you may come across in C are shown here:

c	char	p		pointer
i	int	s		string
l	long	w		word (unsigned int)

Sometimes the prefixes can be several characters deep, where more complicated entities are used, which can make the names quite long.

We won't be going the whole hog in the examples in this book, but we will be using the prefix **p** for pointer names, and as you will see later, pointers have a particular potential for misuse.

Data Types

The kind of data your variable is going to store is obviously very important. Recording the number of persons in a string quartet requires a rather different kind of capacity to that required to hold the current gross national product. There are three basic kinds of data values that you can store in C variables: whole numbers (usually referred to as **integers**), **characters**, and **floating point numbers**.

Integers

The basic integer type in C is specified by the keyword **int**. You specify a variable of this type in a **declaration** statement, for example:

```
int my_number;
```

This statement declares a variable called **my_number**, that is of type **int**, and therefore can only be used to store whole numbers. All variables must be declared before you use them. A variable of type **int** will normally occupy 2 bytes of memory, however it can be more on some machines.

long

Since a 2-byte integer contains 16 bits, it can store values between -32,768 and 32,767 (assuming that we're using a machine featuring 2's complement representation for negative numbers - the majority do, and we will continue to assume so throughout this book).

> Most computers represent such numbers using the two's complement notation, where the left-most bit denotes the *sign* bit. If this bit is 1 then the number is negative, and if the bit is 0 then the number is positive. This method of representation makes it a lot easier for the CPU to perform arithmetic operations.

In a machine that doesn't use 2's complement arithmetic, the difference is slight - the range of values being between -32,767 and 32,767. In either case, the range isn't enough for many purposes, so the type **long int** is also available, which can be and usually is abbreviated to **long**. You can declare a variable of type **long** in a similar way to that of type **int**, but using the **long** keyword instead:

```
long BigNumber;
```

A variable of type **long** occupies at least 4 bytes, and so it will be able to store values in the range of -2,147,438,648 to 2,147,438,647. This gives us a little more breathing space, but it's still not enough for the GNP of the USA (we'll discuss how we can do that a little bit later).

short

A third variation on integer variable types is **short   int**, usually abbreviated to **short**. This is normally the same as **int**, except when **int** is the same as **long**, in which case **short** will be shorter, if you see what I mean. The essential idea is that a **short** variable should be smaller than a **long**. An example of a short variable declaration is:

```
short SmallNumber;
```

The range of values that you can store in a short variable is implementation dependent. Commonly, a **short** variable will occupy 2 bytes, which would allow for values from -32,768 to 32,767, but sometimes it's only 1 byte in which case you would have a miserly range of just -128 to 127.

An Example of Using Integer Variables

Let's try a simple example of using integer variables:

```
/* EX2-01.C  Using integer variables */
#include <stdio.h>              /* For input and output */

int main()
{
    int Apples;                /* Declare the integer variable Apples */
    int Oranges;               /* Declare the integer variable Oranges */
    int TotalFruit;            /* Declare the integer variable TotalFruit */

    Apples = 10;               /* Set the value of Apples as 10 */
    Oranges = 25;              /* Set the value of Oranges as 25 */
    Apples = Apples + 5;       /* Increase the value of Apples by 5 */
    TotalFruit = Apples + Oranges;              /* Calculate the total */

    /* Now display the total number of fruit */
    printf("\nTotal number of fruit = %d", TotalFruit );

    return 0;                  /* Return from the function */
}
```

Program Analysis

Apart from the explanatory initial comment, the example starts with a pre-processor directive, causing the library header file, **STDIO.H**, to be included in the program. This **include file** contains all the necessary definitions for our program to display output to the screen, and receive input from the keyboard.

The rest of the program file consists of the single function **main()**. Note how each statement in the body of the function is terminated by a semi-colon. You will find it very easy to forget semi-colons when you first use C, but you'll soon get the hang of it.

The function **main()** starts off by declaring three **int** variables, **Apples**, **Oranges**, and **TotalFruit** in separate statements. Next are four **assignment statements**, so called because they 'assign' a value to a variable. The first two of these assign integer values to the variables **Apples** and **Oranges**. The next takes the current value stored in **Apples**, adds 5 to it, and stores the result back in the variable **Apples**. The last assignment adds the values in the variables **Apples** and **Oranges** together, and stores the result in the variable **TotalFruit**.

After a comment line the function **printf()** is called, which allows you to print text and variables to the screen.

If you compile and execute the previous program example, it will produce the output:

Total number of fruit = 40

We will take a look at how we actually get this output, and how the **printf()** function works, a little later on.

Integer Constants

We used the integer constants **10**, **25**, and **5** in the previous example. If a number is written without a decimal point (e.g. **92**) then it's taken to be an **int**; if it has an '**L**' appended to it (e.g. **92L**) then it's a **long**. You could use a lower case letter **l**, but it's easily confused with the digit 'one', so it's better to consistently use the upper case version.

Note that the commas you would normally use to write a number such as 99,999 aren't used in writing C constants, and will cause an error. You would write this number as **99999L**.

An integer written with a leading zero, **0123** for example, is understood to be an octal constant in C. Thus it has the decimal value 83. Octal is rarely used now - modern computers invariably have a word length which is a multiple of 8 bits, although some special purpose microprocessors still use octal representation.

Integer constants can also be specified in hexadecimal form, that is base 16. A hexadecimal number can have digit values from zero to fifteen, written using the standard representation of **0** to **9**, and **A** to **F** (or **a** to **f**). A hexadecimal constant is also preceded by **0x** (or **0X**) to distinguish it from a decimal value. For example, the decimal value 123 could be represented as the hexadecimal constant **0x7B**. For a crash course in hexadecimal number representation, see Appendix B.

Declaring Several Variables

All the examples of variable declarations so far have specified just one variable to name. You can also declare several variables of the same type in a single statement. For example:

```
long Value1, Value2, BigNumber;
```

Some programmers prefer to declare each variable in a separate statement because it can be a little clearer, particularly when comments are needed to document what they are for. However, there is no hard and fast rule on this - it's purely a matter of taste.

Initializing Variables

You can assign an initial value to a variable when you actually define it. For example, to declare a long variable, **Distance**, and initialize it with the value 93,000,000, you would write:

```
long Distance = 93000000L;      /* Distance from the earth to the sun */
```

Where multiple variables are declared and initialized, they're separated by commas in the normal manner:

```
int Quartet = 4, Octet = 8;
```

This type of declaration that also initializes a variable is called a **defining declaration**, because it causes memory to be allocated for that variable, and its value to be defined. Variables that aren't initialized will contain a 'garbage value'.

> When you switch on your computer, everything that you need to reside in memory is automatically loaded. Those areas of memory that aren't used will contain values that no one can predict - garbage values. Such values are wildly unpredictable.

It's usually rather unhelpful to have garbage floating around in your program, so it's good practice to initialize variables every time. This avoids leaving spurious values around, and makes it easier to discover what is wrong if your program doesn't work.

Character Variables

Variables that can hold a character are specified using the keyword **char**. The **char** data type serves a dual purpose; it can specify a one byte integer variable or a variable storing a single character. On most, but not all computers, this will be an **ASCII** character.

> ASCII is the acronym for the American Standard Code for Information Interchange. Pronounced 'asskey', this 7-bit standard code was adopted to facilitate the interchange of data between different types of data processing and equipment.

We will assume that we're programming a machine supporting the ASCII character set throughout this book, but we'll also address the implications of non-ASCII environments in Chapter 10. The ASCII character set appears in all its glory in Appendix B.

Declaring Character Variables

We can define a character variable with the statement:

```
char letter = 'A';
```

Note here that we specify a constant which is signified by single quotes, not double quotes.

Since a value of type **char** occupies 1 byte, it can store integer values from -128 to 127. A **char** variable can be treated as a character or an integer value interchangeably. Because the character 'A' is represented as the decimal ASCII value 65, we could have written:

```
char letter = 65;                    /* Equivalent to A */
```

to produce the same result.

We can also use hexadecimal constants to initialize **char** variables (as other integer types). Thus we could rewrite the last statement as:

```
char letter = 0x41;                  /* Also equivalent to A */
```

A character is always two hexadecimal digits, because two hexadecimal digits define 8 bits.

An Example of Character Variables

Here's an example of how we can use character variables:

```
/* EX2-02.C Using char variables */
#include <stdio.h>                    /* For input and output */

int main()
{
   char First = 0x41;
   char Second = 'B';
   char Third = Second + 1;

   printf("\nUsing character variables is as easy as %c%c%c,
                                    First, Second, Third );

   return 0;
}
```

Program Analysis

Here we have defined three **char** variables, initializing each in a different way. As you can see, we are able to use expressions as well as constants to initialize variables when they are being declared, as long as the expression evaluates to a constant.

The **printf()** function (which we will be discussing shortly) will display the specified text in the format string, followed by the values of the three variables.

The values generated here can only be guaranteed on ASCII-based systems. If you want your program to be portable between different kinds of computers, then you need to avoid this built-in ASCII dependency.

Integer Type Modifiers

Variables of the integral types **char**, **int**, and **long** can contain signed values by default, so they can store both positive and negative values. This is because the type modifier **signed** is assumed for these types by default. So wherever we wrote **char**, **int**, or **long**, we could have used **signed char**, **signed int**, or **signed long** respectively. If you're sure that you don't need to store negative values in a variable, then you can specify a variable as **unsigned**, where the sign bit is used as part of the data value allowing a larger maximum value to be stored. For example:

```
unsigned long mileage = 0UL;
```

In this case the minimum value that can be stored is zero, and the maximum is increased to 4,294,967,295. You can also apply the **unsigned** modifier to **int** as well, where such variables may assume values from 0 to 65,535. Note how a **U** (or a **u**) is appended to **unsigned** constant values.

> Both **signed** and **unsigned** are keywords in C, so you can't use them as variable names.

In the previous example we have '**L**' appended as well to indicate that the value is also **long**. You can use either upper or lower case for **U** and **L** and the sequence is unimportant too, but it's a good idea to adopt a consistent way of specifying such constants.

Floating Point Variables

Values which aren't integral are stored as **floating point** numbers. A floating point number has two parts, a decimal fractional part with a fixed number of digits called the **mantissa**, and an **exponent** which is the power of 10 by which the mantissa is multiplied. For example, the number 123.45 can be written as $.12345 \times 10^3$, so the mantissa here is .12345 and the exponent value is 3. The number of digits in the mantissa, and the range of possible values for the exponent are dependent upon the capacity of the computer system that you're using.

You can write a floating point number as just a decimal value such as 112.5, or with an exponent, such as 1.125E2, where the decimal part is multiplied by the power of 10 specified after the E (for Exponent). Our example therefore can be represented by 1.125E2 which is simply 112.5. Note that a floating point constant must contain a decimal point, an exponent or both. If you write neither then it's an integer.

double Variables

You can specify a floating point variable using the **double** keyword, as in the statement:

```
double Speed_of_Light = 670619880;      /* In miles per hour */
```

A **double** variable typically occupies 8 bytes in memory and stores values accurate to 15 decimal digits, so we still have room for a much more precise value for the speed of light.

The range of values stored is much wider than that indicated by the 15 digits accuracy, because it's also determined by the range of possible exponent values. The precise range is dependent on the kind of hardware you are using, but for an IBM compatible PC it's from 1.7×10^{-308} to 1.7×10^{308}, positive and negative. We're now able to deal with the GNP with room to spare. The number 10^{100} is called a googol, so here we're fully googol enabled. Unfortunately, the googolplex is out though - since it's 10 to the power of a googol, or 10^{googol}.

float Variables

If you don't require 15-digit precision, and you don't need the massive range of values provided by **double** variables, then you can opt to use the **float** keyword to declare floating point variables occupying 4 bytes (on a PC). For example:

```
float Pint_to_Go = 2.6274f;
```

This isn't, as you might have imagined, the volume of a takeaway beer, but the conversion factor from a US pint to the Japanese 'go' unit of measure. In case you ever need it, there are 10 '**shakus**' to the 'go'. The **f** at the end of the constant specifies it to be of a **float** type. Without the **f**, the constant would have been represented as a **double**. Note that if you want to write a float value with an exponent, then the suffix must go at the very end, as in:

```
float LY_to_AU = 6.327147E4f;    /* Light years to Astronomical Units */
```

Variables declared as **float** are of 7-decimal-digit precision on an IBM compatible PC, and can have values from 3.4×10^{-38} to 3.4×10^{38}, both positive and negative.

long double Variables

Another floating point type that can provide even more precision on some computers is a **long double**. In some implementations (Borland C++ 4.0 for instance), variables of this type provide 19-digit precision, and support numbers in the range of 3.4×10^{-4932} to 1.1×10^{4932} .

You define constants of this type with the suffix '**L**', and as with all suffices - it can be in lower case as well. An example of defining a variable of this type is:

```
long double Pi = 3.1415926535889793238L;
```

This defines a value for the ratio of the circumference of a circle to its diameter, with 19-digit precision.

Named Constants

Usually, circumstances can arise quite frequently when you want some variables to have a fixed value that shouldn't be changed during the execution of a program. The last example is a case in point. Having defined the value for **Pi** you'll probably never want to change it. Prefixing the **const** keyword does the trick, for example:

```
const long double Pi = 3.1415926535889793238L;
```

You can use the **const** qualifier in the declaration of any variable that you don't want be changed. Naturally, any **const** variable must have an initial value assigned to it, because it's impossible to assign anything to it later.

Boolean Types

C doesn't provide a standard boolean (or logical) type, so you must find another way of representing them. You could use integers to represent them (i.e. 1 and 0), which are faster than characters, but characters could save you some data space. For this reason, the designers of C decided that this space/time trade-off should be left up to the programmer.

Apart from using messy variables, you could use any of the following:

```
#define  TRUE  1             #define  YES  1
#define  FALSE  0            #define  NO  0
enum  boolean{false,  true};  enum  boolean{no,  yes};
```

We will be discussing True and False in greater detail in the next chapter.

Enumeration

You will sometimes be faced with the need for variables that have a limited set of possible integer values, for instance the days of the week or the months in the year. We have a specific facility in C to handle this situation called an **enumeration**. Let's take the example of a variable that can assume values corresponding to days of the week. We can define this as:

```
enum Week (Mon, Tues, Wed, Thurs, Fri, Sat, Sun) This_week;
```

This declares an enumeration type called **Week**, and the variable **This_week** that is an instance of **Week**, so that it can only assume the values in parentheses.

> Note that if you try to assign to an enumeration variable such as **This_week** anything other than the set of values specified, then your compiler won't necessarily flag this as an error.

39

Enumeration Constants

The symbolic names listed between the parentheses are known as **enumeration constants**. In fact, the names of the days will be defined as having fixed integer values. The first name in the list, **Mon**, will have the value 0, **Tues** will be 1, and so on. If you would prefer the implicit numbering to start at a different value then you can just write:

```
enum Week (Mon = 1, Tues, Wed, Thurs, Fri, Sat, Sun) This_week;
```

and they will be equivalent to 1 through to 7. Having defined the form of an enumeration, you can define another variable thus:

```
enum Week   Next_week;
```

This defines a variable **Next_week** as an enumeration that can assume the values previously specified.

Assigning Specific Values

You can also assign specific values if you wish. We could define this enumeration for example:

```
enum Punctuation (Comma=',', Exclamation='!', Question='?' );
```

Here we've defined the possible values for enumeration variables of type **Punctuation** as the numerical equivalents of the appropriate symbols. If you look in the ASCII table in Appendix B, you'll be able to see that in decimal they are 44, 33, and 63 respectively.

Obviously the values assigned don't have to be in ascending order. If you don't specify all the values explicitly, then incrementing values continue to be assigned from the last specified value, as in our second **Week** example.

Defining Boolean Variables

You could also use an enumeration to define the idea of logical variables, take the following for example:

```
enum Boolean (False, True) B1, B2, B3;
```

This defines three variables as having the ability to possess the values of False or True.

Printing Text and Variables

The simplest way of printing data to the screen is to use the **printf()** function, from the **STDIO.H** library. We have already seen a brief example of this, and it worked like this:

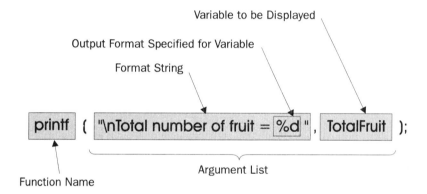

The **argument list** specifies what is passed to the function, and the arguments are separated by commas. In this example there are two arguments, a **format string** which specifies how the output is to be presented, and the variable **TotalFruit** which contains the value that we want to display.

The format string is a sequence of characters enclosed within double quotes. It can contain two sorts of information: text to be displayed, and **format specifiers** which determine how the values of variables which appear in the argument list are to be presented. A format specifier always begins with a **%** symbol. In our example, the format specifier is **%d** which indicates that the value to be displayed is a decimal integer of type `int`. To output a value of type `long` you would need to use the format specifier `%ld`. The `l` specifier is called a **length modifier**. For a short variable, the length modifier is **h** so you would use the format specifier `%hd`.

> Note that the `printf()` function deduces the type of data that you are passing to it from the format specifier. If the format specifier doesn't match the variable type, then you won't get the correct value displayed.

The format specifiers are matched in sequence with the variables to be displayed, so there should be the same number of format specifiers in the format string, as there are variables in the argument list. Of course, the format specifiers always need to be appropriate to the type of value to be displayed.

Note that if you ever want to display the percent symbol, then you must use `%%` in the format string.

Escape Sequences

The `\n` at the beginning of the format string is called an **escape sequence.** This is because the \ character escapes from the standard interpretation of the string to interpret the following character in a special way. Here the `\n` pair enable the representation of a newline character.

There are several escape sequences you can use. Some of the particularly useful ones are:

`\a`	sound a beep	`\b`	backspace
`\n`	newline	`\t`	tab
`\'`	single quote	`\"`	double quote
`\\`	backslash		

Obviously, if you want to be able to include a backslash or a double quote as a character to be output, then you must use the escape sequences to represent them. Otherwise the backslash would be interpreted as another escape sequence, and a double quote would indicate the end of the character string.

Arithmetic Operations

All of the computational aspects of C are fairly intuitive, so we should slide through this like a hot knife through butter. The C arithmetic operators are:

+   Addition

-        Subtraction

*   Multiplication

/   Division

%   Remainder or Modulus (integers only)

++   Increment (integers only)

– –   Decrement (integers only)

Arithmetic Expressions

The first four arithmetic operators in this table are similar to what you're used to using in normal arithmetic. For example, the expression:

```
2*2.5  +  8/2
```

evaluates to 9. The multiply and divide operations are executed before the addition, just like normal arithmetic, because they are said to be of a higher **precedence** than addition or subtraction. We will come back to the question of operator precedence before the end of this chapter.

The Remainder Operator

The remainder operator only works with integers. It calculates the remainder when the left integer operator is divided by the right integer operator, so if **A** and **B** are integer variables with the values 10 and 3 respectively, the expression:

```
A%B
```

has the value 1. The remainder operator has the same precedence as multiply and divide. Where more than one of these occur in the same expression, they are evaluated from the left to the right. The multiply, divide, and remainder operators have left to right **associativity**.

The Divide Operator

When the divide operator is used with integer values, the result is rounded down to an integer. With variables **A** and **B** having the values 10 and 3 respectively, the expression produces the value 3:

    A/B

The Increment and Decrement Operators

These operators don't apply to floating-point variables. The increment operator increases the value of a variable by 1, and the decrement operator decreases a value by 1. So if **A** starts out as 10, after executing the expression **++A**, it will have the value 11. Within an expression, their effect is slightly unusual. The operators can be placed before or after the value to which they apply, that is as either a **prefix** operator or a **postfix** operator. If the operator prefixes a variable, as in the expression:

    2*(++A)

then assuming that **A** starts out as 10, it will first be incremented to 11, so that the value of the expression is 22. If, on the other hand, the postfix form is used, as in the expression:

    2*(A++)

then the value of **A** will be incremented after the value of the expression has been calculated. So if, as in the previous example, **A** starts out as 10, it will still end up as 11, but the value of the expression will be 20. If you omit the parentheses and just use the expression **2*A++**, then the value of the expression will still be 20, and **A** will be incremented to 11 after the value of the expression has been calculated.

Using Parentheses

You can always use parentheses in an arithmetic expression to ensure that the calculation proceeds in the order that you want it to. In any expression containing parentheses, all the sub-expressions are evaluated starting with the innermost and working to the outermost. This is easy to see with an example:

```
( 2*( A + B ) - C )*( D - E )
```

The value of (A + B) will be calculated first. The result will then be used to evaluate the sub-expression (2*(A + B) - C). Next, the value of (D - E) will be calculated and finally be multiplied by the previous result to generate the final value for the whole expression.

The Assignment Statement

An assignment statement assigns the value of the expression to the right of the equals sign, to the variable appearing to the left of the equals sign. A typical arithmetic assignment statement would look like:

```
whole = part1 + part2 + part3;
```

In this statement, the **whole** is exactly the sum of its parts, and no more. However, recalling the odd behavior of the increment and decrement operators, we could write:

```
whole = (part1−) + (part2−) + (part3−);
```

After the execution of this statement the variable **whole** will be three more than the sum of the variables **part1**, **part2** and **part3**, since each of these will be decremented after the overall expression on the right of the equals sign.

Multiple Assignments

You can also write repeated assignments such as:

```
A = B = 1;
```

This is equivalent to assigning the value 1 to **B**, then assigning the value of **B** to **A**.

An Arithmetic Exercise

We can exercise basic arithmetic in C, along with a few of the other things we have covered so far in this chapter, by calculating how many standard rolls of wallpaper are needed to paper a room. This is done with the following example:

```
/* EX2-03.C A wallpaper planner */

/* This program calculates how many rolls of wallpaper   *
 * are required for a room, based on the room dimensions  *
 * and a standard width and length for a roll.            */

#include <stdio.h>
int main()
{
    /* Room dimensions and perimeter */
    double height = 0.0, width = 0.0, length = 0.0;
    double perimeter = 0.0;

    /* A roll of wallpaper is 33 feet long and 21 inches wide */
    const double ROLLWIDTH = 21.0;
    const double ROLLLENGTH = 12.*33.;

    /* Some working variables for use in the calculations */
    int Strips_per_Roll = 0;
    int Strips_Reqd = 0;
    int Nrolls = 0;

    /* Ask for the room height, and read it in */
    printf("\n Enter the height of the room in inches: ");
    scanf("%lf", &height);

    /* Do the same for the height and width */
    printf("\n Now enter the length and width in inches: ");
    scanf("%lf%lf", &length, &width);

    /* Find the number of strips in a roll, and the perimeter
       of the room */
    Strips_per_Roll = ROLLLENGTH/height;
    perimeter = 2.0*(length + width);

    /* That gives us the number of strips we need, so we can
       work out the number of rolls */
    Strips_Reqd = perimeter/ROLLWIDTH;
```

```
    Nrolls = Strips_Reqd/Strips_per_Roll;

    /* Now print the result */
    printf("\nFor your room you need %d rolls of wallpaper.", Nrolls );

    return 0;
}
```

Program Analysis

One thing needs to be clear from the outset. No responsibility is assumed for you running out of wallpaper as a result of using this program. All errors in the estimate of the number of rolls required are due to the way C works, as we shall soon see, and due to the wastage that inevitably occurs when you hang your own wallpaper - usually 50%+.

We have a block of declarations for the variables used in the program right at the beginning of the body of **main()**. These statements should be fairly familiar by now. Two of them define constant variables:

```
const double ROLLWIDTH = 21.0;
const double ROLLLENGTH = 12.*33.;
```

Because they have been declared as constants, the compiler can check that they are used properly, and in particular, it will complain about any attempts to change their values.

Note that the variable names declared as **const** are written here with capital letters. This is a common convention to distinguish them from variables. It can be very useful defining constants by means of **const** variable types, particularly when you use the same constant many times.

Constant Expressions

The **const** variable **ROLLLENGTH** is also initialized with an arithmetic expression **(12.*33.)**. Being able to use a constant expression as an initializer saves having to work out the value yourself, and can also be a lot more meaningful, since 33 feet multiplied by 12 inches is much clearer than simply writing 396. The compiler will generally evaluate constant expressions accurately, whereas if you do it yourself, depending on the complexity of the expression and your ability to number crunch, there's a possibility that you may be wrong.

You can use any expression that can be calculated as a constant at compile time, including **const** objects you've already defined. So for instance we could declare the area of a standard roll of wallpaper as:

```
const double ROLLAREA = ROLLWIDTH * ROLLLENGTH;
```

This statement would obviously need to be placed after the declarations for the two **const** variables used in the initialization of **ROLLAREA**.

Reading Floating Point Values

The next four statements in the program handle the user input:

```
printf("\n Enter the height of the room in inches: ");
scanf("%lf", height);

printf("\n Now enter the length and width in inches: ");
scanf("%lf%lf", length, width);
```

We've used **printf()** to display prompts, and then we use the function **scanf()** to input the height, length and width. In a practical program we would need to check for errors, and possibly make sure that the values entered are sensible, but we will look at that a little later.

Note the format specification, **%lf**, for reading a variable of type **double**. Here we don't have the option of using a capital 'L' in the format specifier. The specification **%Lf** is for reading values of type **long double**. To read a value of type **float** you would just use plain old **%f**.

Notice that the names of the variables in the argument list to **scanf()** are prefixed by an ampersand. Exactly why this is we'll discover later, but for the meantime, just make sure that you use an '**&**' with variable names in **scanf()**.

Calculating the Result

We have four statements involved in calculating the number of standard rolls of wallpaper required for the size of room given. First we calculate the number of room-height strips we can get out of a single roll:

```
Strips_per_Roll = ROLLLENGTH/height;   /* Get no. of strips in a roll */
```

Note that the result is stored as an integer, which will mean that the result is rounded down, effectively discarding partial strips, which is actually what we want. For example, if the room is 8 feet (96 inches) high, we divide 96 into 396, giving us a result of 4.125 - four strips with a little left over.

The perimeter of the room is equal to twice the sum of the length and breadth, parentheses being used to make sure that the addition is carried out before the multiplication:

```
perimeter = 2.0*(length + width);       /* Calculate room perimeter */
```

The last arithmetic statement calculates the number of rolls required, by dividing the number of strips required (integer), by the number of strips in a roll (also integer):

```
Nrolls = Strips_Reqd/Strips_per_Roll;   /* Calculate number of rolls */
```

Because we are dividing one integer by another, the result has to be an integer and any remainder is ignored. The result we obtain is essentially the same as if we produced a floating point result and rounded down to the nearest integer. This isn't really what we want, so you'll need to fix this too, if you want to use this program in practice.

> As a rule you should only use the floating point types when you need to. If you have to use floating point types to hold integer values, you must not rely on their values being exact. In floating point, 0.9999999 is as good as 1.0 and in most instances it will make no difference. However, if you round down to an integer, it isn't one at all, it's zero.

The op= Version of Assignment

It's often necessary to modify the existing value of a variable, such as incrementing or doubling it. We could increment a variable **count** using the statement:

```
count = count + 5;
```

This simply adds five to the current value stored in **count**, and stores the result back in **count**, so if **count** started out at 10, then it would end up as 15. In addition, you also have an alternative shorthand method of writing the same thing in C:

```
count += 5;
```

We can also use other operators with this same notation as well. For example:

```
count *= 5;
```

has the effect of multiplying the current value of **count** by 5, and storing the result back in **count**.

Operators and Syntax

In general we can write statements of the form (where **lhs** and **rhs** stand for left-hand and right-hand side respectively):

```
rhs op= lhs;
```

where **op** is any one of the following operators:

```
+        -        *        /        %        &        ^        |        <<        >>
```

The general form of the statement is equivalent to:

```
rhs = rhs op ( lhs );
```

This means that we can write statements such as:

```
A /= B + C;
```

which will in effect be identical to:

```
A = A/(B + C);
```

Bitwise Operations

The bitwise operators treat their operands as a series of individual bits rather than a numerical value. They only work with integer variables or constants, so only the data types **short**, **int**, **long**, and **char** can be used. They are particularly useful in programming hardware devices, where the status of a device is often represented as a series of individual flags or bits in a word.

There are six bitwise operators:

  &   bitwise AND

  | bitwise OR

  ^   bitwise exclusive OR

  ~   bitwise NOT

  >>   shift right

  <<   shift left

We won't be discussing the shift operators here since they are rarely used, but let's take a look instead at how each of the first four work.

The Bitwise AND

The bitwise AND, &, is a binary operator that combines corresponding bits in its operands. We can represent this in a table, often referred to as a **truth table**:

	0	1
0	0	0
1	0	1

Let's see how this works in an example.

A Simple Example

Bitwise operators are commonly used to test the properties (or attributes) of files. For example if a certain file had a bit field in the format '00010010', representing its attributes, we could perform a variety of operations. Supposing that we wanted to check whether this file is writable, where the writable attribute is represented in bit 2.

```
int fileInfo                    /* 0001 0010 for example */
int isWritable                  /* 0000 0010 for example */

int nResult = fileInfo & isWritable
```

If **nResult** becomes 0 then the specified file isn't writable. You can confirm this by looking at how corresponding bits combine with **&** in the truth table.

Masking

Because the **&** produces zero if either bit is zero, we can use this operator to make sure any unwanted bits are zero. We can achieve this by creating what is called a **mask**, which is combined with the original variable using **&**. We create the mask by putting 1's where we want to keep bits, and 0's where we don't. The result will be 0's where the mask bit is 0, and the same value as the original bit in the variable where the mask is 1.

Suppose that we have a **char** variable **Letter** where, for the purposes of illustration, we want to eliminate the 4 high order bits, but keep the 4 low order bits. This can easily be achieved by setting up a mask as **0x0F** (00001111 in binary), and combining them using **&**, like thus:

```
Letter = Letter & 0x0F;
```

If **Letter** started out as **0x41**, then it would end up as **0x01** as a result.

The Bitwise OR

The bitwise OR, **|**, is sometimes called the inclusive OR. The truth table for the bitwise OR is:

	0	1
0	0	1
1	1	1

The OR can be used to turn bits on. If we want to be sure that the fifth bit in a **char** variable **flag** is on, but we want to leave the other bits alone then we could use the statement:

```
flag |= 0x08h;
```

The value ORed with **flag** is 0000 1000 in binary, which forces the fifth bit to be 1, and leaves the others as they were.

The Bitwise Exclusive OR

The exclusive OR (abbreviated to EOR or XOR), ^, is so called because its operates in a similar way to the inclusive OR but produces 0 when both operand bits are 1. Its truth table is therefore:

	0	1
0	0	1
1	1	0

The ^ operator has a rather surprising property. Suppose that we have two **char** variables, **First** with the value `'A'`, and **Last** with the value `'Z'`, corresponding to the binary values 0100 0001 and 0101 1010. If we write the statements:

```
First ^= Last;        /* Result First is 0001 1011 */
Last  ^= First;       /* Result Last is 0100 0001 */
First ^= Last;        /* Result First is 0101 1010 */
```

then the results show that **First** and **Last** have exchanged values without using any intermediate memory location. This also works with any integer values.

The Bitwise NOT

The bitwise NOT, ~, takes a single operand for which it inverts the bits. Thus, take the following statement:

```
Result = ~Letter1;
```

If **Letter1** is 0100 0001, then **Result** will have the value 1011 1110, which is **0xBE** or 190 as a decimal value.

Variable Types and Casting

In spite of the impression you may have gained so far, calculations in C, or any other programming language for that matter, can only be carried out between values of the same type. Your computer can't work any other way.

To override this, when you write an expression involving variables or constants of different types, you must tell the compiler to convert one of the types of operands to match that of the other. This conversion process is called **casting**. For example if you want to add a **double** value to an integer, then the integer value is first converted to **double**, and then the addition is carried out. Of course the variable which contains the value which must be cast isn't changed. The compiler will store the converted value in a temporary memory location which will be discarded when the calculation is finished.

Conversion Rules

There are rules that govern which operand is selected to be converted in any operation.

Any expression to be calculated can be broken down into a series of operations between two operands. For example, the expression **2*3-4+5** amounts to the series:

- **2*3** resulting in **6**
- **6-4** resulting in **2**
- and finally **2+5** resulting in **7**

Thus, the rules for casting operands where necessary only needs to be defined in terms of decisions about pairs of operands. So for any pair of operands, the following rules are checked in the sequence that they are written until one applies, and then that rule is used:

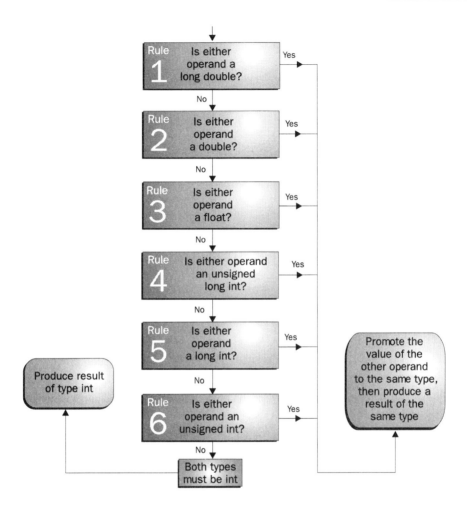

A Simple Example

We could try these rules on a hypothetical expression to see how they work. Let's suppose that we have a sequence of variable declarations as follows:

```
double value = 23.0;
int count = 8;
float many = 2;
char num = 4;
```

Let's also suppose that we have the following statement:

```
value = (value - count)*(count + num)/many + num/many;
```

We can now work out what casts the compiler will apply.

1 The first operation is to calculate **(value - count)**. Rule 1 doesn't apply but Rule 2 does, so the value of **count** is converted to **double** and the **double** result, 15.0 is calculated.

2 Next **(count + num)** must be evaluated, and here the first rule in sequence which applies is Rule 5, so **num** is converted from **char** to **int** and the result 12 produced as type **int**.

3 The next calculation is the product of the first two results, a **double** 15.0 and an **int** 12. Rule 2 applies here and the 12 is converted to 12.0 as **double**, and the **double** result 180.0 is produced.

4 This result now has to be divided by **many**, so Rule 2 applies again and the value of **many** is converted to **double** before generating the **double** result 90.0.

5 The expression **num/many** is calculated next, and here Rule 3 applies to produce the **float** value **2.0f** after converting the value of **num** from **char** to **float**.

6 Lastly the **double** value 90.0 is added to the **float** value **2.0f** for which Rule 2 applies, so after converting the **2.0f** to 2.0 as **double**, the final result of 92.0 is stored in **value**.

Casts in Assignment Statements

As we saw in example **EX2-03.C**, you can cause an implicit cast by writing an expression of the right hand side of an assignment that is of a different type to the variable on the left hand side. This can cause values to be changed and information to be lost. For instance, if you assign a **float** or a **double** value to an **int** or a **long** variable, then the fractional part will be lost and just the integer will be stored, assuming that it doesn't exceed the range of values available for the integer type concerned.

For example, after executing the following code fragment:

```
int number;
float decimal = 2.5f;
number = decimal;
```

the value of **number** will be 2. Any constant containing a decimal point is floating point, and if you don't want it to be double precision then you need to append the **f**. A capital **F** would do just as well. We can also define **long** integer constants by appending an **l**, or better still an upper case **L** to avoid confusion, to the integer value. Thus, **99** is a 2-byte integer, and **99L** is a 4-byte integer.

Explicit Casting

Sometimes though, the default cast rules can be inconvenient. Suppose you have an expression:

```
result = x+i/j;
```

where **x** is double and **i** and **j** are integers. Because of the way integer division works, you won't get an exact result here unless **i** is a multiple of **j**. The variable **i** will be divided by **j** and any fractional part in the result will be discarded.

You can use an explicit type cast to convert a value from one type to another. We can rewrite the last statement as:

```
result = x + (double)i/j;
```

The **(double)** in the right hand side expression causes **i** to be converted to a **double**. As a result, the value of **j** must also be converted to type **double** before the division occurs, so we now get an exact result.

Syntax of Explicit Casting

In general:

```
( type )expression
```

causes the value of **expression** to be converted to **type**, before the value is used further.

Operator Precedence

Operator **precedence** orders the operators in a priority sequence. Operators with the highest precedence are always executed before operators of a lower precedence. The precedence of the operators in C is shown in the following table:

Precedence	Operators	Associativity

High	`Function call`
	`Array indexing`
	`->   .`
		Left to right

	`!   ~   ++   —`
	`The unary operators + - & *`
	`(typecast) sizeof`
		Right to left

	`*   /   %`	Left to right
	`+   -`	Left to right
	`<<   >>`	Left to right
	`<   <=   >   >=`	Left to right
	`==   !=`	Left to right
	`&`	Left to right
	`^`	Left to right
	`|`	Left to right
	`&&`	Left to right
	`||`	Left to right
	`?:`(conditional operator)	Right to left
	`=   *=   /=   %=   +=   -=` `&=   ^=   |=   <<=   >>=`	Right to left
Low	`,` (**comma operator**)	Left to right

Here, operators in the same row are all of equal precedence. If there aren't any parentheses in an expression, then operators of equal precedence are executed in a sequence determined by their **associativity**. Thus, if the associativity is 'left to right', then the leftmost operator in an expression is executed first, progressing through the expression to the rightmost. There are a few operators you haven't seen yet, but you'll know most of them by the end of this book.

Note that where an operator has a unary (working with one operand) and a binary (working with two operands) form, the unary form is always of a higher precedence and is therefore executed first. The unary `+` and `–` apply to constants or expressions, as in `-1.234`, or `-(A+B)` for example. We will see the unary `*` in Chapter 4.

Rather than spend hours with your family and friends doing memory tests to remember the precedence table, you can always override them using parentheses. Since there are so many operators in C, sometimes it can be hard to be sure what actually takes precedence over what. In such cases it's a good idea to insert parentheses just to make sure. A further plus is that parentheses often make the code easier to read.

Variable Scope

The range of a program where you can use a certain variable is called the variable's **scope**. All variables are limited in scope. They come into existence from the place where you define them, and then at some point, when your program terminates, they disappear. Obviously they can only be used while they exist, and for some variables their scope is more limited than this.

Automatic Variables

All of the variables that we've declared thus far have been declared within a block, that is within the extent of a pair of curly braces. These are called **automatic** variables, and are said to have **local** or **block scope**. They are born when they are declared and they automatically cease to exist at the end of the block containing their declaration. You can declare variables at the beginning of any block, immediately after the opening brace.

An Example to Demonstrate Variable Scope

We can demonstrate how automatic variables behave with this example:

```
/* EX2-05.C Demonstrating variable scope */
#include <stdio.h>
int main()
{
   /* Function scope starts here - these variables last until the end
      of the program */
   int count1 = 10;
   int count3 = 50;

   printf("\nValue of outer count1 = %d", count1);

   {                                       /* New block starts here.. */
      int count1 = 20;                     /* This hides the outer count1 */
      int count2 = 30;

      printf("\nValue of inner count1 = %d", count1);

      count1 += 3;                         /* This affects the inner count1 */
      count3 += count2;
   }                                       /* ...and ends here. */

   printf("\nValue of outer count1 = %d", count1);
   printf("\nValue of outer count3 = %d", count3);

   /* Decomment the following to get an error */
   /* printf("\nValue of count2 = %d", count2); */
   return 0;
}                                          /* Function scope ends here */
```

Program Analysis

The output from this example will be:

```
Value of outer count1 = 10
Value of inner count1 = 20
Value of outer count1 = 10
Value of outer count3 = 80
```

Two variables are declared at the start of the main routine; then a new block is started, and two new local variables are declared, one of which hides the original **count1**. When that block ends, the local variables no longer exist, and you can see that changes made within the block haven't affected the value of the original **count1**.

The output statement shows by the value in the second line that we're using the `count1` in the inner block. The variable `count1` is incremented, and the increment applies to the variable in the inner block since the outer one is still hidden. However, `count3,` which was defined in the outer block, is incremented without any problem, showing that the variables defined at the beginning of the outer block are accessible within the inner block.

After the closing brace, `count2` and the inner `count1` cease to exist. The variables `count1` and `count3` are still there in the outer block, and the values displayed show that `count3` was indeed incremented in the inner block. If you de-comment the line:

```
/* printf("\nValue of count2 = %d", count2); */
```

the program will no longer compile correctly because it attempts to output a non-existent variable. You should get some kind of error message indicating that `count2` is undefined at this point.

Global Variables

Variables declared outside of all blocks and functions are called **global variables** or **globals**, and have **file scope**. This means that they're accessible throughout all the functions in the program file, after the point where they were declared. If you declare them at the very beginning, then they will be accessible throughout the file.

Since global variables are declared outside of all the blocks in a program, they continue to exist as long as the program is running. This might raise the question in your mind, 'why not make all variables global and avoid all this messing about with local variables that disappear?'. This sounds like a very attractive proposition at first, but like the Sirens of mythology they bring serious disadvantages with them that completely outweigh any advantages that you might gain.

Real programs are generally composed of a large number of statements, a significant number of functions, and a great many variables. Declaring all variables of global scope greatly magnifies the possibility of accidentally modifying a variable, as well as making the job of sensibly naming them a little difficult. By keeping variables local to a function or a block, they have almost complete protection from external effects, and the whole development process becomes much easier to manage.

There are also significant advantages in memory management when you use local variables. The memory occupied by a local variable is automatically made available for other purposes at the end of the block where the local variable is defined. This allows the same memory area to be used for many different purposes during the execution of a program.

Static Variables

It's quite conceivable that you might want to have a variable that's defined and accessible locally, but continues to exist after exiting the block in which it is declared. This will become more apparent when we come to deal with functions specifically in Chapter 5. The **static** specifier provides this. To declare a **static** variable **count** you would write:

```
static int count;
```

Although a variable declared as **static** will continue to exist for the duration of a program, if it's declared within a block, its scope will be limited to just that block. Static variables, that retain their value during subsequent visits, are always initialized to zero if you don't provide an initializer yourself. The variable **count** declared here will be initialized with 0.

Register Variables

You can indicate that you want a variable to be placed in a register in your computer, rather than in conventional memory. Operations using registers are faster than using conventional memory. They are integer variables, and only 16 are allowed on a PC. They are defined using the **register** keyword. For example, the declaration:

```
register int number;
```

declares an integer variable **number**, and requests that it be placed in a register. However, the compiler reserves the right not to put your variable in a register if it doesn't have one available.

This kind of declaration isn't used very frequently because the limited availability of registers in most contexts means that it doesn't usually produce a substantial improvement in the performance of a program.

Defining Your Own Data Type Names

If you don't like standard type names such as **long** or **double**, you can change them using the **typedef** keyword. For example, if you wanted to use **BigOne** instead of **long**, you could define **BigOne** as an alternative, with the statement:

```
typedef long BigOne;      /* Define BigOne as equivalent to long */
```

You can now use **BigOne** just as you would have used **long**. For example we can now declare a variable **Number** as type **long** with the statement:

```
BigOne Number;
```

Of course, you can still use the **long** keyword in your program too.

This may seem quite trivial at this point, since we aren't defining a new type, just an alias for an existing type. We will see later that this can become quite an asset in two contexts; in providing a simple means of expressing a complex type, and as an aid to portability where the meaning of integer types can differ on various kinds of computer.

Summary

In this chapter you've learnt all the basic types of data that you can handle in C, and almost all of the operations that you can carry out on them. The only ones missing are those associated with comparing and testing values, and we will get to those in the next chapter. You should now feel comfortable with writing a program consisting of a function **main()**, and using all of the operators we have discussed so far.

In the next chapter we will take a giant leap forward, since we will add decision making capability to the computational skills we have just gained.

Programming Exercises

1 Write a program to convert a Fahrenheit temperature value read from the keyboard to Centigrade, and display the result. The formula to do this is:

Centigrade = 5*(Fahrenheit - 32)/9

Try to do this with integers first. You should be able to get a result to the nearest degree. Then try it with floating point values.

2 Write a program to read in values of each of the types you've learnt about, and then display them. Find out what happens when you have the following sorts of errors:

The format specifier doesn't match the type of value being displayed.
You omit the **&** in front of the name of a variable in a **scanf()** argument.

3 Write a program to allow a capital letter to be entered and display the letter and its sequence number in the alphabet - A is 1, B is 2 and so on. See what happens when characters other than letters are entered.

4 Write a program to read in a **long** integer value, and then:

Alter the rightmost 8 bits of the value to 1, and display the result as an integer.
Change the 1 bits to 0 and vice versa, displaying the result as an integer.
Change the 1 bits to 0 and vice versa, add 1, and display the result.
Run the program with both positive and negative numbers as input.

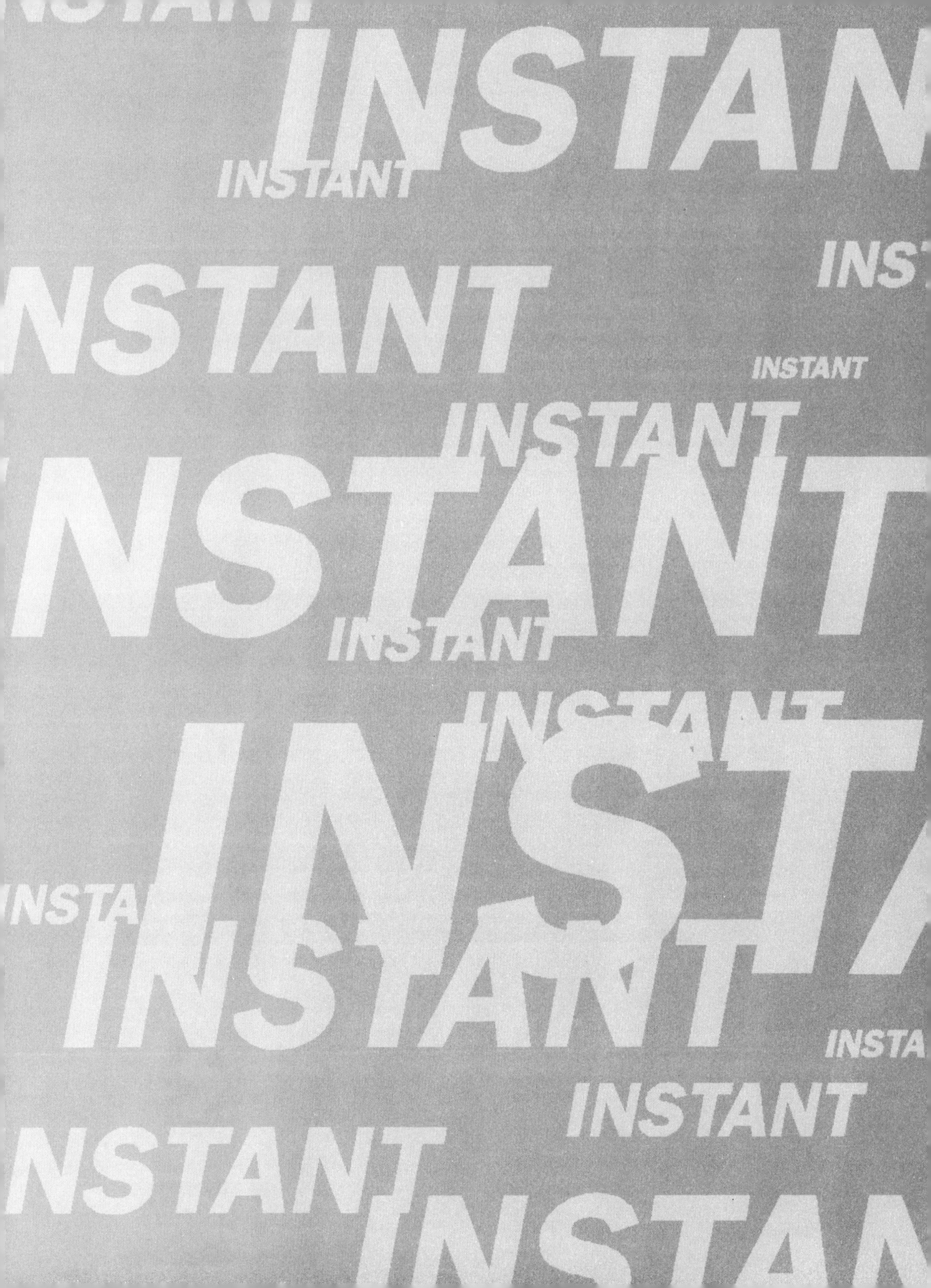
INSTANT
INSTANT
INSTANT
INSTANT
INSTANT
INSTANT
INSTANT

Chapter

Logic and Loops

In the last chapter we saw how to calculate in C. In this chapter we are going to add the potential for intelligence in a program. The language elements in this chapter, on top of those we saw in the last, provide the potential for writing chess playing programs, programs to predict the weather or possibly even the result of the next presidential election. All you have to do is figure out how.

By the end of this chapter you will have learnt:

- How to compare values, and affect the sequence of execution based on the result of a comparison.

- How to assemble multiple comparisons into a single logical expression for decision-making purposes.

- What statements are provided in C for repeating one or more statements until a given condition is satisfied, and how to apply them.

- Some additional capabilities for reading input from the keyboard and writing output to the screen.

Making Decisions

The ability to compare values and alter the course of a program based on the result is what gives your computer the power to solve problems rather than just being a big calculator. There are two aspects to decision making in your program: the means of making comparisons between items of data, and the program statements that alter the sequence of execution based on the result. We will start by comparing data values.

Relational Operators

To determine how one item of data compares to another we're going to use **relational operators**. Since character information is ultimately represented by numeric codes, we're always dealing with numbers in one way or another, so comparing numerical values is integral to all decision making. We have available to us six operators for comparing two values:

<	less than	<=	less than or equal to
>	greater than	>=	greater than or equal to
==	equal to	!=	not equal

The == Operator

The 'equal to' comparison operator has two successive equal signs. This is because a single equals sign is treated as the assignment operator. You will find that using one equals sign instead of two is a common mistake that most C programmers make. Bear this in mind because it won't necessarily cause a compiler error, but your program will behave rather differently than intended.

> Remember, you use == when you are asking whether two variables are exactly the same. You use = when you are telling them to be the same.

If you do find that you are forever typing a single equals sign instead of a pair, then try putting the constant, assuming that there is one, first. For example:

```
if (x == 10)          /*  The right version */
if (x = 10)           /*  Wrong, but valid code; the compiler
                          won't complain, and will always
                          evaluate to true! */
if (10 = x)           /*  Wrong, and illegal; the compiler
                          will complain */
```

True and False

When we make a decision in C, one action is taken if an expression is **True** (represented by 1), and another action is taken if an expression is **False** (represented by 0). In fact, this isn't strictly accurate, since in C, any non-zero integer, including -1, will be interpreted as True for decision-making purposes. We can see how this works by having a look at a few simple examples of comparisons. Let's assume that we define the following variables:

```
char First = 'A', Last = 'Z';
int i = -10, j = 20;
double x = 1.5, y = -0.25E-10
```

We can now write some examples of comparing values. Take a look at the following expressions and their equivalent values:

Expression	Value
`First == 65`	True
`First < Last`	True
`'E' <= First`	False
`First != Last`	True
`-1 < y`	True. The variable y has a very small negative value -0.000000000025, and so it's greater than -1.
`j < (10 - i)`	False
`2.0*x >= (3 + y)`	True. The expression `3 + y` is slightly less than 3, and `2.0*x` is exactly 3.

69

We can use the relational operators to compare values of any of the basic data types, so all we need now is a practical way of using the results of a comparison to modify the behavior of a program.

The if Statement

The **if** statement allows you to execute a single statement or a block of statements enclosed within curly braces if a given expression results in the value True. If the expression results in 0, which is False, then the statement or block isn't executed. This is illustrated here:

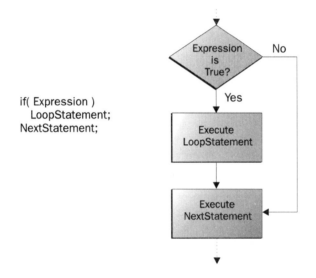

```
if( Expression )
    LoopStatement;
NextStatement;
```

A simple example of an **if** statement is:

```
if( Letter == 'A' )
    printf("\nThe first capital, alphabetically speaking.");
```

The condition to be tested appears in parentheses immediately following the keyword, **if**. Note the position of the semi-colon here. It appears after the statement following the **if**, not after the condition in parentheses. You can also see how the statement following the **if** is indented, to indicate that it's associated with the **if**.

The output statement will only be executed if the variable **Letter** has the value `'A'`. We could extend this example to change the value of **Letter,** if it contains the value `'A'`:

```
if( Letter == 'A' )
{
   printf("\nThe first capital, alphabetically speaking.");
   Letter = 'a';
}
```

Here, if the condition is True, we execute these statements in the block. Without the braces, only the first statement would be the subject of the **if**, and the statement assigning the value `'a'` to **Letter** would be executed, irrespective of the condition. Note that there is only a semi-colon after each of the statements in the block, not after the closing brace at the end of the block. Now, as a result of **Letter** having the value `'A'`, we change its value to `'a'` after outputting the same message as before. If the condition is False, there will be no message and the values aren't changed.

The else Keyword

The **if** statement we have so far used executes a statement if the expression specified results in the value True. Program execution then continues with the next statement. We also have an extended version of the **if** statement which allows one statement to be executed if the result is True, and another if the result is False. Execution then continues with the next statement after the two choices:

```
/* EX3-01.C  Using the extended if */
#include <stdio.h>
int main()
{
   long number = 0;                              /* Store input here */
   printf("\nEnter a number less that 2 billion: ");/* Prompt for input */
   scanf("%ld", &number);                        /* Read a value */

   if( number%2L )              /* Test remainder after division by 2 */
      /* Execute this if the remainder is 1 */
      printf("\nYour number is odd.");
   else
      /* Execute this if the remainder is 0 */
      printf("\nYour number is even.");

   return 0;
}
```

Note that **number%2** returns True, equivalent to **number%2 == 1**.

The **if-else** combination provides a choice between two options:

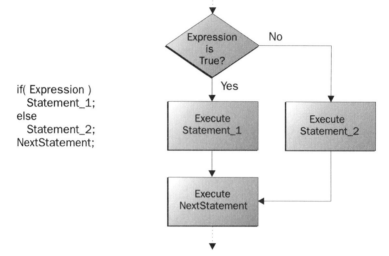

```
if( Expression )
    Statement_1;
else
    Statement_2;
NextStatement;
```

Nesting if-else Statements

You can nest **if** statements within **if** statements, **if-else** statements within **if**s, **if**s within **if-else** statements and **if-else** statements within **if-else** statements. This gives us plenty of room for serious confusion, so let's look at these with a few examples.

An Example of if-else Nesting

Taking the second case, an example of a nested **if-else** within an **if** might be:

```
if( coffee == 'y' )
    if( donuts == 'y' )
        printf("\nWe have coffee and donuts.");
    else
        printf("\nWe have coffee at least...");
```

This assumes that we have a variable **coffee,** which has the value **'y'** when there is coffee, and a variable **donuts**, indicating the similar presence (or absence) of donuts. The test for **donuts** is executed if the result of the test for **coffee** is True, so the messages reflect the correct situation in each case. However, it's easy to get this confused - if we write much the same thing with incorrect indentation we can be trapped into the wrong conclusion:

```
if( coffee == 'y' )
   if( donuts == 'y' )
      printf("\nWe have coffee and donuts.");
else                           /* This else is indented incorrectly */
   printf("\nWe have no coffee...");                        /* Wrong! */
```

This mistake is easy to see here. In spite of how it looks, the **else** doesn't belong to the first **if**; it will only be executed if there *is* coffee and there *aren't* any donuts, so when it's executed the message will always be False.

The if-else Ownership Rule

Whenever things look a bit complicated, you can apply the following rule to sort things out:

> **When you are looking at nested ifs, you need to bear in mind the rule about which if owns which else; an else always belongs to the nearest preceding if that isn't already spoken for by another else.**

When you're writing your own programs, you can always use braces to make the situation clearer.

It's not really necessary in such a simple case, but we could write the last example as:

```
if( coffee == 'y' )
{
   if( donuts == 'y' )
      printf("\nWe have coffee and donuts.");
   else
      printf("\nWe have coffee at least...");
}
```

73

Now that we know the rules, understanding the case of the `if` within the `if-else` becomes easy:

```
if( coffee == 'y' )
{
   if( donuts == 'y' )
      printf("\nWe have coffee and donuts.");
}
else
   if( tea == 'y' )
      printf("\nWe have tea at least...");
```

Here the braces are essential. If we leave them out, then the `else` would belong to the `if` which is looking out for `donuts`. In this kind of situation it's easy to forget to include them and create a logic error, which may be quite hard to locate.

The last case can get very messy even with just one level of nesting. Coffee and donuts are always welcome, so let's have some more:

```
if( coffee == 'y' )
   if( donuts == 'y' )
      printf("\nWe have coffee and donuts.");
   else
      printf("\nWhat only coffee, no donuts?");
else
   if( tea == 'y' )
      printf("\nWe have tea at least...");
   else
      printf("\nNo tea or coffee, but maybe donuts...");
```

This is starting to look slightly muddled. As the rule will verify that this is correct, no braces are necessary, but having them makes things clearer:

```
if( coffee == 'y' )
{
   if( donuts == 'y' )
      printf("\nWe have coffee and donuts.");
   else
      printf("\nWhat only coffee, no donuts?");
}
else
{
   if( tea == 'y' )
      printf("\nWe have tea at least...");
   else
      printf("\nNo tea or coffee, but maybe donuts...");
}
```

If you combine enough nested **if**s, you can almost guarantee a mistake somewhere.

Logical Operators

As we have just seen, where we have two or more related conditions, using **if**s can be a little cumbersome. We have tried our 'iffy' talents on the important question of whether there is coffee and donuts, but in practice you may want to check more complex conditions. You could be searching a personnel file for someone who is over 21 but under 35, is female with a college degree but not in psychology, and who is unmarried and fluent in Quechua or Waica. Defining a test for this could involve an **if** to make your eyes water.

Logical operators provide a neat and simple solution. We can combine a series of comparisons using logical operators within a single expression, ending up with just one **if**, virtually regardless of the complexity of the conditions. We have just three logical operators at our disposal:

```
&&    logical AND
||    logical OR
!     logical negation (NOT)
```

Let's consider how each of these are used.

AND

You would use the logical AND operator, **&&**, where you have two conditions and you want both to be True, giving a True result. This is the case when testing for upper case. For example, the value being tested must be greater than or equal to `'A'`, *and* less than or equal to `'Z'`. If either or both conditions aren't True, then the value isn't a capital letter. If we take the example of a value stored in a **char** variable **Letter**, we could write the test that originally used two **if**s as a single **if**:

```
if( (Letter >='A') && (Letter<='Z') )
    printf("\nThis is a capital letter.");
```

Here the output statement will only be executed if both of the conditions combined by the operator **&&** are True. The effect of logical operators is often shown using a truth table, just as we did in the previous chapter. Please refer back to those if you need a reference.

OR

The OR operator, ||, applies when you have two conditions and you want a True result if either (or both) of them are True. For example, you might be considered creditworthy for a loan from the bank if your income was at least $100,000 a year, or if you had $1,000,000 in cash. This could be tested using the following `if`:

```
if( (Income >= 100000) || ( Capital >= 1000000) )
   printf("\nHow much would you like to borrow?");
```

The response emerges when either or both of the conditions are True. A better response might be *"Why* do you want to borrow?".

NOT

The third logical operator, !, takes one operand with a logical value, True or False, and inverts its value. So if the value of `Test` is True, then `!Test` becomes False. For example, if `x` has the value 10, then

```
!( x > 5 )
```

is False, since `x > 5` is True.

Using Several Logical Operators

You can combine conditional expressions and logical operators to the degree that you feel comfortable with. For example, we could construct a test for whether a variable contained a letter, just using a single `if`.

An Example

Let's write it as a working example:

```
/* EX3-02.C  Testing for a letter using logical operators */
#include <stdio.h>
int main()
{
   char Letter = 0;

   printf("\nEnter a character: ");
   scanf("%c", &Letter);
```

```
    /* Test for alphabetic */
    if( ((Letter>='A')&&(Letter<='Z')) || ((Letter>='a')&&(Letter<='z')) )
      printf("\nYou entered a letter.");
    else
      printf("\nYou didn't enter a letter.");
    return 0;
}
```

Program Analysis

The interesting part of this program is in the **if** statement condition, consisting of two logical expressions combined with the OR operator.

```
if( ((Letter>='A')&&(Letter<='Z')) || ((Letter>='a')&&(Letter<='z')) )
```

Each combines a pair of comparisons with the operator AND, so both must be True if the logical expression combining them is to be True. The first logical expression is True if the input is upper case, and the second is True if the input is lower case.

The Conditional Operator

The **conditional operator**, sometimes called the **ternary operator**, enables you to choose to execute one of two expressions, depending on the value of a True or False condition.

Syntax of the Conditional Operator

The conditional operator can generally be written as:

```
condition ? expression1 : expression2
```

If **condition** evaluates as True, then the result is the value of **expression1**, and if it evaluates to False, then the result is the value of **expression2**. It's best understood by looking at an example.

A Conditional Operator Example

Suppose we have two variables, **a** and **b**, and we want to assign the maximum value between them to a third variable, **c**. We can do this with the statement:

```
c = a>b ? a : b;                    /* Set c to the maximum of a and b */
```

77

The conditional operator has a logical expression as its first argument, in this case a very simple one, **a>b**. If this expression has the value 1 (True), then the second operand, **a** in this case, is returned as a value. If it's False, then the third operand, **b** in this case, is returned instead. Thus the result of the conditional expression is **a**, if **a** is greater than **b**, and **b**, if **a** is less than **b**. This value is stored in **c**. The equivalent **if** statement is:

```
if( a> b )
    c = a;
else
    c = b;
```

However, the conditional operator doesn't give you the same flexibility as an **if**. It will only allow you to choose between two different expressions. If you need to do several things with either choice, then the way to go is with an **if** statement.

The switch Statement

The **switch** statement enables you to select from a number of choices based on a fixed set of values for a given expression. We can examine how the **switch** statement works with the following example of a program that was an early contender for the home market, but didn't sell very well:

```
/* EX3-03.C  Using the switch statement */
#include <stdio.h>
int main()
{
   int choice = 0;

   printf("\nYour electronic recipe book is at your service."
          "\nYou can choose from the following delicious dishes: "
          "\n\n\t1 Boiled eggs"
          "\n\t2 Fried eggs"
          "\n\t3 Scrambled eggs"
          "\n\t4 Coddled eggs"
          "\n\n\tEnter your selection number: ");
   scanf("%d", &choice);

   switch( choice )
   {
      case 1: printf("\nBoil some eggs.");
               break;
      case 2: printf("\nFry some eggs.");
               break;
```

```
        case 3: printf("\nScramble some eggs.");
                    break;
        case 4: printf("\nCoddle some eggs.");
                    break;
        default: printf("\nYou entered a wrong number, try raw eggs.");
    }

    return 0;
}
```

Program Analysis

The first **printf()** statement introduces something new - the output of several lines of text, all in one batch:

```
printf("\nYour electronic recipe book is at your service."
        "\nYou can choose from the following delicious dishes: "
        "\n\n\t1 Boiled eggs"
        "\n\t2 Fried eggs"
        "\n\t3 Scrambled eggs"
        "\n\t4 Coddled eggs"
        "\n\n\tEnter your selection number: ");
```

Each line appears between double quotes, and there is no comma separating one from the next. When you write two or more strings between quotes with just whitespace separating them, they will be treated as though they were one long string by an ANSI C compiler. This allows you to space them out in a readable fashion, without having to write multiple **printf()** statements. Note how a **\t** (a tab character) is used to indent the choices when they are displayed.

The **switch** keyword is followed by a test condition in parentheses, which must evaluate to an integer value. The possible choices in the **switch** are identified by **case** labels, whose expressions should match the expected values taken by the test condition.

The break Statement

The statements to be executed for a particular **case** are written following the colon after the **case** label and are normally terminated by a **break** statement which transfers execution to the statement after the **switch**. The **break** isn't mandatory, but it stops the switch from continuing down the list of cases.

Note that breaking out of the normal flow of a program is considered to be bad programming style. It is best to try and avoid using **break** in every circumstance, and only use it when you deem it necessary.

The Flow of a switch Statement

If the value of **choice** doesn't correspond with any of the **case** values specified, then the statements preceded by the non-mandatory **default** label are executed. In its absence the **switch** is exited and the program continues with the next statement after the **switch**:

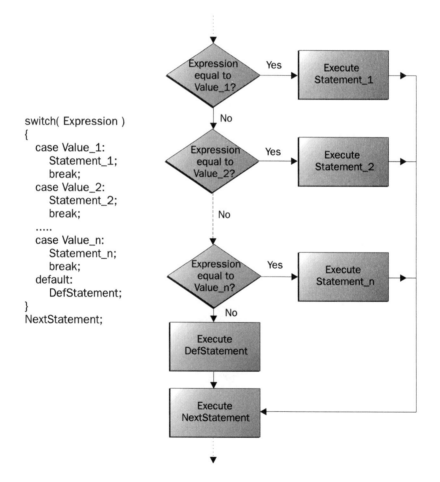

```
switch( Expression )
{
   case Value_1:
      Statement_1;
      break;
   case Value_2:
      Statement_2;
      break;
   .....
   case Value_n:
      Statement_n;
      break;
   default:
      DefStatement;
}
NextStatement;
```

Each of the **case** constant expressions must be constant and unique. If two **case** constants are the same, the compiler would have no way of knowing which should be executed for that value.

Sharing case Actions

However, different **case**s don't need to have a unique action; several **case**s can share the same action, as is shown in the following example:

```c
/* EX3-04.C  A case of multiple case actions */
#include <stdio.h>
int main()
{
    char Letter = 0;
    printf("\nEnter a lower-case letter: ");
    scanf("%c", &Letter);

    switch( Letter*( Letter>='a' && Letter <='z' ) )
    {
        case 'a':
        case 'e':
        case 'i':
        case 'o':
        case 'u': printf("\nYou entered a vowel.");
        break;

        case 0: printf("\nIt is not a lower-case letter.");
        break;

        default: printf("\nYou entered a consonant.");
    }
    return 0;
}
```

Program Analysis

In this example, we have a more complex expression in the **switch**. If the given character isn't a lower case letter then the expression:

   (Letter>='a' && Letter <='z')

will result in the value 0. This will then cause the statements following the label **case   0** to be executed. As long as the character entered is lower case, the variable **Letter** will be multiplied by 1, and will retain its original value.

If a lower case letter is entered for all values corresponding to vowels, the same output statement is executed. This is achieved by writing each of the **case** labels corresponding to the five vowels one after the other, before the statements to be executed. If a lower case consonant is entered, since there are no **case** labels corresponding to this situation, the **default** label statement is executed.

The goto Statement

The **if** statement provides you with the flexibility to choose to execute one set of statements or another depending on a specified condition, so the statement execution sequence is varied depending on data values in the program. In contrast, the **goto** statement is a blunt instrument, providing the possibility to branch to a specified program statement, *unconditionally*.

The statement to be branched to must be identified by a **statement label**. These identifiers are defined according to the same rules as a variable name, but are distinct from the labels of other entities. The statement label is followed by a colon and placed before the statement requiring labeling. Here is an example:

```
MyLabel: x = 1;
```

This statement has the label **MyLabel**, and an unconditional branch to this position, in the same function of the program, would be written as:

```
goto MyLabel;
```

Using **goto**s (like **break**s) in your program should be avoided as much as possible. They tend to encourage very convoluted code that can be extremely difficult to follow, and if you ever get the program working it can become a nightmare to maintain. As the **goto** is theoretically unnecessary there is always an alternative approach, and a significant cadre of programmers say that it should never be used.

Repeating a Block of Statements

The ability to repeat a group of statements is fundamental to most applications. This programming mechanism is called a **loop**. Without loops, an organization would need to modify the payroll program every time an extra employee was hired. Without loops, you would need to restart your word processor every time you wanted to open another document. So let's first understand how a loop works.

What is a Loop?

A loop is basically the execution of a sequence of statements until a particular condition is True (or False). We can actually write a loop with the C statements we have met so far. We just need an **if** and the dreaded **goto**.

An Example of a Loop

For example:

```
/* EX3-05.C  Creating a loop with an if and a goto */

#include <stdio.h>
int main()
{
   int i = 0, sum = 0;
   const int MAX = 10;

   i = 1;                      /* i is the loop counter - starting at 1 */
   loop:
      sum += i;                /* Add current value of i to sum */
      if (++i <= MAX)          /* Execute the loop MAX number of times */
         goto loop;            /* Go back to loop until i > MAX */

   printf("\nSum = %d\ni = %d", sum, i );

   return 0;
}
```

Program Analysis

This program accumulates the sum of integers from 1 to **MAX**, where **MAX** has been initialized to 10. The first time through the sequence of statements beginning with the statement label **loop**, **i** is 1 and it's added to **sum** which is zero. In the **if**, **i** is incremented by 1, and as long as it's less than or equal to **MAX**, then the unconditional branch to **loop** occurs. The cycle begins again and the value of **i**, now 2, is added to **sum**. This continues with **i** being incremented and added to **sum** each time until finally, **i** is incremented to 11 in the **if**, and the branch back won't be executed. If you run this example, you will get the output:

```
sum = 55
i = 11
```

This quite clearly shows how the loop works, but it has two serious disadvantages. It uses a **goto**, and it introduces another label into our program, both of which we really should be avoiding.

We can achieve the same thing and more with the next statement that we are going to have a look at, which is specifically used for writing a loop.

Using the for Loop

The **for** loop works in a way that looks like an analog of the loop we created using an **if** and a **goto** in the last example.

Syntax of the for Loop

The general form of the **for** loop is:

```
for( initializing_expression ; test_expression ;
increment expression )
    loop_statement;
```

Of course, **loop_statement** can be a block of code between braces. The sequence of events in executing the **for** loop is shown here:

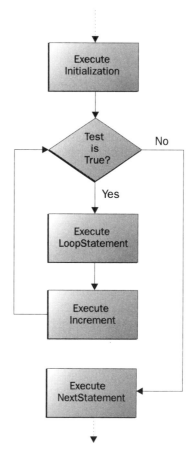

```
for( Initialization ; Test ; Increment )
   LoopStatement;
NextStatement;
```

An Example of the for Loop

So let's get a preliminary understanding of how a **for** loop works by
rewriting the last example to use it:

```c
/* EX3-06.C  Summing integers with a for loop */
#include <stdio.h>
int main()
{
   int i = 0, sum = 0;
   const int MAX = 10;
```

```
    for ( i = 1 ; i <= MAX ; i++ )       /* Loop specification */
      sum += i;                          /* Loop statement */

    printf("\nSum = %d\ni = %d", sum, i );

    return 0;
}
```

Program Analysis

This program gives exactly the same output as the previous example, but has accomplished it without a label and using only two lines of code:

```
    for ( i = 1 ; i <= MAX ; i++ )       /* Loop specification */
      sum += i;                          /* Loop statement */
```

The conditions determining the operation of the loop appear in the **for** statement, and there are three expressions that appear within the parentheses after the keyword **for**. The first sets **i** to 1 as the initial condition, the second specifies the condition that must be True in order to continue to loop, in this case as long as **i** is less than or equal to **MAX**, and the third is the action to be taken each time the loop executes.

> Any time you find yourself repeating something more than a couple of times, then it's worth considering a **for** loop. They will usually save you time and memory.

Actually, this loop isn't exactly the same as the version in **EX3-05.C** - it can behave differently. You can demonstrate this if you set the value of **MAX** to 0 in both programs and run them again. You will find that the value of **sum** is 1 in **EX3-05.C**, and 0 in the **for** loop version, and the value of **i** differs too. The reason for this is that the **if** version of the program always executes the loop at least once, since the condition isn't checked until the end. The **for** loop doesn't, so the condition is evidently checked at the beginning.

The Infinite for Loop

If you omit the test condition, the value is assumed to be True, so the loop will continue indefinitely unless you provide some other means of exiting from it. In fact, if you like, you can omit all the expressions in the parentheses after the **for**. This may not seem very useful, but in fact quite the reverse is true. Have a look at the following example:

```
/* EX3-07.C  Using an infinite for loop to compute an average */

#include <stdio.h>

int main()
{
    double value = 0.0;        /* Value entered stored here */
    double sum = 0.0;          /* Total of values accumulated here */
    int i = 0;                 /* Count of number of values */
    char indicator = 'n';      /* Continue or not? */

    for( ;; )                  /* Infinite loop */
    {
        printf("\nEnter a value: ");    /* Prompt for input */
        scanf("%lf", &value);           /* Read a value */

        ++i;                            /* Increment count */
        sum += value;                   /* Add current input to total */

        printf("\nDo you want to enter another value ( enter n to end )?");
        scanf(" %c", &indicator);       /* Read indicator */

        /* Now test for no indicator - n or N */
        if ( (indicator == 'n') || ( indicator == 'N') )
            break;                      /* Exit from loop if no */
    }

    printf("\nThe average of  the %d"
           " values you entered is %f", i, sum/i);

    return 0;
}
```

Program Analysis

This program will compute the average of an arbitrary number of values. After each value is entered, you need to indicate if you want to enter another value.

Typical output is:

Enter a value: 10
Do you want to enter another value (enter n to end)? y

Enter a value: 20
Do you want to enter another value (enter n to end)? y

Enter a value: 30
Do you want to enter another value (enter n to end)? n

The average of the 3 values you entered is 20.000000

After declaring and initializing the variables we need, we start a **for** loop with no expressions specified, so there's no provision for ending it here. The block immediately following is the subject of the loop which is to be repeated, and if the program is ever to end, a means of ending the loop must appear in this block (note the '**break**' statement, which is used to exit from the loop if the user decides not to continue).

Infinite loops are not considered to be very good practice - they are dangerous, because of the restrictive nature of their structure. Unless you include a suitable number of good opt-out clauses, then a user of your software (which may unwittingly be yourself) would be unable to exit from the loop, and thus unable to leave your program. For now though, because you're just in the cocoon stage of C programming you should be aware of such tricks and all their dangers.

Input/Output Tips

You should compare the format specifiers used in the last example for inputting a **double** value using **scanf()**, and outputting a **double** value using **printf()**. On input, **%f** specifies that you want to read a **float** value, and **%lf** specifies that you're inputting a value into a **double** variable. It's important to use the correct specifier, otherwise the value stored will be incorrect and may actually overwrite important parts of memory.

So how do we get more digits displayed if we're dealing with a **double** value? First of all, we can specify a field width for the output value in a similar manner to the way integer output is used, so **%15f** specifies a field width of 15. The default number of output digits after the decimal point is 6, but you can increase this by specifying a precision value after the field width, separated from it by a decimal point. So, to display a **double** value in a field width of 15, with 10 digits after the decimal point, you would use the specifier **%15.10f**. Try out a few variations of this example to get the feel of how field width and precision work when outputting floating point values.

Please refer to Appendix A for more information on input and output formatting.

The continue Statement

Besides **break,** there is another statement that is used to affect the control of a loop - the **continue** statement, written simply as:

```
continue;
```

Executing **continue** within a loop immediately starts the next loop iteration, skipping any remaining statements in the current one.

A continue Example

We can demonstrate this with the following code fragment:

```
int i = 0, value = 0, product = 1;
for( i = 1 ; i <= 10 ; i++ )
{
  scanf(" %d", &value);

  if( value == 0 )               /* If value is zero */
     continue;                   /* skip to next iteration */

  product *= value;
}
```

This loop reads 10 values with the intention of producing the product of the values entered. The **if** checks whether the value entered was zero, and if it was, the **continue** statement skips to the next iteration. Obviously, if this occurred on the last iteration then the loop would end.

Using continue

The **continue** statement provides a very useful capability, particularly with complex loops, where you may need to skip to the end of the current iteration from different points in the loop.

The effect of the **break** and **continue** statements on the logic of a **for** loop is illustrated here:

```
for( Initialization ; Test ; Increment )
{
   .....
   if(Expression1)
      break;
   if(Expression2)
      continue;
   .....
}
NextStatement;
```

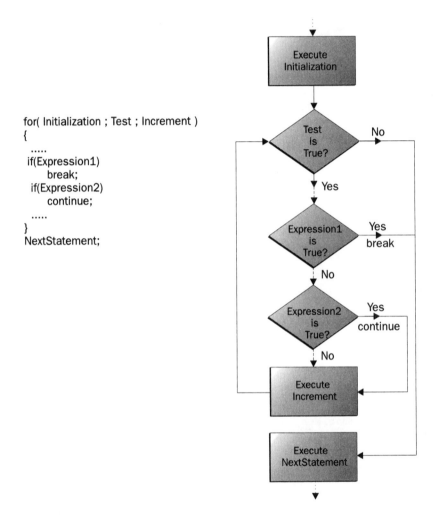

The **break** and **continue** statements can also be used with other kinds of loop, which we'll be investigating in the next few sections.

Alternative Iteration Count Variables

So far, we have only used integers to count loop iterations. You are in no way restricted as to which type of variable you use to count iterations. Look at the following example:

```
/* EX3-8.C  Display ASCII codes for alphabetic characters */
#include <stdio.h>
int main()
{
    /* Declare variables, pointing to the start of the alphabet */
    char capital = 'A', small = 'a';

    /* Display headings, appropriately spaced */
    printf("\n\tCharacter    Hex        Dec"
            "\tCharacter    Hex        Dec");

    /* Loop through the alphabet, displaying each one in three
        formats - as a character, a hex digit, and a decimal digit */

    for(; capital<='Z'; capital++,small++)
        printf("\n\t     %c%10X%10d\t     %c%10X%10d",
                    capital, capital, capital, small, small, small);

    return 0;
}
```

Program Analysis

The way in which a value is displayed is determined entirely by the format specifier. A value is displayed as a character by using %c, preceded by four spaces to align it with the heading. A value is displayed as a hexadecimal value in a field 10 characters wide, with the specifier %10X. This will display hexadecimal digits with values from 10 to 15, as A to F. If you prefer lower case 'a' and 'f', then you can use the specifier %10x. By default, the value will be right justified. If you wanted it to be left justified, you would use %-10X. The decimal versions of **capital** and **small** are displayed using the specifier %10d, which we have already seen. This is also in a field width of 10 characters. Remember that Appendix A summarizes how input and output is formatted.

You can also use a floating point value as a loop counter. An example of a **for** loop with this kind of counter is as follows:

91

```
double a = 0.3, b = 2.5;              /* Equation coefficients */
double x = 0.0;                       /* Equation variable */
for( ; x <= 2.0 ; x += .25 )
   printf("\n\tx = %f\ta*x + b = %f", x, a*x + b);
```

This calculates the value of **a*x + b** for values of **x** from 0.0 to 2.0 in steps of 0.25.

> Note that there are potential problems with using floating point values to control a loop. Decimal floating point numbers don't always have an exact binary representation. For example, if you start with **x** as zero and increment it repeatedly by 0.1, you may never reach the exact value of 1.0. You should therefore avoid checks for *exact* equality when using floating point values to control a loop, or you may end up with an infinite loop when you least expect it.

The while Loop

Now that we're expert **for** loop coders, let's look at a different kind of loop - the **while** loop. With a **while** loop, the mechanism for repeating a set of statements allows execution to continue as long as a specified expression has the value True.

Syntax of the while Loop

This loop will continue as long as the specified expression is True:

```
while( expression )
   loop_statement;
```

The **loop_statement** will be constantly repeated as long as **expression** has the value True. Once the value becomes False, the program continues with the statement following straight after the loop. Of course, a block of statements between braces could replace the single loop statement. The logic of the **while** loop is represented in this diagram:

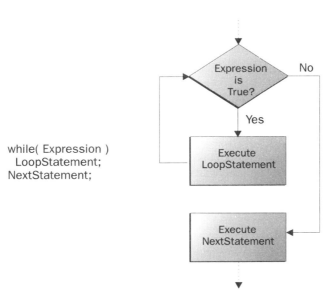

```
while( Expression )
    LoopStatement;
NextStatement;
```

A while Loop Example

We could rewrite our program to compute an average using the **while** form of loop:

```c
/* EX3-9.C  Using a while loop to compute an average */

#include <stdio.h>
int main()
{
    double value = 0.0;         /* Value entered stored here */
    double sum = 0.0;           /* Total of values accumulated here */
    int i = 0;                  /* Count of number of values */
    char indicator = 'y';       /* Continue or not? */

    while( indicator == 'y' ) /* Loop as long as y is entered */
    {
        printf("\nEnter a value: ");
        scanf(" %lf", &value);          /* Read a value */
        ++i;                            /* Increment */
        sum += value;                   /* Add current input to total */

        printf("\nDo you want to enter another value ( enter n to end )?");
        scanf(" %c", &indicator);       /* Read indicator */
    }
```

```
    printf("\nThe average of  the %d"
          " values you entered is %f.", i, sum/i);

    return 0;
}
```

Program Analysis

For the same input, this version of the program will produce exactly the same output as before. It was necessary to initialize **indicator** with a 'y' in place of an 'n', otherwise the **while** loop would terminate immediately. As long as the condition in the **while** is True, the loop continues.

It would be better if the loop condition were extended to allow 'Y' to be entered, as well as 'y'. At the moment, the loop will end if you enter 'Y' - it's easy to overlook such simple limitations. Modifying the **while** loop like this would do the trick:

```
while( indicator=='y' || indicator=='Y' )
{
    ...
}
```

The Infinite while Loop

You can also create an infinite **while** loop by using a condition that's always True:

```
while( 1 )
{
    ...
}
```

Naturally, the same requirements that applied to the infinite **for** loop, should be adopted here as well - in other words, there *must* be some way to exit within the loop.

The do-while Loop

The **do-while** loop is similar to the **while** loop in that it continues as long as the specified expression remains True. The main difference is that the condition is checked at the end of the **do-while** loop, not at the beginning. Thus the loop statement is always executed at least once.

Syntax of the do-while Loop

The general form of the **do-while** loop is:

```
do
{
    ...
}while( expression );
```

The logic of this form of loop is shown in this illustration:

```
do
{
    LoopStatement;
}while(Expression);
NextStatement;
```

A do-while Example

We could replace the **while** loop in the last version of the program to calculate an average with a **do-while** loop:

```
do
{
  printf("\nEnter a value: ");
  scanf(" %lf", &value);                 /* Read a value */
  ++i;                                   /* Increment */
  sum += value;                          /* Add current input to total */

  printf("\nDo you want to enter another value ( enter n to end )?");
  scanf(" %c", &indicator);              /* Read indicator */
}while( (indicator=='y') || (indicator=='Y') );
```

There is little to choose between them except that, for correct operation, this version doesn't depend on the initial value set. As long as you want to enter at least one value - which isn't unreasonable for the calculation in question - then this version is preferable.

> Notice the semi-colon after the `while` statement in a `do-while` loop. There isn't one in the `while` loop.

The `do-while` loop is rarely used compared with the other two forms. Keep it in the back of your mind though, because when you need a loop that executes at least once, it delivers the goods.

Summary

In this chapter we've assembled all of the essential mechanisms for making decisions in C, and we've also gone through all the facilities for repeating a group of statements. The essentials of what we have discussed are:

- The basic decision-making capability is based on the set of **relational operators**, which allow expressions to be tested and compared, yielding a value of True or False.

- When a condition is tested, True is normally represented by 1, although any non-zero integer will also be interpreted as True, and False is represented by 0.

- The decision-making capability in C is provided by the **if** statement, the **switch** statement and the **conditional operator**.

- There are three basic methods provided for repeating a group of statements. They are:

  The **for** loop which allows the loop to repeat a given number of times.

  The **while** loop which allows a loop to continue as long as a specified condition is True.

  The **do-while** loop which executes the loop at least once and allows continuation of the loop as long as a specified condition is True.

- The **continue** keyword allows you to skip the remainder of the current iteration in a loop and go straight to the next iteration.

- The keyword **break** provides an immediate exit from a loop, and an exit from a **switch** at the end of a group of statements for a given case value.

Programming Exercises

1 Write a program to compute the maximum and minimum of an arbitrary number of values entered from the keyboard. The program should allow more than one sequence of input to be entered. Use an input prompt to control whether more data is to be entered and when the program is to end.

2 Write a program to create and display a multiplication table for two ranges of values entered and defined from the keyboard. Make the range with the least number of values run across the screen in a row.

3 Write a program to display all the ASCII characters in a 16x16 table, which has the first hexadecimal digit of a given character as a row label, and the second hexadecimal digit as a column label.

4 A prime number is an integer that is only exactly divisible by 1 and itself. Write a program to compute all the primes less than or equal to an integer entered from the keyboard.

> (Hint: for each number greater than 2 and less than the number entered, check that it isn't even. Also check that it isn't divisible by any odd number greater than 1, and less than or equal to the number being tested.)

Chapter

Arrays and Pointers

In this chapter we will look at how collections of data can be created and manipulated. The methods involved here for dealing with data indirectly are very characteristic of C, and are a major reason why the language is so powerful. By the end of this chapter you will understand:

- What arrays are, how they are created and used.
- How to use arrays for holding and processing character strings.
- How to declare and use multi-dimensional arrays.
- What the operator **sizeof** is used for.
- What a pointer is and how it works.
- The relationship between pointers and arrays.
- How to process strings using pointers.
- How you can allocate and use memory during the execution of your program.

Collections of Data Values

Each type of variable that we've used up until now has contained only a single item of information (incidentally, such variables are often referred to as **scalar** variables). The most obvious extension necessary to handle applications of a broader scope would be the ability to reference several data elements of a particular type by using a single variable name.

A Simple Scenario

Suppose you had a fanatical interest in the weather and wanted to record the rainfall, together with maximum and minimum temperatures, on a daily basis throughout the year. Since there are a maximum of 366 days in a year, this would involve a maximum of 366 values for each of the three types of data. So we could record these three types of data under the names `TempMax`, `TempMin` and `Rainfall`.

Now, in order to feed your computer with this information and to form some sort of opinion on it, you want to be able to reference any set of the data items by their generic name. You also want to be able to select a particular member of each set by some means, the rainfall figure for day 62, for example.

Arrays

The mechanism in C to do all of this, and more, is called an **array**. An array is simply a block of several contiguous memory locations, each of which can store an item of data of a given type, say **int** or **double**, and be referenced through a common variable name. Each of the recorded data values of rainfall can be stored in a single array, which we have agreed to name `Rainfall`.

Declaring an Array

To declare an array with the name `Rainfall` to store values of type **float**, you would use the declaration statement:

```
float Rainfall[366];                 /* An array to store rain data */
```

The size of the array appears between square brackets immediately after the array name, so here we've declared the array `Rainfall[]` as being able to store 366 separate values, which are normally referred to as **elements** of the array. When referring to an array in the text, we will include the square brackets to make it clear that we're dealing with an array, and not a variable or a function.

Since a single `float` value normally occupies 4 bytes and we have 366 values in the array, the total memory occupied by the array `Rainfall[]` is a significant amount - 1464 bytes.

Index Values

Individual elements in an array are referenced by an **index value**. The first has the sequence number 0, the second 1 and so on. Alternatively, you can envisage the index value as an offset from the first element in the array, so that the second element is offset by 1 from the first, the second element is offset by 2 from the first and so on.

> Remember, the last element always has an index of one less than the number of elements.

An Example of Index Values

Assuming that you're going to store the rainfall figures in sequence, the index value to access the value for day 62 would be 61, and you would reference this element with the expression `Rainfall[61]`. Due to a leaking fire hydrant, which always leaks on this day, you need to apply a correction factor of six inches. A C program statement to do this would be:

```
Rainfall[61] = Rainfall[61] + 6;          /* Correct for leaky hydrant */
```

This demonstrates that you can use an array element reference just like a normal variable.

Using Index Values

An integer was used as the index value, when we applied the hydrant correction factor, but we can use any expression that results in a valid index for the array concerned. If you know that your equipment for recording rainfall consistently produces values that are in error and that they should be 90% of the values recorded, you can correct all the values for the year with a loop:

```
for( i=0 ; i<366 ; i++ )
Rainfall[i] *= 0.9f;
```

It's a very compact piece of code for processing 366 elements, isn't it? This loop will multiply each element of the array **Rainfall[]** by 0.9, starting with the element referenced by an index value of 0, up to the element referenced by 365.

Arrays in Memory

It can sometimes be useful to understand how an array is laid out in memory. Assuming that the array starts at address 0x1000 in memory, the basic structure of an array is:

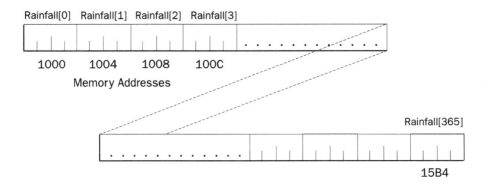

float Rainfall[366];

Arrays are usually stored in memory in ascending address order, so successive elements will be at regular increments of 4 bytes (since each **float** value occupies 4 bytes).

It's your responsibility to make sure that the index values in your program stay within the valid range for your array. Attempts to reference memory locations outside of an array will cause an error on machines with memory protection in operation, or worse, let your program continue for a while, only to trip you up later on.

Initializing Arrays

Arrays can be initialized when they're declared, just like scalar variables. In the case of an array, initial values are given in braces, like this:

```
int tempMax[12] = { 50, 45, 52, 60, 66, 69, 67, 84, 85, 71, 67, 53 };
```

Each value is assigned to an individual array element, starting from element zero, so that `tempMax[0]` is '50', `tempMax[2]` is '52' and so on.

Be careful that you don't include more values than there are elements in the array! Of course, you can have fewer values, and those not given values will be initialized with zeros. Note that array elements will only be set to zero if there's some sort of initialization list present. If there isn't, then garbage values are likely to be present and liable to cause serious problems.

An Example of Arrays

Let's suppose that you're able to generate rainfall by firing a 300 pound package containing a secret compound into the air with a giant catapult you have erected in your yard. This only works, however, when the temperature has been below 70 degrees Fahrenheit for the past month, and you only want to risk trying it (because of the unscientific, abusive, unreasonable and unpleasant reaction of neighbors) when the mean rainfall is below the annual average for two successive months. All you need, to be the hero of the weather scene, is a program which will tell you when to fire the catapult. The following program will test out the methodology with data for a whole year:

```
/* EX4-01.C  Determining when to make it rain */

#include <stdio.h>
```

```
#define SAMPLES 12                         /* Number of data samples */

int main()
{
    const int CRITICALT = 70;             /* Critical temperature */

    int TempMax[SAMPLES] = { 50,45,52,60,66,69,67,84,85,71,67,53 };

    float Rainfall[SAMPLES] = { 1.2f, 2.4f, 6.9f, 4.1f, 2.1f, 2.3f, 0.2f,
    1.8f, 3.7f, 3.1f, 2.9f, 1.1f };

    float RainMean = 0.0f;                /* Average rainfall */
    float BiMonthRain = 0.0f;             /* Mean of 2 months rain */
    int i = 0;

    /* Calculate the average rainfall */
    for( i=0 ; i<SAMPLES ; i++)
        RainMean += Rainfall[i];          /* Sum total rainfall and */
    RainMean /= SAMPLES;                  /* divide by number of samples */

    for( i=0 ; i<SAMPLES-1 ; i++)
    {
        BiMonthRain = (Rainfall[i] + Rainfall[i+1])/2.0f;
        if( (BiMonthRain<RainMean) && (TempMax[i+1]<CRITICALT) )
            printf("\nFire the catapult for month %d!", i+2);
    }

    return 0;
}
```

Program Analysis

This program works extremely well, producing the output:

Fire the catapult for month 2!
Fire the catapult for month 6!
Fire the catapult for month 7!
Fire the catapult for month 12!

This means that you would have had four rainmaking opportunities in the year. In all probability, it also means that the neighbors will insist that you dismantle the catapult and take dancing lessons, but let's see how it works anyway.

We have something new in the line of code:

```
#define SAMPLES 12          /* Number of data samples */
```

This is a pre-processor command that will be processed before the program is compiled. It defines the string **SAMPLES** as being equivalent to 12, so wherever **SAMPLES** appears, it'll be replaced by 12. The **#define** command enables you to avoid the use of explicit numbers by enabling you to use a more meaningful mnemonic instead. There are quite a few more pre-processor commands, and we will be looking at these in Chapter 9.

Both arrays, **TempMax[]** and **Rainfall[]**, are declared with **SAMPLES** number of elements, and their values are included in an initializing list for each.

Because we're dealing with pairs of months, corresponding to index values **i** and **i+1**, the **for** loop index runs from 0 to **SAMPLES-1**:

```
for( i=0 ; i<SAMPLES-1 ; i++)
```

The average of two successive months is stored in the variable **BiMonthRain**, and this is used in the following **if** statement to determine when the rainmaking should take place:

```
BiMonthRain = (Rainfall[i] + Rainfall[i+1])/2.0f;
   if( (BiMonthRain<RainMean) && (TempMax[i+1]<CRITICALT) )
      printf("\nFire the catapult for month %d!", i+2);
```

The **if** expression uses a logical **&&** to combine the conditions that **BiMonthRain** should be less than the annual average, and the maximum temperature for that month should be less than the critical temperature. The message will only be output by the **printf()** function when both conditions are fulfilled.

You could avoid the need for the variable **BiMonthRain** by substituting the expression actually in the **if** statement, but it makes the program a little less clear, and hardly seems worth it just to save 4 bytes.

Character Arrays and String Handling

An array of type **char** is called a character array and is generally used to store a **string**. A character array is handled a little differently from an array of numeric values, since you frequently want to treat it as a single entity, whereas a numeric array is almost always a set of distinct values.

A character array of a given number of elements may be used to store strings of different lengths at different times. For these reasons, a character string in C is a sequence of characters, with a special character appended to indicate the end of the string. The string-terminating character is defined by the escape sequence `'\0'` and is referred to as a null character. The representation of a string in memory is shown here:.

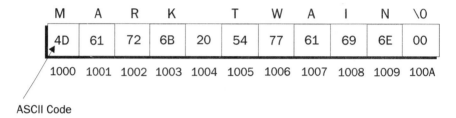

The diagram assumes that the string is stored at memory location 0x1000. It also shows the ASCII code of each character in the string as a hexadecimal value. Each character occupies one byte, so, together with the null character, a string requires a number of bytes that is one greater than the number of characters it is composed of. In this case the string occupies 11 bytes.

We can declare a character array and initialize it with a string constant between quotes:

```
char Author[11] = "Mark Twain";
```

Note that the terminating `'\0'` is supplied automatically by the compiler, so there is no need to include one yourself.

> Remember, you must declare the array one bigger than the number of characters you want to store, allowing room for the computer to automatically add `\0`.

You can even let the compiler work out the length of an initialized array for you. Consider the following declaration:

```
char Scientist[] = "Richard Feynman";
```

Because the dimension is unspecified, the compiler will allocate enough
space to hold the initializing string plus the terminating null, in this case 16
elements. Of course, if you want to use this array for storing a different
string later, the length of the new string must not exceed 16 bytes.
Generally, it's your responsibility to ensure that the array is large enough
for any string you might subsequently want to store.

String Input

So far, we've used the function **scanf()** for reading all our input from the
keyboard. We can also use it to read in a character string. It supports the
format specifier, **%s** in order to do this, but has one rather serious limitation
- it won't read a string containing blanks, and any whitespace character
signals the end of input. If we tried to read the name of the physicist
Richard Feynman using **scanf()**, we would only get 'Richard'.

The gets Function

Fortunately, the header file **STDIO.H** contains definitions of a number of
other functions for reading characters from the keyboard. The one that we
shall look at here is the function **gets()**, which reads a string into a
character array and is typically used with statements such as:

```
char Name[80];
...
gets(Name);
```

These statements first declare a **char** array **Name[]** with 80 elements, and
then read characters from **stdin**, normally the keyboard.

Characters are read from **stdin** until the **'\n'** (newline) character is read -
the **'\n'** character is generated when you press the *Return* key. After the
input string is stored into memory, a **'\0'** replaces the newline character.

A String Reading Example

We now have enough knowledge to write a simple program to read a string
and then count how many characters it contains:

```
/* EX4-02.C  Counting characters in a string */
#include <stdio.h>

#define MAX 80                          /* Maximum buffer size */

int main()
{
    char buffer[MAX];                   /* Input buffer */
    int count = 0;                      /* Character count */

    printf("\nEnter a string less that %d characters:\n", MAX);
    gets( buffer );                     /* Read a string */

    while( buffer[count] != '\0' )      /* Increment count as long as the */
        count++;                        /* current character is not null */

    printf("The string \"%s\" has %d characters", buffer, count);

    return 0;
}
```

Program Analysis

The **while** loop continues as long as the current character referenced by **buffer[count]** isn't **'\0'**. This sort of checking on the current character while stepping through an array is a common technique in C, although there are better ways of performing this particular operation (primarily via library functions). The only action in the loop is to increment **count** for each non-null character entered.

Finally, let's note a couple of points about displaying the string and character count. The string output uses the specifier **%s** to output string characters until a **'\0'** character is found. If we only wanted to output the first 10 characters of the string and ignore the rest, we could use a width specification after the **%** symbol, like **%10s**.

> In order to output a double quote character in the **printf()** format string argument, we need to use the escape character **\"**, because a bare quote character would instead signal the end of the format string.

There is a serious flaw in this program: nothing prevents you from entering more than 79 characters. This would cause serious problems, not least that a terminating null would be missing. How can we protect against this?

Managing String Input

In order to gain control of the situation, we can deal with string input by reading one character at a time, where we can check that we don't exceed the capacity of the intended array. Another function, **getchar()**, is available from the standard library, which will enable us to do this:

```
/* EX4-03.C  String input with some security */
#include <stdio.h>

#define MAX 80                          /* Maximum buffer size */

int main()
{
   char buffer[MAX];                    /* Input buffer */
   char ch;                             /* Single char store */
   int count = 0;                       /* Character count */

   printf("\nEnter a string less than %d characters:\n", MAX);

   /* Read characters from the keyboard.... */
   while(
          ((ch=getchar()) != '\n')      /* while the character isn't */
                                        /* end-of-line and there's */
        && (count < MAX-2)              /* enough space left to include */
        )                               /* the NULL on the end, */
      buffer[count++] = ch;             /* add it to the buffer and */
                                        /* increment the counter. */

   /* Finished reading - why has the loop finished? */
   /* If it was because the string finished, add the null terminator */
   if( ch == '\n' )
      buffer[count] = '\0';

   /* But if we ran out of space, print an error message */
   else
   {
      printf("\nToo many characters. Program aborted.");
      return 0;
   }

   while( buffer[count] != '\0' )       /* Increment count as long as the */
      count++;                          /* current character is not null */

   printf("The string \"%s\" has %d characters", buffer, count);

   return 0;
}
```

Program Analysis

This looks like quite a long piece of code, but remember, since we're reading one character at a time, we have to look out for the end of the string, as well as check that the number of characters doesn't exceed the capacity of the array.

The maximum legal index value for the array is **MAX-1**, so the second condition, **(count<MAX-2)**, makes sure that the maximum index used to store a character is one less than this value, so as to allow space for the **'\0'** at the end.

When the loop ends, it may be because **'\n'** has been read, or because **count** is equal to **MAX-2**, or both. The **if** statement following the loop:

```
if( ch == '\n' )
    buffer[count] = '\0';
```

tests the variable **ch** for **'\n'**, and if it's encountered then **'\0'** is stored in the current free position in **buffer[]** and marks the end of the string; there will always be at least one free element in **buffer[]** if **'\n'** is found.

If **ch** doesn't contain **'\n'**, then it means that the loop must have ended because **count** is equal to **MAX-2,** indicating that there's only one free element in **buffer[]**. Since we need at least two - for the current character and for **'\0'** - there's insufficient space, so the program ends with an error message.

Multi-dimensional Arrays

The arrays we have defined so far, with one index for accessing elements, are referred to as **one-dimensional arrays**, or **vectors**. An array can also have more than one index value though. If an array has two index values it is called a two-dimensional array, and so on.

A Multi-dimensional Example

Suppose our enthusiasm for nature and the weather extends into farming, and that we have a field where we grow bean plants in rows of ten. We could declare an array to record the weight of beans produced by each plant with the statement:

```
double beans[12][10];
```

This declares the two-dimensional array **beans**, the first index being the row number, and the second the number within the row. An equivalent way of envisaging this is as an array of 12 objects, each of which has an array of 10 **double** elements. Referring to any particular element requires two indices, each enclosed in their own pair of square brackets. For example, we could set the value of the element reflecting the performance of the fifth plant in the third row with the statement:

```
beans[2][4] = 10.7;
```

With our meteorological skills to help us, we are successful bean farmers so we can add several identical fields. Assuming we have five fields cultivated, we could use a three-dimensional array like this:

```
double beans[5][12][10];
```

If we ever get to bean farming on an international scale we'll be able to use a four-dimensional array, with the extra dimension designating the country. Producing this sort of quantity of beans for human consumption, however, may start to damage the ozone layer.

Multi-dimensional Arrays in Memory

Arrays are stored in memory such that the rightmost index value varies most rapidly. You can visualize the array **data[3][4]** as 3 one-dimensional arrays, with 4 elements each:

1000	1004	1008	100C
data[0][0]	data[0][1]	data[0][2]	data[0][3]

1010	1014	1018	101C
data[1][0]	data[1][1]	data[1][2]	data[1][3]

1020	1024	1028	102C
data[2][0]	data[2][1]	data[2][2]	data[2][3]

long data[3][4];

111

The diagram also shows the memory address of each element as a hexadecimal value, assuming that the array is stored at location 1000.

Initialization of a Multi-dimensional Array

To initialize a multi-dimensional array, you use an extension of the method used for a one-dimensional array. For example, you can initialize a two-dimensional array, `data[]`, with the declaration:

```
long data[3][4] =
                {
                    {  1,  2,  3,  5 },
                    {  7, 11, 13, 17 },
                    { 19, 23, 29, 31 }
                };
```

Thus the initializing values for each row are contained within their own pair of braces.

Incomplete Rows

When the values in any row are exhausted, the remaining array elements will be assigned zero. For example, with the declaration:

```
long data[3][4] =
                {
                    {  1,  2,  3       },
                    {  7, 11          },
                    { 19, 23, 29, 31 }
                };
```

the elements `data[0][3]`, `data[1][2]` and `data[1][3]` have no initializing values and will therefore be initialized as zero. If you wanted to initialize the whole array with zeros, you could simply write:

```
long data[3][4] = {0};
```

If you are initializing numeric arrays with even more dimensions, then remember that the braces are nested to the same number of levels as there are dimensions in the array.

Storing Multiple Strings

You can use a two-dimensional array of type **char** to store multiple strings. The first dimension defines the number of strings in the array, and the second the maximum number of characters in each string. So the declaration:

```
char Names[5][50];                    /* Array of five names */
```

provides storage for 5 strings, with up to 50 characters in each string.

Improving Our Output

We could use this to improve the output for our first example in this chapter:

```
/* EX4-04.C  Determining which month to make it rain */

#include <stdio.h>

#define SAMPLES 12                    /* Number of data samples */

int main()
{
   const int CRITICALT = 70;          /* Critical temperature */

   int TempMax[SAMPLES] = { 50,45,52,60,66,69,67,84,85,71,67,53 };

   float Rainfall[SAMPLES] = { 1.2f, 2.4f, 6.9f, 4.1f, 2.1f, 2.3f,
                               0.2f, 1.8f, 3.7f, 3.1f, 2.9f, 1.1f };

   char Month[][10] = { "January","February","March","April",
                        "May","June","July","August",
                        "September","October","November","December"};

   float RainMean = 0.0f;             /* Average rainfall */
   float BiMonthRain = 0.0f;          /* Mean of two months rain */
   int i = 0;                         /* Loop counter */

   /* Calculate the average rainfall */
   for( i=0 ; i<SAMPLES ; i++)
      RainMean += Rainfall[i];        /* Sum total rainfall and */
   RainMean /= SAMPLES;               /* divide by number of samples */
```

```
for( i=0 ; i<SAMPLES-1 ; i++)
{
    BiMonthRain = (Rainfall[i] + Rainfall[i+1])/2.0f;
    if( (BiMonthRain<RainMean) && (TempMax[i+1]<CRITICALT) )
        printf("\nFire the catapult in %s!", Month[i+1]);
}

return 0;
}
```

Program Analysis

The lone output statement possibly contains the only modification difficult to understand:

```
printf("\nFire the catapult in %s!", Month[i+1]);
```

We just index the first dimension of the array **Month[]** with **i+1** (not **i+2**, which we used to get the month number starting with January as 1), and use that as the output argument. We don't need to specify the second index to the array **Month[]**, since we're referring to a complete string. A reference such as **Month[1][2]** refers to a single letter - in this case the letter '**b**'.

The program is now more explicit in its recommendations:

```
Fire the catapult in February!
Fire the catapult in June!
Fire the catapult in July!
Fire the catapult in December!
```

The sizeof Operator

The **sizeof** operator comes in very handy when working with arrays. It's applied to a single operand and so is a **unary** operator. It returns the size of any object in bytes as an unsigned integer. If we've declared a variable **number** of type **long**, then the expression:

```
sizeof number
```

will have the value 4, since the variable **number** occupies 4 bytes. Alternatively, you could use parentheses.

Generic Sizes

You can also obtain the size of a generic type, by placing the type name as the operand of **sizeof**. So we could use the statement:

```
intSize = sizeof( int );
```

to record in the variable **intSize**, how many bytes are occupied by an integer. Note that when you are using **sizeof** with a data type, you must use parentheses.

Using sizeof to Aid Array Flexibility

If we declare an array, such as:

```
long numbers[][3] = { {20, 30, 40}, {40, 50, 60} };
```

from time to time you may well want to be able to add or delete rows, just by adding or deleting some of the values that initialize it. Ideally, you don't want to be ferreting around the program, looking for all the places where you've fixed the number of rows - the **sizeof** operator can help you with this:

```
NumRows = sizeof numbers/sizeof numbers[0];
```

The expression **sizeof numbers** will generate the number of bytes in the whole array, whilst the expression **sizeof numbers[0]** produces the number of bytes in one row of the array. Dividing the first by the second produces the number of rows in the array, so you can use the variable **NumRows** to control loop counts and row indexing of the array. If you add rows to the array, the value of **NumRows** will adjust automatically.

If you need to know how many elements the array has, you could use the statement:

```
NumElmnts = sizeof numbers/sizeof numbers[0][0];
```

Dividing the number of bytes in the array by the number of bytes in a single element will give you the number of elements in the array.

Indirectly Accessing Data

The variables we have dealt with so far provide you with the ability to name a memory location where you can store data of a particular type. The contents of a variable are either entered from an external source, such as the keyboard, or calculated from other values. There's another kind of variable in C which doesn't store data that you enter or calculate, but greatly extends the power and flexibility of your programs. This kind of variable is called a **pointer**.

What is a Pointer?

Each memory location that you use to store a data value has an address, which provides the means by which your computer references a particular data item. A **pointer** is a special kind of variable that can store the address of another variable. They have names just like any other variable, and they have an associated type which designates what kind of variables its contents can refer to. So, a pointer of type `double` can only store an address of a variable of type `double`.

Of course, since a pointer is a variable, it can store the addresses of different variables of a given type at different times during the execution of your program.

Declaring Pointers

The declaration for a pointer is similar to that of an ordinary variable, except that the pointer name has an asterisk in front of it. For example, to declare a pointer **pnumber** of type **long**, you could use the statement:

```
long *pnumber;
```

The asterisk identifies it as a pointer, and the type is read as a 'pointer to **long**'. We will use the prefix **p** for pointer names, in order to distinguish them from other variables and make them more readily recognizable as pointers.

You can mix declarations of ordinary variables and pointers in the same statement. For example:

```
long *pnumber, number = 99;
```

This declares both the variable **pnumber** of type 'pointer to **long**' as before, and also the variable **number**.

Let's take an example to see how a pointer works without worrying about what it's for at this stage. Suppose we have the above **long** integer variable **number**, containing the value 99. We also have the pointer, **pnumber**, of type **long** which we could use to store the address of our variable **number**. But how can we obtain the address of a variable?

The Address Operator

What we need is a new operator, the **address operator**, **&**, which we first met when we used **scanf()** to get input. To set up the pointer we could write the assignment statement:

```
pnumber = &number;                /* Store address of number in pnum */
```

You can use the address operator to obtain the address of any variable, but you need a pointer of the same type to store it (there is one exception, which we will see later). For example, if you want to store the address of a **double** variable, then the pointer must have been declared as type 'pointer to **double**'.

Using Pointers

Taking the address of a variable and storing it in a pointer is tremendous fun, but the really interesting question is, what can you actually do with it? Fundamental to making a pointer useful, is the mechanism for accessing the data value in the variable to which it points. This is done using the indirection operator.

The Indirection Operator

The **indirection operator**, *****, is used with a pointer variable to access the contents of the variable pointed to. The name 'indirection operator' stems from the fact that the data is accessed indirectly. It is also called the **dereference operator**, and the process of accessing the data in the variable pointed to via a pointer is termed '**dereferencing**' the pointer.

One aspect of this operator that can sometimes be confusing is that we now have several different uses for the asterisk symbol - it's the multiply operator, the indirection operator and is also used in the declaration of a pointer. Fortunately, the compiler is able to distinguish the meaning by its context. When you multiply two variables, **A*B** for instance, there is no meaningful interpretation of this expression for anything other than a multiplication operation. Each context has a unique interpretation, so if you have an example that doesn't immediately identify the context, then there's something wrong with your code.

Initialization

Using pointers that haven't been initialized is extremely hazardous - an uninitialized pointer can point to anywhere in memory. You could use it accidentally to write to areas of memory that currently hold your operating system, and change the contents with disastrous results.

To initialize a pointer to the address of a variable that's already been declared is very easy. For example, to initialize the pointer **pnum** with the address of the variable **number,** you just use the operator **&** with the variable name:

```
int number = 0;                    /* Initialized integer variable */
int* pnum = &number                /* Initialized pointer */
```

When initializing a pointer with another variable, the variable must have already been declared prior to the pointer declaration.

The Null Pointer

Of course, you may not want to initialize a pointer with the address of a specific variable when you declare it. In such cases you can initialize it with the pointer equivalent of zero, guaranteed to not point to anything. The standard header file **STDIO.H** defines the mnemonic **NULL** for this, so you can declare and initialize it with the statement:

```
int* pnum = NULL;                  /* Pointer not pointing to anything */
```

A pointer with the value **NULL** is commonly called a 'null pointer'.

Using Null Pointers

Using **NULL** to initialize a pointer ensures that the pointer doesn't contain a valid address and makes it clear that this is a pointer being initialized with zero. It also provides the pointer with a particular value that you can distinguish in expressions. For example:

```
if( pnum == NULL )
   printf("\nThe pointer pnum is null.");
```

This checks whether the pointer **pnum** contains a valid address, and if it doesn't a message is displayed. You could just as easily use the following statement, which achieves the same thing:

```
if( !pnum )
   printf("\nThe pointer pnum is null.");
```

Attempting to store a value in a null pointer will usually result in an error message, although execution won't necessarily stop at the point where the error occurred.

String Pointers

A pointer of type **char** has the interesting property that it can be initialized with a string constant. For example, we can declare and initialize such a pointer with the statement:

```
char* pproverb = "The higher the fewer.";
```

This looks very similar to initializing a **char** array, but differs in that it will create a pointer to variables of type **char**, which is initialized with the address of the constant array containing the characters "**The higher the fewer.**" The address of the array will be stored in the pointer **pproverb**. If you were to just declare an array:

```
char proverb[] = "The higher the fewer.";
```

this would then produce a somewhat different result. Here only the minimum memory necessary to accommodate the string is allocated:

char proverb[] = "The higher the fewer.";

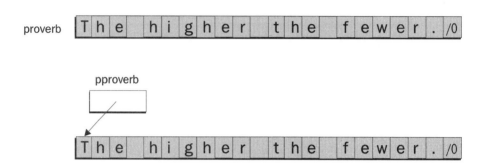

char *pproverb = "The higher the fewer.";

This shows the extra memory allocated for the pointer **pproverb**, which will contain the address of the beginning of the string, as opposed to the **char** array declaration which just allocates the space for the array **proverb[]**.

Arrays of Pointers

We can declare an array of pointers in the same way that we declare a normal array.

An Example of Pointer Arrays

We could use a pointer array to manage the month names in the previous example. Only one statement in the program needs to be changed - you just need to replace the declaration of the **Month[]** array with the following declaration:

```
char *Month[] = { "January","February","March","April",
                  "May","June","July","August",
                  "September","October","November","December"};
```

This declares **Month[]** as a one-dimensional array of pointers, where each element is initialized with the address of a constant string. The program will run exactly the same as before, so what's the difference?

The original two-dimensional **char** array had a fixed row length of ten characters. Here we have 12 independent string constants, each of which occupies the minimum amount of space - the length of the string plus one byte for the '\0' character, plus an array of twelve pointers containing the addresses of the string constants. Using the array of pointers, the strings are stored without any wasted space. Take the following example:

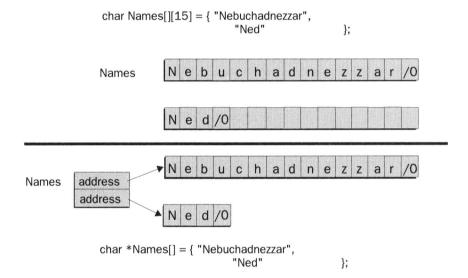

```
char Names[][15] = { "Nebuchadnezzar",
                     "Ned"              };
```

```
char *Names[] = { "Nebuchadnezzar",
                  "Ned"              };
```

Whether memory is saved by using a pointer array instead of the **char** array will depend on how variable the string lengths are. In this case the **char** array at the top occupies 30 bytes, whereas the definition using a pointer array at the bottom only requires 27 bytes, allowing 4 bytes for each pointer.

> The memory occupied by a pointer will vary from one type
> of machine to the next and even between different
> circumstances on the same machine, but it isn't usually more
> than 4 bytes. Of course, if all the strings are the same length,
> then the pointer array will require more memory, but this isn't
> the typical situation.

There's also another difference between these two definitions. The **char**
array declaration allocates a fixed block of memory which has been
initialized with the two-name strings. You cannot change the memory area
to which the array **Names[]** refers, but you are free to change the contents
to different strings within your program in any way that you wish. On the
other hand, using the pointer-based approach you can change the addresses
in the pointer array, but you can't legally change the strings they point to.

Pointers and Arrays

Arrays and pointers work in a surprisingly similar way, and you can
normally interchange array or pointer notation. You can use array names in
your programs as though they were pointers (with certain limitations), and
you can also use an index value with a pointer. In most circumstances, if
you use the name of a one-dimensional array by itself, it's automatically
converted into a pointer to the first element of the array. The exceptions are
if the array name is the operand of the address operator, **&**, or of the
operator **sizeof**.

A Example of Pointers and Arrays

If we have the declarations:

```
double* pdata;
double data[10];
```

then we can write the assignment:

```
pdata = data;              /* Initialize pointer with the array address */
```

This assigns the address of the array **data** to the pointer **pdata**. If we use
the array name **data** with an index value, then it defines the contents of
the element corresponding to that index value. So, if we want to store the
address of that element in the pointer, we have to use the address operator:

```
pdata = &data[1];
```

Here, **pdata** contains the address of the second element of the array.

Pointer Arithmetic

Pointer arithmetic implicitly assumes that the pointer points to an array and that the arithmetical operation is on the address contained in the pointer. You are limited to addition and subtraction, but you can also perform comparisons.

A Simple Arithmetic Example

For example, the pointer **pdata** could be assigned the address of the third element of the array **data** with the statement:

```
pdata = &data[2];
```

In this case, the expression **pdata+1** would refer to the fourth element (the address of **data[3]**). This is very important - pointer arithmetic isn't simple arithmetic. It always operates in units determined by the type of the involved pointer, so our expression doesn't add 1 to the address value in **pdata**, it adds enough to make it point to the next element of type **double**. We could make the pointer point to this element by writing the statement:

```
pdata += 1;                    /* Increment pdata to the next element */
```

This is different from the expression **pdata+1** in that the expression doesn't change the value of the pointer, but the assignment does. Here, the address contained in **pdata** has been incremented by the number of bytes occupied by one element of the array **data**.

Using Arithmetic

In general, the expression **pdata+n**, where **n** can be any expression resulting in an integer, will refer to an address offset by **n*sizeof(double)** bytes from the pointer **pdata**, since it was declared to be of type pointer to **double**. This is illustrated here:

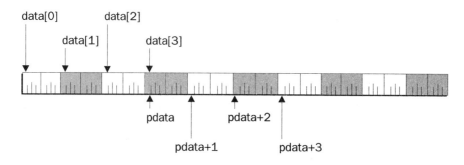

```
double data[10];
double pdata;
pdata = &data[3];
```

In other words, incrementing or decrementing a pointer works in terms of the type of the object pointed to. The change is in terms of a number of elements of the given type. The most common notation for incrementing a pointer is using the increment operator. For example:

```
pdata++;                        /* Increment pdata to the next element */
```

This is equivalent to, and more usual than, the **+=** form. However, the **+=** form was used in the earlier statement just to make it clear that the increment value is actually specified as 1, whereas the effect is usually otherwise, except in the case of a pointer to **char**.

The address resulting from an arithmetical operation on a pointer can be anything from a value representing the address of the first element of the array, to the address which is one beyond the last element. Outside of these limits however, the behavior of the pointer is generally undefined.

Dereferencing

You can of course dereference a pointer that you have performed arithmetic on. There wouldn't be much point to it otherwise. For example, assuming that **pdata** is still pointing to **data[3]**, the statement:

```
*(pdata+1) = *(pdata+3);
```

is equivalent to:

```
data[4] = data[6];
```

The parentheses are necessary when you want to dereference a pointer after incrementing the address it contains, since the precedence of the indirection operator is higher than that of the arithmetic operators, **+** or **-**. If you write the expression ***pdata+1** instead of ***(pdata+1)**, then this would add one to that value stored at the address contained in **pdata**, which is equivalent to executing **data[3]+1**. Since the result of this expression isn't an address, its use in the assignment statement above would cause the compiler to generate an error message. The difference between these two expressions is illustrated in the diagram here:

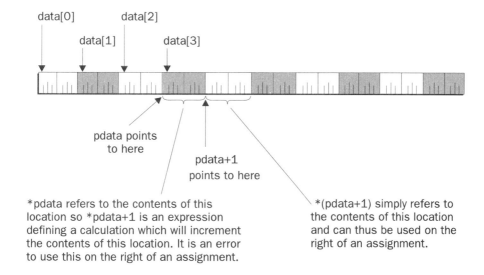

*pdata refers to the contents of this location so *pdata+1 is an expression defining a calculation which will increment the contents of this location. It is an error to use this on the right of an assignment.

*(pdata+1) simply refers to the contents of this location and can thus be used on the right of an assignment.

Using Array Names

We can use an array name for operations on its elements as though it were a pointer. So we can also write the last statement as:

```
*(data+4) = *(data+6);            /* The same as data[4]=data[6]; */
```

This kind of notation can generally be applied so that the corresponding elements `data[0]`, `data[1]`, `data[2]`, etc. can be written as `*data`, `*(data+1)`, `*(data+2)`, etc.

An Example of Array Naming

We could exercise this aspect of array addressing with a program to calculate prime numbers:

```
/* EX4-05.C  Calculating primes using pointers */
#include <stdio.h>
#define MAX 100                        /* Number of primes required */
int main()
{
   long primes[MAX] = { 2L,3L,5L };  /* First three primes defined */
   long trial = 5L;                    /* Candidate prime */
   int count = 3;                      /* Count of primes found */
   int found = 0;                      /* Indicates when a prime is found */
   int i = 0;                          /* Loop counter */

   do
   {
      trial += 2L;                     /* Next value for checking */
      found = 0;                       /* Set found indicator */

      /* Try division by existing primes */
      for ( i=2 ; i<count ; i++ )
      {
         /* found will be 1 for exact division          */
         /* and if division is exact, it's not a prime */
         if(found = (( trial % *(primes+i)) == 0L) )
            break;                      /* it's not a prime so exit the for loop */
      }

      if (!found)                       /* We got one... */
                                        /* ..so save it in primes array */
         *(primes + count++) = trial;
   }while (count < MAX );

   /* Output primes 5 to a line */
   for( i=0 ; i<MAX ; i++)
   {
      if( (i%5)==0 )                    /* New line on 1st, and every 5th line */
         printf("\n");
      printf("%10ld", *(primes+i));
   }
   return 0;
}
```

Program Analysis

The **primes** array which stores the results is seeded with the first three primes:

```
long primes[MAX] = { 2L,3L,5L };        /* First three primes defined */
```

All the work is done in the **do-while** loop, which continues until **MAX** primes have been found.

The algorithm is very simple and based on the fact that if a number isn't prime, then it must be divisible by one of the primes found so far, all of which are less than the number in question (in fact, only division by primes less than the square root of the number in question needs to be checked, so this example isn't as efficient as it might be).

Dividing the value to be tested by each of the known primes is done in the nested **for** loop. Since the value to be tested, held in the variable **trial**, is always odd, we don't need to test for division by 2. The **for** loop only contains the **if** statement:

```
if(found = (( trial % *(primes+i)) == 0) )
   break;                       /* it's not a prime so exit the for loop */
```

This first divides the value in **trial** by the current prime, ***(primes+i)** (equivalent to **primes[i]**). If the result is zero, then this signifies that the division is exact, so the specified number cannot be a prime. In this case, the variable **found** will be set to 1, and the **break** statement is executed to end the **for** loop. If the division isn't exact, then **found** will be set to zero and the loop will continue until **trial** has been divided by all of the primes found up until now.

If the loop ends, it may be due to the **break** being executed, or possibly because all primes have been exercised. Therefore it's necessary to decide whether or not the value in **trial** was prime. This is indicated by the value saved in the variable **found**. If **trial** does contain a prime, then **found** will be zero and **!found** will be True, so the statement:

```
*(primes+count++) = trial;            /* ...so save it in primes array */
```

will be executed. This stores the new prime number in **primes[count]**, and then increments **count** through the postfix increment operator (**++**).

If you compile and execute this example with **MAX** defined as 50, you should get the output shown here:

2	3	5	7	9
11	13	17	19	23
29	31	37	41	43
47	53	59	61	67
71	73	79	83	89
97	101	103	107	109
113	127	131	137	139
149	151	157	163	167
173	179	181	191	193
197	199	211	223	227

In this example, pointers provide a very convenient and compact notation for programming operations with arrays.

Handling Strings with Pointers

Programming operations with character strings are almost invariably done with pointers, because pointers tend to provide the most natural way of handling strings, with extremely compact but nonetheless readable code.

An Example of Copying a String with Pointers

We can illustrate the technique with a simple example of copying a string:

```
/* EX4-06.C  Copying a string using pointers */
#include <stdio.h>

int main()
{
   char StringIn[80];                  /* Input string */
   char StringOut[80];                 /* Output string */
   char *pSIn = StringIn;              /* Pointer to input string */
   char *pSOut = StringOut;           /* Pointer to output string */

   printf("\nEnter a string of less than 80 characters:\n");
   gets(StringIn);                     /* Read input string */

   /* Copy string to output array */
   while(*pSOut++ = *pSIn++);

   puts(StringOut);                    /* Now output the copy */
   return 0;
}
```

Program Analysis

The complete copying process is accomplished in a single line:

```
while(*pSOut++ = *pSIn++);
```

The loop contains no statements - everything is done by the expression controlling the loop. This diagram illustrates the position at the start of the loop:

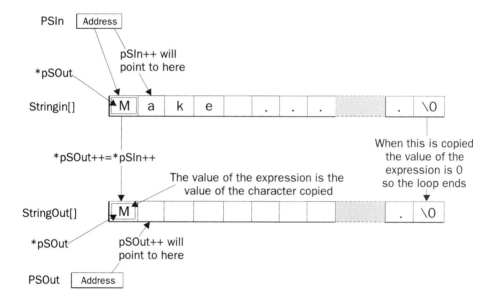

Here, **pSIn** and **pSOut** point to the first element of the corresponding array. The condition within the **while** loop is an assignment which copies the contents of the location pointed to by **pSIn** to the location pointed to by **pSOut**, that is, from an element of **StringIn[]** to the corresponding element in **StringOut[]**. After the copy, the addresses stored in both pointers are incremented to point to the next element in each array. The value of the **while** loop expression is the value of the character copied. As long as the contents of **pSOut** after each copy operation aren't zero, the loop continues. When the '\0' character is copied, ***pSOut** will be zero, and so the loop will end.

> Note that we need to use StringOut as the argument, since pSOut no longer points to the beginning of the string, because the address it contains is modified in the loop.

void Pointers

You can declare a pointer to be of type **void**, with a statement such as:

```
void *pGeneral;
```

This results in a pointer of no particular type, useful when you don't know in advance what type of pointer you are going to be dealing with. These are primarily used with functions, and particularly with the memory allocation functions in the standard library which we shall see later in this chapter. We will be discussing functions in general in Chapter 5.

Note that assigning the address in a pointer to a pointer of a different type, requires an explicit typecast, unless the destination pointer is of type **void**. Any type of pointer can be assigned to a pointer of type **void**, and subsequently recovered. Note that even with a typecast, assigning a pointer to another of a different type that isn't **void** can cause problems and should be avoided.

A void Pointers Example

Here's an example, showing how void pointers can be cast:

```
void *pVoid;
int *pInt *pInt2;
int i;

/* Store the address of i in pInt */
i = 3;
pInt = &i;

/* Copy the pointer around. We don't need the casts to and */
/* from void*, but it doesn't hurt, and shows how casting works */
pVoid = (void *)pInt;
pInt2 = (int *)pVoid;
```

Pointer Notation with Multi-dimensional Arrays

Some care is needed to keep your mind clear as to what is happening when you use pointer notation with multi-dimensional arrays. By way of illustration we can use an array **beans**, with the pointer **pbeans** declared as:

```
double beans[3][4];
double *pbeans=&beans[0][0];
```

The pointer will contain the address of the first element of the array. We could quite easily have declared and initialized the pointer as:

```
double *pbeans=beans[0];
```

Using a two-dimensional array name with a single subscript returns the address of the row of the array defined by the subscript, so **pbeans** will be initialized with the address of the first element of the first row of the array. This is the same as the previous declaration.

Suppose we now initialize it with just **beans**:

```
double *pbeans=beans;
```

With some compilers you'll get a warning message, because although **beans** will refer to an address, that address will contain the address of **beans[0]**, which, as we've just seen, also contains an address. So here we are initializing **pbeans** with an address of an address, or in other words, a pointer to a pointer. This is said to be a different level of indirection so our declaration is wrong, in spite of the fact that many compilers won't complain about it. A correct initialization using just the array name would be either of the following:

```
double *pbeans=*beans;
double **pbeans=beans;
```

so that **beans** is dereferenced to just an address. A pointer of the form **double** ** is a pointer to a pointer and can be used to point to an object like '**beans**', which is an address containing an address...

131

Referencing

You can reference each element of the array in three ways:

- Using the array name with two index values.
- Using the array name in pointer notation.
- Using a separate pointer.

Therefore the following are equivalent:

```
beans[i][j]        *(*(beans+i)+j)         *(pbeans+4*i+j)
```

It's also possible to mix array and pointer notation, such as `*(beans[i]+j)` or `(pbeans+4)[j],` but this has no obvious advantages and is best avoided.

Dynamic Memory Allocation

Working with a fixed set of variables in a program can be very restrictive. The need often arises to adjust the amount of space available for storing different types of variables at execution time, depending on the input data for the program. You can create variables dynamically, as your program actually executes, by allocating a piece of memory and then accessing it through a pointer. The allocation of memory for variables at execution time is achieved through functions defined in the standard library, **STDLIB.H**.

The Heap

In most instances, there is unused memory in your computer when your program is executed. In C, this unused memory is usually called the 'heap'. You can allocate space on the heap using four functions defined in **STDLIB.H**:

malloc()   Allocates a block of memory on the heap with a size given in bytes by the integer value passed to the function. The function returns the address of the block of memory allocated, or **NULL** if the allocation fails.

`calloc()`	This function allocates a block of memory on the heap based on the two arguments passed to it. The first argument specifies that the number of arguments for which memory is required, and the second specifies their size (in bytes).
`realloc()`	This function changes the size of a block of memory that has previously been allocated. The first argument is a pointer to the block concerned, and the second specifies a new size (in bytes) for the block.
`free()`	This function de-allocates a previously allocated block of memory specified by a pointer passed as an argument.

You can allocate space on the heap for variables in one part of a program and then release that space, returning it to the heap and making it available for reuse later in the same program. This enables you to efficiently use memory, and enables programs to handle much larger problems, involving considerably more data than might otherwise be possible. The pointer to a memory area allocated will be of type **void** *, which can store the address of any kind of variable, but you should cast the pointer to the type of data you're going to store.

The best way of understanding how dynamic memory allocation works is by looking at a couple of examples.

Using malloc() for Dynamic Memory Allocation

Let's take a very simple example of a program that will read in an arbitrary number of strings, and then display them:

```
/* EX4-07.C  Allocating memory dynamically for strings */
#include <stdio.h>                    /* For input and output */
#include <stdlib.h>                   /* For memory management functions */

#define MAXLENGTH 80
#define MAXSTRINGS 100

int main()
{
```

```
     char StringIn[MAXLENGTH];              /* Input string */
     char *pSIn=StringIn;                   /* Pointer to input string */
     char *pSOut=NULL;                      /* Pointer to new memory */

     char *pString[MAXSTRINGS];             /* Pointers to strings */
     int NumStr=0;                          /* Number of strings read */
     int i=0;                               /* Loop counter */

     printf("\nEnter a string of less than 80 characters:\n");

     do
     {
        gets(StringIn);                     /* Read input string */

        pSIn=StringIn;                      /* Get pointer to input */

        /* Find the end of the input */
        while(*pSIn++)
          /* Do nothing */;

        /* Now get sufficient memory for input and save the address */
        pSOut=(char *)malloc(pSIn-StringIn);

        if(!pSOut)                          /* Verify we've got some memory */
        {                                   /* If not - report and exit */
           printf("\nMemory allocation failed - exiting program.");
           return 1;
        }

        pString[NumStr]=pSOut;              /* Store address in array */

        pSIn=StringIn;                      /* Reset pointer to start */
        while(*pSOut++=*pSIn++);            /* Copy input to new memory */

        printf("\nDo you want to enter another (y or n)?:");
        gets(StringIn);

     }while( (++NumStr < MAXSTRINGS)&&
             ((StringIn[0]=='y') || (StringIn[0]=='Y')) );

     /* Done - so output all the strings */
     for( i=0 ; i<NumStr ; i++ )
        puts(pString[i]);                   /* Now output the copies */

     /* Lastly - release the memory back to the heap */
     for( i=0 ; i<NumStr ; i++ )
        free(pString[i]);

     return 0;
}
```

Program Analysis

The idea here is to read a string, find out how long it is (including the '\0' character) and then, after getting sufficient memory allocated on the heap, copy the string into it. This will repeat as long as you want to enter more strings and as long as the total number of strings doesn't exceed **MAXSTRINGS**.

After reading a string in the **do-while** loop, we find the address immediately after the end of the string that was entered, with the loop:

```
while(*pSIn++);
```

The pointer **pSIn** starts out containing the address of the first character of the string. The loop adds one to the address stored in **pSIn** up to and including the point where **pSIn** is pointing to a location that contains '\0'. Thus **pSIn** will end up pointing to the address one beyond the '\0' at the end of the string. We then call the library function **malloc()** to allocate memory in the statement:

```
pSOut=(char *)malloc(pSIn-StringIn);
```

The expression passed as an argument to **malloc()** is the difference between two pointers. For the difference between two pointers to be meaningful, they need to point to members of the same array. In this case, it defines the number of characters in the string, since **StringIn** is the address of the first character of the input and **pSIn** contains the address of the position one character beyond the end of the input.

After casting the address returned from the function **malloc()**, to the type pointer to **char**, we save it in **pSOut** so that we can use it in the copying process. We then check that the pointer returned by **malloc()** isn't **NULL** with the statements:

```
if(!pSOut)                          /* Verify we got some memory */
  {                                 /* If not - report and exit */
     printf("\nMemory allocation failed - exiting program.");
     return 1;
  }
```

If the pointer value returned by **malloc()** is **NULL**, the expression in the **if** will be True and the program will end after displaying the message. The value returned from the program is handed over to the operating system.

> By choosing different values for different kinds of problems, the value returned can be used to indicate the condition causing the program to be terminated.

If the address we got from **malloc()** isn't **NULL**, then we also store it in the current free position in the array **pString[]**. The copying is then done using a **while** loop, but because we've modified the contents of **pSIn**, it's necessary to reset it back to point at the beginning of the array **StringIn[]**.

Using calloc() for Dynamic Memory Allocation

Many programmers prefer to use the **calloc()** library function rather than **malloc()** for obtaining space in the heap, because apart from the fact that **calloc()** will allocate memory as a multiple of objects of a particular type, it will also initialize the memory to zero. We could use **calloc()** in an alternative version of our primes program, which will produce as many primes as available memory will allow:

```
/* EX4-08.C  Calculating primes using memory dynamically */
#include <stdio.h>                    /* For input and output */
#include <stdlib.h>                   /* For memory management functions */

int main()
{
   long *pPrimes=NULL;                /* Pointer to primes array */
   long trial = 5L;                   /* Candidate prime */
   unsigned int count = 3;            /* Count of primes found */
   unsigned int NumPrimes=0;          /* Count of primes required */
   int found = 0;                     /* Indicates when a prime is found */
   unsigned int i = 0;                /* Loop counter */

   printf("\nHow many primes do you want?:");
   scanf(" %u", &NumPrimes);          /* Read the number of primes ..... */

   /* Get enough memory for the number required, and validate pointer */
   if((pPrimes=(long*)calloc(NumPrimes, sizeof(long)))==NULL)
   {
      printf("\nMemory allocation failure - program terminated.");
      return 1;
   }

   pPrimes[0]=2L,pPrimes[1]=3L,pPrimes[2]=5L;      /* Set up seed primes */
```

```
   do
   {
      trial += 2L;                        /* Next value for checking */
      found = 0;                          /* Set found indicator */

      /* Try division by existing primes */
      for ( i=2U ; i<count ; i++ )
      {
         /* found will be 1 for exact division */
         /* and if division is exact, its not a prime */
         if(found = (( trial % *(pPrimes+i)) == 0) )
            break;                /* it's not a prime so exit the for loop */
      }

      if (!found)                         /* We got one... */
         *(pPrimes+count++) = trial;   /* ..so save it in primes array */
   }while (count < NumPrimes );

   // Output primes 5 to a line
   for( i=0U ; i<NumPrimes ; i++)
   {
      if( (i%5U)==0U )                 /* New line on 1st, and every 5th line */
         printf("\n");
      printf("%10ld", *(pPrimes+i));
   }

   free(pPrimes);                        /* Release the memory before we go */

   return 0;
}
```

Program Analysis

This is very similar to the original, so let's just look at the changes. The primes are now to be stored on the heap, so we've the pointer **pPrimes** which will store the address of the space that is allocated:

```
long *pPrimes=NULL;                     /* Pointer to primes array */
```

This value is used as the first argument to **calloc()**, with the second argument being **sizeof(long)**, so the function will provide space for **NumPrimes** elements of type **long**:

```
if((pPrimes=(long*)calloc(NumPrimes, sizeof(long)))==NULL)
```

Both arguments to **calloc()** need to be of type **unsigned   int**.

The type **size_t** is defined in the standard library as **unsigned int**, and values of this type are returned by the operator **sizeof**. The variables **count** and **NumPrimes**, and the loop counter **i**, have all been declared as type **unsigned int** for consistency and to avoid compiler warnings which you may get if they're different. So the maximum number of primes the program will generate is limited to the maximum value of an **unsigned int**, although it may also be limited by the maximum value of a type **long** number and the amount of time you are prepared to wait for output.

Extending a Memory Area

The **realloc()** function allows you to increase the size of a memory block that you've already created on the heap. Assuming that you've already created an initial area of say 100 bytes, to store a string and its address in a pointer **pArea**, you can increase the area with:

```
pArea=(char *)realloc( (void *)pArea, 200);
```

The new area will be 200 bytes. The first argument to **realloc()** is a cast of type 'pointer to **void**' because, this is the type the function expects. The second argument specifies the size of the new area, and its address is returned by the function. Any data stored in the original area on the heap pointed to by **pArea** will remain, but the additional space won't be initialized. The size of a memory area on the heap can also be reduced by this function, in which case the data originally stored in the smaller area is also retained.

If the function **realloc()** can't reallocate the memory, then it will return **NULL**, and in this situation leave the first argument unchanged. If you wanted to retain the original memory area in these circumstances, you would need to save the address returned from **realloc()** in a different pointer from that containing the address of the original memory area.

Summary

We have seen how arrays are declared and used and how they relate to pointers. While they have a role in many numerical calculations, pointers are by far the most common basis for processing and managing data in C. It's therefore most important that you hone your knowledge and skill in the use of pointers. They are essential to good programming in C.

The important points we have discussed in this chapter are:

- Arrays enable you to define a number of elements of one type and manage them through a single variable name. Individual elements in an array are referenced using one or more index values.

- A pointer is a variable that can store the address of another variable or value of a specified type. You can obtain the address of a variable using the **&** operator, and you can use the value stored at the location pointed to with a pointer by using the dereference operator *.

- You can perform arithmetic on pointers. You can add or subtract a constant integer value, in which case the change in the address is in terms of a number of units of the pointer type. You can also subtract one pointer from another when they point to elements of the same array - the difference will be in terms of the number of elements.

- Pointers and arrays are quite strongly related. You can use array notation with a pointer and vice versa, but remember - an array name is *not* a pointer, so you can't modify it. You can only use it in expressions to access an element of the array, whereas you can modify the address stored in a pointer.

- You can allocate memory for your data using functions provided by the standard library. In order to use them you must include the header file **STDLIB.H** in your program.

Programming Exercises

1 Write a program to read a string into an array, and then reverse the sequence of characters in the string and display the result You can exercise the program with palindromes such as:

Madam I'm Adam
A man a plan a canal Panama
Ned I am a maiden

2 Write the same program, but this time use pointers.

3 Write a program using pointers to compare two strings. Do this by making character by character comparisons. The string with the first character that has a code value greater than the other, is greater. If one string is longer than the other, and the characters in the shorter strings are identical to the corresponding characters in the longer string, then the longer string is the greater.

4 Write a program using pointers to read a string, and to capitalize the first letter of each word. Assume the string begins with a word, and that each succeeding word is preceded by a space. Don't forget to allow for the possibility that the first letter of a word may already be a capital.

5 Write a program using pointers to count the frequency of different letters in a string.

Chapter

Using Functions

Now that we understand the computational aspects of C, and the kinds of data that we can deal with, we are going to look into how the components of a C program are put together. To successfully produce a program of significant complexity, it's essential to be able to break the program up into manageable units. Defining these units is the subject of this chapter. By the end of this chapter, you will have learnt:

- The concept and structure of a C function.

- What a function prototype is, and why it's necessary.

- How information is passed to a function and how you can get results back.

- How pointers are used to transfer information to and from a function.

- How static variables can be used within a function.

- What a recursive function is and how recursion works.

- How to process command-line arguments in your program.

Functions

Functions are the basic building blocks for creating a program. All the examples we have written have consisted of a single function, **main()**, but as we saw in Chapter 1, a real world C program usually comprises many functions. A function is a self-contained block of code with a specific purpose. It can have data passed to it and it can return a value. It has a unique name to identify it, governed by the same rules as those for a variable, and that function name is used to call it for execution.

> Note that a function name only needs to be unique among the functions in your program. A variable or a statement label can have the same name as a function without interfering with it, although using the same name for a variable, label and function isn't a particularly good habit.

Executing a function is referred to as a **function call**, or **calling** a function. When a function is called, execution transfers to the first statement of the function, and on its completion, the function returns control to the calling point. A function can be called as many times as necessary from different points in a program. Therefore, if you have a computation used several times in a program, packaging it into a function will save considerable memory space because this will avoid duplicating code.

The Structure of a Function

The first line of a function, specifying its name, is called the **function header**. This is followed by the function's executable code, called the **body** of the function, which is situated between curly braces. The structure of a function is illustrated in this diagram:

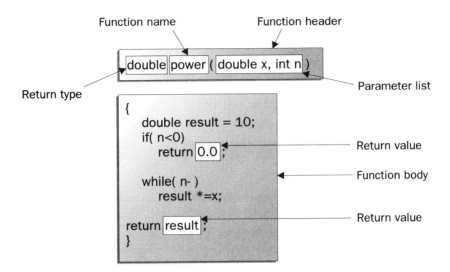

Function name   Function header

double power (double x, int n)

Return type   Parameter list

```
{
    double result = 10;
    if( n<0)
        return 0.0 ;

    while( n- )
        result *=x;

    return result ;
}
```

Return value

Function body

Return value

The diagram also shows the components of the function header, which we'll discuss later. All the variable names that are declared within the body of a function are local to that function, so you don't have to worry about avoiding unnecessary duplication.

Program Analysis

Let's look at the example shown in the illustration in a little more detail. It will raise a value of type **double** to a given positive integral power, such as compute x^n. Here is a commented version:

```
/******************************************************
 *  A function which will compute the positive     *
 *  integral power, n, of a double value, x,       *
 *  and return the result as double.               *
 ******************************************************/
double power( double x, int n )        /* Function header */

{                                      /* Function body starts here */
    double result = 1.0;               /* Result stored here */

    if( n<0 )                          /* Check that n is not negative */
        return 0.0;                    /* Error return */

    while( n-- )
        result *= x;                   /* Calculate x*x..*x with n terms */

    return result;                     /* Return value to calling point */
}                                      /* ...and ends here */
```

To understand how this works, let's look at it one part at a time.

The Function Header

Typically, we won't include the initial description of functions in our examples, in order to avoid overly inflating the page count. You should, however, get into the habit of including a description in your examples.

The return value is returned to the calling function when execution of the function is finally completed. The value to be returned is specified within the body of the function by a **return** statement. As you can see here, there can be more than one **return** statement in a function.

When our function is called by using it within an arithmetic expression, the **double** value returned will be used in the expression's evaluation. Any function that has a return type other than **void** must have a **return** statement specifying the value to be returned.

Our function has two parameters - the first is **x**, the value to be raised to a given power (of type **double**) and the second is **n**, the value of the power to which **x** is to be raised (of type **int**). Note that no semi-colon is required at the end of the function header. If you include one, then it becomes a prototype and the code that follows it becomes erroneous.

Function Header Syntax

The general form of a function header can be written as:

```
return_type  FunctionName( parameter_list )
```

The **return_type** can be any legal type. If the function doesn't return a value, then the keyword **void** should be specified. The **void** keyword is also used to indicate the absence of parameters, so a function that has no parameters and doesn't return a value would have a header like this:

```
void  MyFunction( void )
```

If nothing is specified for the parameter list, then this also an indication that the function has no parameters.

You mustn't use a function with a return type specified as **void** in an expression combining it with other variables or constants in your program. Since it doesn't return a value, it can't participate in any calculation defined by an expression. You can only use it in a statement by itself.

The Function Body

The computation is performed by the statements in the block following the function header. This is called the **function body**. In our example, the first statement declares a variable **result**, initialized with the value 1.0, because any number raised to the power 0 is equivalent to 1. The variable **result** is local to the function, as are all variables declared within the function body. This means that the variable **result** is automatically created and initialized each time the function is called, and ceases to exist after the function has completed its execution. For this reason, variables local to a function are sometimes called **automatic variables**. Once execution of the function is finished, the memory that the variable **result** occupies may well be used for something else.

After the declaration of the variable result, the **if** statement checks whether **n** is negative. If it is, then a value of 0.0 is returned arbitrarily, since the function isn't intended to deal with negative values for **n**. You could easily add code here to deal with a negative exponent, but you would need to check that **x** wasn't zero.

147

As we have said, the names of all the variables declared within the body of a function are local. This includes the parameter names too. There is nothing to prevent you from using the same names for variables in other functions. Indeed, this is just as well. It would be extremely difficult to ensure that variable names are always unique with a program containing a large number of functions, particularly if they weren't all written by the same person.

The return Statement

The first **return** statement returns 0.0 if **n** is negative, and the second **return** statement returns the value of **result**. The value is returned to the point where the function was called. The thought that might immediately strike you is that we just said **result** ceases to exist on completing execution of the function - so how is it returned? The answer is that a copy is made of the value being returned, and this copy is made available to the return point in the program.

The general form of the return statement is:

```
return   expression;
```

where **expression** must evaluate to a value of the type specified in the function header for the return value. The **expression** can be any expression, as long as you end up with a value of the required type.

If you've specified the type of return value as **void**, then there must be no expression appearing in any **return** statement within the function. It must simply be written as:

```
return;
```

With a return type of **void**, you aren't obliged to include a **return** statement in your function at all - when execution of the body of such a function reaches the closing brace, it will automatically return to the calling point in your program.

Using Functions

Before you can use a function in a program, you must declare it using a statement called a **function prototype**. This enables the compiler to check that the usage of the function is correct.

Function Prototypes

A prototype for a function provides the compiler with basic information about how the function is used. It specifies the parameters to be passed, the function name and the type of the **return** value, essentially the same information as the function header, with the addition of a semi-colon. The compiler is able to check the types of the arguments passed to a function and to verify that they correspond with the types of parameters appearing in the prototype. If they don't match, then if possible, the compiler will automatically cast the arguments you use to the required type, or else it will issue an error message.

The prototypes for the functions used in a program must always appear before the functions are called, and are usually grouped together at the beginning of a program. The header files we've been including for standard library functions include the prototypes of all the functions provided by that library.

Prototypes are only necessary if a function is used before it is declared; if, in your source file, you put all your functions before the main routine, then the compiler has all the information it needs and prototypes aren't necessary. However, it takes little effort and is always good practice to put them in.

Function Parameter Naming

For our `power()` example we could write the prototype as:

```
double power( double value, int index );
```

Note that we've specified different names for the parameters, just to show that this is possible. Normally, in the definition of the function, the same names are used in the prototype as in the function header, but it doesn't have to be so. You can choose the parameter names in the function prototype to help you understand exactly what they're used for.

You can also omit the names altogether if you like, and just write:

```
double power( double, int );
```

This is just enough for the compiler to do its job, but it's better practice to use some descriptive labels in a prototype, and in some cases it can make all the difference. If you have a function with two parameters of the same type and you omit the names from the prototype, you'll have no information about which parameter comes first.

A Simple Function Example

We can exercise the options available with a function, by trying out our **power()** function in an example:

```
/* EX5-01.C  Declaring, defining, and using a function */
#include <stdio.h>

double power( double x, int n );       /* Function prototype */

int main()
{
    int index = 3;              /* Raise to this power */
    double x = 3.0;             /* Different x from that in function power */
    double y = 0.0;             /* Store return value here */

    y = power( 5.0, 3 );                /* Passing constants as arguments */
    printf("\n5.0 cubed is %f", y);     /* Display the result */

    /* Calling the function in an argument to printf() */
    printf("\n3.0 cubed = %.3f", power( 3.0, index ));

    /*Calling the function in an argument to a call of the same function */
    x = power( power( x, 2 ), index ); /* Computes x to the power 6 */
    printf("\nx = %.2f\n\n", x);

    /* Using a function in a loop */
    for(index=0;index<=8;index++)
        printf("%6.0f", power(2.0, index));
```

```
    return 0;
}

/**********************************************
 *   A function which will compute  the     *
 *   integral power, n, of a double value,  *
 *   x, and return the result as double.    *
 **********************************************/
double power( double x, int n )        /* Function header */
{                                      /* Function body starts here */
   double result = 1.0;                /* Result stored here */

   if( n<0 )                           /* Check that n is not negative */
      return 0.0;                      /* Error return */

   while( n-- )
      result *=x;                      /* Calculate x*x..*x with n terms */

   return result;                      /* Return value to calling point */
}                                      /* ...and ends here */
```

Program Analysis

This program shows some of the ways in which we can use the function
power() in the way that arguments are specified. If you run this example,
you will get this output:

```
5.0 cubed is 125.000000
3.0 cubed = 27.000
x = 729.00

    1    2    4    8    16   32   64   128   256
```

You will have already gathered from some of our previous examples that
using a function is very simple. To use the function **power()** to calculate 5^3
and store the result in a variable **y** in our example, we have written:

```
y = power( 5.0, 3 );            /* Passing constants as arguments */
```

The values **5.0** and **3** are called **arguments**. They happen to be constants,
but any expression can be used as an argument, as long as, ultimately, a
value of the correct type is produced. The arguments substitute for the
parameters x and **n**, which were used in the definition of the function. The
computation is performed using these values and a copy of the result, 125.0,

will be returned to the calling function, **main()**, and stored in **y**. You can think of the function as having this value in the statement or expression in which it appears.

The next call of the function is actually used within the output statement:

```
printf("\n3.0 cubed = %.3f", power( 3.0, index ));
```

so the value returned from the function is used as the argument to **printf()**. Since we haven't stored the returned value anywhere, we can't access it or use it for any other purpose.

The **power()** function is next used in the statement:

```
x = power( power( x, 2 ), index );         /* Computes x to the power 6 */
```

where the function will be called twice. The first call of the function will be the rightmost in the expression, appearing as the first argument to the second call of the function. The **double** result, 9.0, will be returned and inserted as the first argument in the call of the next function, with **index** as the second argument. Since **index** has the value 3, the value of 9.0^3 will be computed and the result 729.0 stored in **x**. This sequence of events is illustrated here:

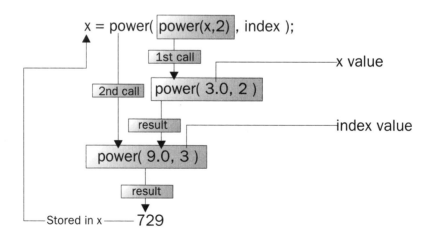

Passing Arguments to a Function

It is most important to understand how arguments are passed to a function in C, as it will affect how you write functions and how they will ultimately operate. There are also a number of pitfalls to be avoided, so we'll look at this mechanism more closely. The arguments specified when a function is called should usually correspond in type and sequence with the parameters appearing in the definition of the function. If they don't, then your compiler should convert them so that they do, or generate an error message if this isn't possible.

In C, a function has no access to the original values you use as arguments. All argument values are copied, and the copies are passed on to the function. Because the function is working with copies, we were able to decrement the parameter **n** quite safely, without affecting the original argument. This mechanism is called the **pass-by-value** (or **pass-by-copy**) method of transferring data to a function.

The Pass by Value Mechanism

With this method, the values of the variables or constants you specify as arguments aren't passed to a function at all. Consequently, a function cannot directly modify the arguments passed. We can demonstrate this by deliberately trying to do so in this example:

```
/* EX5-02.C  A futile attempt to modify caller arguments */
#include <stdio.h>

int AddTen( int value );                    /* Function prototype */

int main( void )
{
   int value = 3;                           /* Argument value to be passed */

   printf("\nvalue starts as %d", value);
   printf("\nAddTen(value) returns %d", AddTen(value));
   printf("\nvalue is now %d", value);

   return 0;
}
```

```
/*********************************************
 * Function to increment a variable by 10 *
 * This works best executed in a fairy     *
 * ring in the presence of a leprechaun.   *
 *********************************************/
int AddTen( int value )     /* Using the same name might help... */
{
    value += 10;            /* Increment the caller argument - hopefully */
    return value;           /* Return the incremented value */
}
```

Program Analysis

Of course this program is doomed to fail due to a shortage of leprechauns. If this program modifies the caller argument on your computer, then the most likely explanation is that a leprechaun sold you a dubious compiler. If you compile this example and run it, you should get this output:

```
value starts as 3
AddTen(value) returns 13
value is now 3
```

This confirms that the original value of **value** remains untouched. The incrementation occurred on the local copy of **value**, which was eventually discarded when we exited from the function.

Clearly the pass-by-value mechanism provides a high degree of protection from having caller arguments mauled by a rogue function, but it is conceivable that we might actually want to modify caller arguments. There is, of course, a way to do this. Didn't you just know that pointers would turn out to be incredibly useful?

Pointers as Arguments to a Function

When you use a pointer as an argument, the pass-by-value mechanism still operates as before. However, a pointer is an address of another variable, and if you take a copy of this address, the copy still points to the same variable.

Specifying a pointer as a parameter enables your function to get at a caller argument. If we change the last example to use a pointer, we can demonstrate this effect:

```
/* EX5-03.C  Modifying caller arguments through a pointer */
#include <stdio.h>

int AddTen( int* pvalue );                    /* Function prototype */

int main( void )
{
   int value = 3;                             /* Argument value to be passed */

   printf("\nvalue starts as %d", value);
   printf("\nAddTen(value) returns %d", AddTen(&value));
   printf("\nvalue is now %d", value);

   return 0;
}

/*********************************************
 * Function to increment a variable by 10 *
 * This works without the aid of a fairy  *
 * ring or a leprechaun.                  *
 *********************************************/
int AddTen( int *pvalue )                     /* Using a pointer should help... */
{
   *pvalue += 10;          /* Increment the caller argument - confidently */
   return *pvalue;                            /* Return the incremented value */
}
```

Program Analysis

In this version of the program, the function **AddTen()** has been modified to accept a pointer as an argument, and to work through the address passed as an argument. The prototype for the function now has the parameter type specified as a pointer to **int**, and in the function **main()**, the address of the variable **value** is passed to the function. The function **AddTen()** will still receive a copy of the address passed, but the copy will still point to the same memory location, so the variable **value** in **main()** is modified by the function. This is confirmed by the output from the program.

In the rewritten version of the function **AddTen()**, both the statement incrementing the value passed to the function, and the return statement, now need to dereference the pointer in order to use the value.

You can now see why **scanf()** needs to have the arguments determining where the input is to be stored, to be specified as addresses. The only way **scanf()** can modify variables in your program is if pointers are passed as arguments. Equally, you should be able to see why forgetting to prefix a variable name in the argument list to **scanf()** with **&**, causes such problems. The function treats whatever you pass as an argument as an address, and since it has no way to authenticate it, it will attempt to store all the input there, regardless of its validity - perhaps writing a string where your operating system is stored, causing an inevitable system crash!

Arrays as Function Arguments

You can also pass an array to a function. In this case, however, the array isn't copied, even though a pass-by-value method of passing arguments still applies. The array name is specified as the argument, converted to a pointer, and a copy of this pointer to the beginning of the array is passed to the function. This is quite advantageous, since copying a large array for each call of a function could be very time-consuming, and expensive on memory. We can illustrate the ins and outs of this by writing a function to compute the length of a string that is passed to a function in a **char** array:

```c
/* EX5-04.C  Passing an array to a function */
#include <stdio.h>
int StrLength( char array[] );                    /* Function prototype */

int main(void)
{
   char Quote[] =
         { "Sir, I have found you an argument;"
           " but I am not obliged to find you an understanding." };

   printf("\nThe string:\n\t%s\nhas %d characters.",
                                    Quote, StrLength(Quote)-1);

   return 0;
}


/***********************************************
 * Function to compute the length of a string *
 * including the '\0'.                         *
 ***********************************************/
int StrLength( char array[] )
{
   int Length = 0;                         /* Store string length in here */
   while(array[Length++]);

   return Length;                          /* Return the string length */
}
```

Program Analysis

The function **StrLength()** will work with a character array of any length. As you can see from the prototype, there's only one parameter, **array[]**, which appears without a specified dimension. When specifying a parameter as a one-dimensional array there is little point in actually specifying a dimension, since only the address of the first element is passed as an argument. Multi-dimensional arrays are a little different, as we shall see later.

The initializing string, a quote from Samuel Johnson, defines the length of the array **Quote[]**. The initializing string is defined as two concatenated string constants, simply because as a single string constant, it's too long to fit on the page.

The value returned from **StrLength()** includes the **'\0'**, so we subtract 1 in the argument to **printf()** to obtain the character count, excluding the **'\0'**.

When **array[Length]** contains **'\0'**, **Length** will be incremented once more and the loop will end. The final value of **Length** is returned as the count of the number of characters, including the **'\0'**.

If you run the example it will output the length of the string as 85, confirming that everything works as we anticipated.

Example Modification

However, we haven't exhausted all the possibilities here. As we determined at the outset, the array name is passed as a pointer, in fact as a copy of a pointer, so within the function we don't have to deal with the data as an array at all. We could modify the function to work with pointer notation throughout, despite the fact that we started out with an array in **main()**, and that the pointer passed to the function contains the address of an array.

```
/* EX5-05.C  Passing an array to a function and using it as a pointer */
#include <stdio.h>

int StrLength( char *array );               /* Function prototype */

int main(void)
{
```

```
      char Quote[] =
            { "Sir, I have found you an argument;"
              " but I am not obliged to find you an understanding." };

      printf("\nThe string:\n\t%s\nhas %d characters.",
                                      Quote, StrLength(Quote)-1);

      return 0;
}

/*************************************************
 * Function to compute the length of a string *
 * including the '\0'.                         *
 *************************************************/
int StrLength( char *array )
{
   char *pArray = array;              /* Store address passed in here */
   while(*array++);

   return array-pArray;               /* Return the string length */
}
```

Program Analysis

The prototype and the function header have been changed, although neither is absolutely necessary. If you change both back to the original version, with the first parameter specified as an array, and leave the function body written in terms of a pointer, then it'll work just as well.

The most interesting aspect of this version is the **while** loop statement:

```
while(*array++);
```

where we apparently break the rule about being unable to modify an address specified as an array name. In fact, we aren't actually breaking the rule. You may recall that the pass-by-value mechanism makes a copy of the original array address and passes that to the function, so here we're modifying the copy, and the original array address will be unaffected. As a result, whenever we pass a one-dimensional array to a function, we're free to treat the value passed as a pointer and to change the address in any way that we wish.

The length of the string is computed in the **return** statement as the difference between the two pointers. We saw this method of obtaining the length of a string in the previous chapter (**EX4-07.C**). Of course, this version of the program produces exactly the same output.

Passing Multi-dimensional Arrays to a Function

Passing a multi-dimensional array to a function is quite straightforward. For instance:

```
char Strings[10][80];
```

You could write the prototype of a hypothetical function **SortStrings()**, as:

```
int SortStrings(char Strings[10][80]);
```

You may be wondering how the compiler can know that it's defining an array of the dimensions shown as an argument, and not a single array element. Well, the answer is simple - you can't write a single array element as a parameter, only as an argument.

When defining a multi-dimensional array as a parameter, you can also omit the first dimension value. Of course, the function will need some way of knowing the extent of the first dimension. For example, you could write:

```
int SortStrings(char Strings[][80], int index );
```

where the second parameter would provide the necessary information about the first dimension. Here, the function can operate with a two-dimensional array with any value for the first dimension, but with the second dimension fixed at 80.

Returning Values from a Function

All the examples of functions we have created up to now have returned a single value. Is it possible to return anything other than a single value? Well, not directly, no, but the single value returned need not be a numeric value. It can also be an address, providing the key to returning any amount of data. You just use a pointer - but this is where the pitfalls start so you need to be very careful.

Returning a Pointer

Returning a pointer value is very easy. A pointer value is just an address, so if you want to return the address of some variable called **value**, you can just write:

```
return &value;                              /* Returning an address */
```

and as long as the function header and prototype indicate the return type appropriately, then we don't have a problem. Of course, if you have a pointer variable with the address already stored, then you can use that in the **return** statement. Assuming that the variable **value** is of type **long**, the prototype of a function containing the above **return** statement might be:

```
long* Factorial( long number );
```

So let's look at a function which will return a pointer.

A Pointer Returning Example

We could try to write a function that produces a factorial of an integer, the product of all integers from 1 to the given number. For example, factorial 4 (usually written 4!) is the equivalent of 1x2x3x4, which is 24. You should know in advance that this first attempt to produce the function doesn't work, but press on - it's educational.

Let's assume that we need a function to return a pointer to the factorial of its argument value. Our first try might look like:

```
/* Function to calculate a factorial - Version 000001 */
long* factorial( long number )
{
   long result = 1;

   do
   {
      result *= number;
   }while(number--);

   return &result;
}
```

We could create a little test program to see what happens:

```
/*EX5-06.C  Testing the factorial function */
#include <stdio.h>

long* factorial( long number );                /* Function prototype */

int main(void)
{
   long num = 5L;                               /* Test value */
   long* ptr=NULL;                              /* Pointer to returned value */

   ptr = factorial( num );

   printf("\nFactorial of 5 should be %ld", 1L*2L*3L*4L*5L;

   printf("\nResult = %ld", *ptr);             /* Display returned value */
}
```

Program Analysis

The function **main()** calls the **factorial()** function and stores the returned address in the pointer **ptr**. This should point to a value which is the factorial of the argument **num**. We then display the result of explicitly computing 5! to check against the result from the function. On my computer I get the output:

Factorial of 5 should be 120
Result = 13172

Well, clearly the second line doesn't reflect the correct value. The error arises because we're returning the address of a variable that is local to the function. The variable **result** in the function **factorial()** is created when the function begins execution and is destroyed on exiting from the function. The memory previously allocated to **result** becomes available for other purposes, and here it has evidently been used for something else. Here you must remember that there is a cast-iron rule:

> **Don't even think about returning the address of a local variable from a function.**

Now we have a function that doesn't work, and we need to think about how we can correct it. One answer lies in dynamic memory allocation. With the library function **malloc()**, we can create a new variable in the free

161

store that will continue to exist until it's eventually destroyed by a call to the function **free()**, or until the program ends. The function would then look like this:

```
/* Function to calculate a factorial - Version 000002 */
long* factorial( long number )
{
   long *result = malloc(sizeof(long));
   if(result == NULL)
   {
      printf("\nMemory allocation error. Program terminated.");
      exit(1);
   }

   *result = 1;
   do
   {
      *result *= number;
   }while(--number);

   return result;
}
```

We need to remember to include the header file **STDLIB.H** to use the **malloc()** function. Rather than declaring **result** as of type **long**, we now declare it as **long*** and store the returned **malloc()** address in it. We then have the necessary check that we got a valid address back, and exit the program if anything is wrong. The function **exit()** that is used here is from the standard library, and is declared in **STDLIB.H**. It provides a means of terminating a program from any point. The integer argument is passed back to the operating system environment as a termination condition. Zero usually indicates a normal program termination.

Since **result** is now a pointer, the rest of the function is changed to reflect this and the address contained in **result** is finally returned to the calling program. You could exercise this version by replacing the function in the previous program with this version. You will see that this now works as you would expect.

However, this is a rather poor implementation of this function. It would be much better to return a value rather than a pointer in this case, but at least it shows that you can return a pointer. You need to remember that with dynamic memory allocation in a function like this, memory is allocated each time the function is called, and it's the responsibility of the calling program to delete the memory when it's no longer required. It's easy to forget to do this in practice, with the result that the heap is gradually eaten up until there's no more memory available and the program will fail. When allocating memory dynamically, it's good practice to free the memory within the scope where it is allocated.

Static Variables in a Function

There are some things that you can't do with automatic variables in a function. For example, you can't count how many times a function is called, because you can't accumulate a value from one call to the next. However, there's more than one way to get around this if you need to. A good solution in most instances is to declare a variable within a function as **static**. You use exactly the same form of declaration for a **static** variable that we saw in Chapter 2. For example, to declare a variable **count** as **static** you could use the statement:

```
static int count = 0;
```

Initialization of a static variable within a function only occurs the first time the function is called. In fact on the first call of a function, the **static** variable is created and initialized. It then continues to exist for the duration of the program execution, and whatever value it contains when execution of the function is complete, is still available when the function is next called. We can demonstrate how this works with a simple example:

```
/* EX5-07.C  Using a static variable within a function */
#include <stdio.h>
void record(void);  /* Function prototype, no arguments or return value */

int main(void)
{
   record();

   for( int i = 0 ; i<= 3 ; i++ )
      record();

   return 0;
}

/* A function that records how often it is called */
void record(void)
{
   static int count = 0;
   printf("\nFunction record() called %d times.", ++count);
   return;
}
```

Program Analysis

Because the increment operation is a prefix, the newly incremented value is displayed by the **printf()** function, thus will be 1 on the first call, 2 on the second and so on. Because the variable **count** is **static**, it continues to exist and retain its value from one call of the function to the next.

Note the **return** statement. Because the return type of the function is **void**, to include a value would be an error. You don't actually need to include a **return** statement in this particular case. Running off the closing brace for the body of the function is equivalent to the **return** statement without a value, so the program will compile and run without the **return**. However, I prefer to include the **return** anyway.

Recursive Function Calls

When a function contains a call to itself, it's commonly referred to as a **recursive function**. This may seem like a recipe for an infinite loop, and if you aren't careful it certainly can be. A prerequisite for avoiding an infinite loop is that the function contains some means of stopping the process. Unless you have come across the technique before, the sort of things to which recursion may be applied may not at first be obvious.

However, situations that need recursion occur surprisingly often. As well as various mathematical functions, such as the factorial of an integer that we saw earlier, analyzing statements in a programming language can often use recursion to good effect. We shall, however, take something a little simpler to start with. Earlier, we produced a function to compute the integral power of a value, that is, compute x^n. We can implement this as an elementary illustration of recursion in action:

```c
/* EX5-08.C   A recursive version of x to the power n */
#include <stdio.h>
#include <stdlib.h>                    /* This for the exit() function */

double power( double x, int n );       /* Function prototype */

int main()
{
    int index = 3;          /* Raise to this power */
    double x = 3.0;         /* Different x from that in function power */
    double y = 0.0;         /* Store return value here */
```

```
      y = power( 5.0, 3 );                /* Passing constants as arguments */
      printf("\n5.0 cubed is %f", y);     /* Display the result */

      /* Calling the function in an argument to printf() */
      printf("\n3.0 cubed = %.3f", power( 3.0, index ));

    /* Calling the function in an argument to a call of the same function */
    x = power( power( x, 2 ), index ); /* Computes x to the power 6 */
    printf("\nx = %.2f\n\n", x);

      /* Using a function in a loop */
      for(index=0;index<=8;index++)
         printf("%6.0f", power(2.0, index));

      return 0;
   }

/*********************************************
 *   A function which will compute  the      *
 *   integral power, n, of a double value,   *
 *   x, and return the result as double.     *
 *********************************************/
double power( double x, int n )
{
   if(n<0)
   {
      printf("\nNegative index, program terminated.");
      exit(1);
   }
   if(n)
      return x*power( x, n-1 );
   else
      return 1.0;
}
```

Program Analysis

We only intend to support positive powers of **x**, so the first action is to check that the value of the second argument, **n**, isn't negative.

```
   if(n<0)
   {
      printf("\nNegative index, program terminated.");
      exit(1);
   }
```

With a recursive implementation this is essential, since a negative value will cause an infinite loop.

The **if** statement provides for the value 1.0 being returned if **n** is zero, or otherwise returning the result of the expression **x*power(x, n-1)**. This causes a further call of the function **power()** with the index value reduced by 1. Clearly, within the function **power()**, if the value of **n-1** is greater than zero, then a further call of the **power()** function will occur. Ultimately, the function **power()** will be called with an index value of 0, so 1 will be returned. This will be multiplied by **x** at the next level, and that value subsequently returned. The recursive calls will continue to unwind until the first level will return **x^n**. For a given value of **n** greater than 0, the function will call itself **n** times. The operation of the function with **n** having the value 3 is illustrated here:

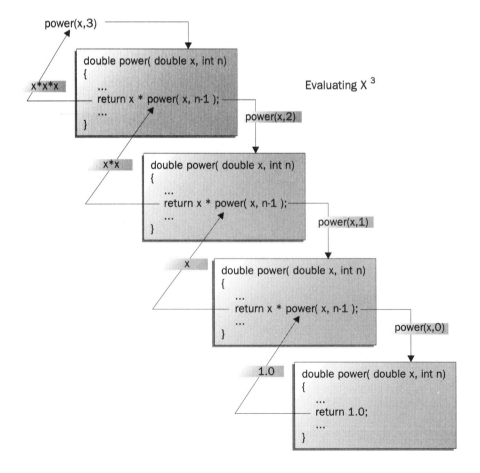

Using Recursion

Unless you have a problem which particularly lends itself to using recursive functions, or if you have no obvious alternative, then it's generally better to use a different approach, such as a loop. This will be much more efficient than using recursive function calls. Think about what happens with our last example to evaluate a simple product, **x*x*...x n** times. On each call, the compiler will generate copies of the two arguments to the function. It also has to keep track of the location to return to when each **return** is executed. It is also necessary to arrange to save the contents of various registers, so that they can be used within the function **power().**Of course, these will need to be restored to their original state at each **return** from the function. With a quite modest depth of recursive call, the overhead will be considerably greater than using a loop.

This isn't to say that you should never use recursion. Where the problem suggests the use of recursive function calls as a solution, the technique can be immensely powerful and can greatly simplify your code.

Pointers to Functions

A pointer stores an address value which, up to now, has been the address of another variable with the same basic type as the pointer. This has provided considerable flexibility by allowing us to use different variables at different times through a single pointer. A pointer can also point to the address of a function. This enables you to call a function through a pointer, and the specific function that will be called will be the function that was last assigned to the pointer.

Obviously, a pointer to a function must contain the address of the function to which it points, but if it's to work properly, more information is necessary. It has to maintain information about the parameter list for the function it points to, as well as the return type. Therefore, when we declare a pointer to a function, the parameter types and the return type of the functions it can point to have to be specified, in addition to the name of the pointer.

Declaring Pointers to Functions

Let's declare a pointer **pfun**, that can point to functions that take two arguments of type **char*** and **int**, and will return a value of type **double**. The declaration would be:

```
double (*pfun)(char*, int);        /* Pointer to function declaration */
```

This may look a little weird at first because of all the parentheses. The parentheses enclosing the pointer name, **pfun**, and the asterisk are necessary, since without them it would be a prototype, rather than a declaration.

You can initialize a pointer to a function by including the name in the declaration of the pointer. Assuming we have a function defined with the prototype:

```
long sum( long num1, long num2);            /* Function prototype */
```

we can declare a pointer to a function with the statement:

```
long (*pfun)(long, long) = sum;             /* Pointer to function */
```

Here, the pointer **pfun** is declared as pointing to any function that accepts two arguments of type **long**, and also returns a **long** value. It is also initialized with the address of the function **sum()**. We could now call the function **sum()** using the pointer with a statement such as:

```
total = pfun( ivalue, jvalue);
```

Here the variables **total**, **ivalue** and **jvalue** are all of type **long**.

Of course, you can also initialize a pointer to a function with an assignment statement. Assuming the pointer **pfun** has been declared as above, and that we've declared and defined the function **product()** accepting two arguments of type **long**, we could set the value of the pointer with the statement:

```
pfun = product;                  /* Set pointer to function product() */
```

As with pointers to variables, you must ensure that a pointer to a function is initialized before you use it to call a function. Without initialization, catastrophic failure of your program is guaranteed.

Using Pointers to Functions

To get a proper feel for how a pointer to a function operates, let's try one out in a program:

```c
/* EX5-09.C  Exercising pointers to functions */
#include <stdio.h>

long sum(long a, long b);              /* Function prototype */
long product(long a, long b);          /* Function prototype */

int main(void)
{
   long (*pdo_it)(long, long);         /* Pointer to function declaration */

   pdo_it = product;
   printf("\n3*5 = %ld", pdo_it(3, 5));  /* Call product thru a pointer */

   pdo_it = sum;                          /* Reassign pointer to sum()   */

   /* Now call sum() through a pointer - twice */
   printf("\n3*(4+5) + 6 = %ld", pdo_it(product(3, pdo_it(4, 5)), 6));

   return 0;
}

/* Function to multiply two values */
long product(long a, long b)
{
   return a*b;
}

/* Function to add two values */
long sum(long a, long b)
{
   return a+b;
}
```

Program Analysis

This is hardly a useful program, but it does show how a pointer to a function is declared, is assigned a value, and is subsequently used to call a function.

After the usual preamble, we declare a pointer to a function, **pdo_it**, that can point to any function with two arguments of type **long,** and returning a value of type **long**. The two functions we've defined, **sum()** and `product()`, are consistent with this. The pointer is used to store the address of the function `product()` in the assignment statement:

```
pdo_it  =  product;
```

When initializing an ordinary pointer, the name of the function is used in a similar manner to that of an array name - no parentheses or other adornments are required. The function name is automatically converted to an address, which is stored in the pointer.

The name of the pointer is used just as if it were a function name, and is followed by the arguments between parentheses exactly as they'd appear if the original function name was being used directly.

Just to show we can do it, the pointer is then changed to point to the function `sum()`. We then use it again in an incredibly convoluted expression to do some simple arithmetic. From this you can see that a pointer to a function can be used in exactly the same way as a function.

A Pointer to a Function as an Argument

Since a pointer to a function is a perfectly reasonable type, a function can also have an argument that's a pointer to a function. This allows the calling program to determine which function is to be called from inside a function. You can pass a function explicitly as an argument in this case.

We can look at this with an example. Suppose that we need a function to process an array of numbers by producing the sum of the squares of each on some occasions, and the sum of the cubes on others. One way of achieving this is by using a pointer to a function as an argument:

```
/*EX5-10.C  A pointer to a function as an argument */
#include <stdio.h>

double squared(double);                        /* Function prototype */
double cubed(double);                          /* Function prototype */

/* Prototype of a function with 3rd parameter as pointer to function */
double sumarray(double array[], int len, double (*pfun)(double));

int main(void)
{
   double array[]=
```

```
            { 1.5, 2.5, 3.5, 4.5, 5.5, 6.5, 7.5 };
   int len = sizeof array/sizeof array[0];

   printf("\nSum of squares = %.3f", sumarray(array,len,squared));

   printf("\nSum of cubes = %.3f", sumarray(array,len,cubed));

   return 0;
}

/* Function for a square of a value */
double squared( double x)
{
   return x*x;
}

/* Function for a cube of a value */
double cubed( double x)
{
   return x*x*x;
}

/* Function to sum functions of array elements */
double sumarray(double array[], int len, double (*pfun)(double))
{
   double total = 0.0;          /* Accumulate total in here */
   int i=0;                     /* Loop counter */

   for(; i<len ; i++)
      total +=pfun(array[i]);   /* Call function through the pointer */

   return total;
}
```

Program Analysis

The first statement of interest is the prototype for the function **sumarray()**. Its third parameter is a pointer to a function. The pointer can store the address of a function that has a single parameter of type **double**, and returns a value of type **double**.

We call the function **sumarray()** twice in **main()**, the first time with **squared** as the third argument, and the second time using **cubed**. In each case the address corresponding to the function name used as an argument will be substituted for the function pointer in **sumarray()**. As a result, the appropriate function will be called within the **for** loop, so that **sumarray()** will return the sum of squares in the first instance, and the sum of cubes in the second.

171

There are obviously easier ways of achieving what this example does. But you can see how using a pointer to a function can provide you with a lot of generality. You could pass any function you care to define to the function **sumarray()**, as long as it takes one **double** argument and returns a value of type **double**.

The example will generate the output:

```
Sum of squares = 169.750
Sum of cubes = 1015.875
```

These answers are just what we'd expect, so obviously the function pointer is doing its job.

Handling Command-line Arguments

Arguments can be passed to your program when you execute it, and you can process these very easily. When you start your program, you access specified arguments on the command-line through parameters to the function **main()**. There can be two parameters to the function **main()**, usually named **argc** and **argv**:

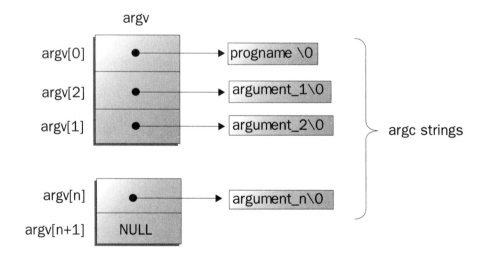

Scope

The first parameter, **argc** (of type **int**), is a count of the number of arguments specified on the command-line invoking the program, including the program name. The second parameter, **argv**, is an array of pointers to character strings. The first string is the name of the program, and the following strings are the command-line arguments. The string containing the last command-line argument will be followed by an empty string containing just the string termination character '\0'. Since the program name is always present, **argc** is always at least 1. In a practical situation, all of the strings may be of various lengths.

We can see how this works using a program that just displays the command-line arguments:

```
/*EX5-11.C  Displaying the command-line */
#include <stdio.h>
int main(int argc, char *argv[])
{
   int i=0;                          /* Loop counter */

   printf("\n");                     /* Start on a new line */

   for(; i<argc; i++)
      printf("%s ",argv[i]);         /* Display a command-line argument */

   return 0;
}
```

Program Analysis

The header for the function **main()** specifies the two parameters **argc** and **argv**. Usually, they are given these names, but you could use your own if you wish. The **for** loop steps through the strings pointed to by **argv[]** up to **argv[argc-1]**, displaying the complete command-line, starting with the program name and followed by each argument.

Another Look at Scope

We briefly looked at variable scope in Chapter 2, but we didn't go through the whole story, so let's rectify that now. We already know that the scope of automatic variables defined within a block extends from the point at which they're declared to the end of that block. Their existence is also limited to the same extent, so that at the end of the block in which they are declared, they are discarded. This applies to any block, including function blocks.

173

A variable defined outside of all the blocks in a program is a global variable. A global variable has a scope which extends from the point of its declaration to the end of the file in which its declaration appears. It's accessible anywhere in the program file, as long as another variable hasn't been declared with the same name in another block elsewhere in the program file. If it has, then the global variable is hidden by the local variable of the same name. We can show how scope is determined graphically in the following illustration:

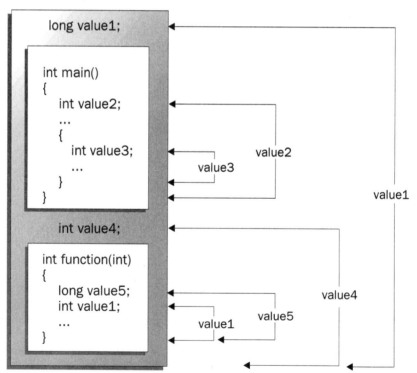

This shows a single program file containing two functions, **main()** and **function()**. The variable **value1** is global, and has a scope which extends from its declaration point to the end of the program file. It can therefore be accessed anywhere in the file, except within **function()**, where it'll be hidden by the local variable of the same name. The variable **value2** is declared in **main()** and has 'function' scope. It exists from its declaration to the end of **main()**. The variable **value3** is declared in a nested block in **main()**, so its scope is limited to the inner block.

The variable **value4** is another global variable with a scope running from its declaration point to the end of the file. Because its declaration appears after **main()**, it can't be accessed in **main()**. The scope of **value5** extends from its declaration to the end of **function()**.

Function names have a scope which extends throughout the entire file, but either the function or its prototype must appear in the file before it is called.

Multiple Source Files

A program divided into two or more source files raises a few additional questions. First of all, how can a function in one file call a function that has its definition in another file? This is quite straightforward. Every function that is used in a file, apart from **main()**, should have a prototype defined in the file. This leads to the idea of a file which contains definitions and declarations for everything that's common across the whole program. So, in programs contained in multiple source files, there is usually one file which contains all the function prototypes. The file normally has the extension **.H** and is copied into a file with a statement:

```
#include "mydefs.h"          /* Standard declarations & definitions */
```

We know that global variables declared outside of a function continue to exist throughout the life of a program. It would seem reasonable to expect that we could access a global variable from anywhere in a program, and indeed we can, but we do need to tell the compiler about it.

External Variables

To access a global variable from a file that is declared in another, we use the **extern** keyword. Assume that we have a variable number of type **long**, that is defined at global scope with the statement:

```
long number;                    /* Global definition */
```

To use the same variable in another file, we must include the declaration:

```
extern long number;            /* Declaration of number as external */
```

This statement simply advises the compiler that the variable **number** isn't defined in this file, but in another. The previous statement defined the global variable **number**. There can only be one definition of a global variable in your program, although external declarations for a global variable can appear as many times as you want, so these are also often aggregated into a common **.H** file.

Private Variables and Functions

Where static is applied to a global variable or function it causes it to have scope only within the file in which it is declared. Where static is applied to a local variable, although stored as a global variable, its scope is restricted to the function in which it is declared. Declaring a global variable as **static** ensures its privacy to the file in which it is defined. The statement:

```
static int number;
```

limits the global variable number to the file in which this statement appears, and **extern** statements in other files for a variable of the same name won't be able to access this variable.

You can also apply the keyword **static** in function prototypes. The prototype:

```
static int myfun(void);                      /* Private function */
```

limits the use of the function to the file in which this statement appears, and obviously the function definition must appear in the same file. The function **myfun()** is now private to one source file, allowing the possibility for other parts of the program to use a different function with the same name.

Summary

You should now be thinking about structuring your programs as sets of functions. Using functions enables you to shorten development time by simplifying the units of code that you need to deal with, making them easier to write and test. It also enables you to reuse functions that provide general processing capability in multiple programs.

The important points we have covered in this chapter are:

- Each function in your program, with the exception of **main()**, requires a function prototype, which should be placed at the beginning of the program file.

- All variables names used within a function definition are local to the function and can be duplicated elsewhere.

- A function with a return type other than **void** must contain a **return** statement. A function with a return type of **void** need not contain a **return** statement, but if it does, a return value mustn't be specified.

- When using a function, arguments should agree in number and type with those appearing in the prototype of the function and the function definition. If an argument type is different from the corresponding parameter type, then the compiler will attempt to convert the argument appropriately.

- You must never return a pointer to a local variable from a function.

- A pointer to a function can store the address of a function and can be used to subsequently call the stored function.

- A recursive function is a function that calls itself. To avoid infinite loops, care must be taken to ensure that a recursive function contains the means of ending a sequence of recursive calls.

Programming Exercises

1 Write a function to compare two strings specified as arguments, and return a value of 1 if the first string is greater than the second, and 0 if otherwise.

2 Use the function from the first example to read a series of strings, and then sort them into descending order and display them.

(Hint: Sort them in order by interchanging pointers.)

3 Write and test a function to accept an argument between 1 and 7, and return the name of the day of the week as a string.

4 Write and test a function to append a string onto the end of another. Use this function to write a program to assemble a series of input lines into a single string, and analyze the composite string for the frequency of occurrence of each letter. Try to write a function to test the frequency of each word as well.

5 Write and test a function to accept two string arguments, and find the initial occurrence of the first within the second. The index value of the first character of the occurrence should be returned, with -1 as the return value if the first string isn't found within the second.

6 Write a program using a recursive function to calculate the factorial of n, that is 1*2*3*...*n.

Chapter

Data Structures

This is the last chapter introducing new methods for organizing data in a C program. The tools we are going to look at in this chapter will enable you to handle any kind of data structure your application may require. In this chapter you will learn:

- What a structure is and how it is defined.
- How you access and process members of a structure.
- How you can use pointers to organize and link a series of structure variables.
- What a linked list is and how it's used.
- What a binary tree is, how it's constructed and used.
- What a union is and how it can be applied.

Structures

Although arrays are very useful, they don't accommodate reality very well since all the elements are essentially the same type. Most things that you want to deal with need a variety of data elements to describe them, often spanning the whole spectrum of data types we have seen so far in C.

If you wanted to describe something quite mundane, such as a TV set, then it has a brand name, a screen size, is color or monochrome, tunes a certain number of channels, has external dimensions, weighs a certain number of pounds, and consumes a certain amount of power, amongst many other things. It would be very useful to be able to handle a varied collection of data items such as this, under a single variable name, perhaps **TVSet**, and be able to access the component elements defining an entity of this kind when necessary. This is exactly what a **structure** enables you to do.

Declaring a Structure

A structure is a group of one or more variables of various types, identified by a single name. The first step in creating a structure is the definition of what it contains. This can then be used as a template for declaring variables which are instances of that particular structure.

Let's take an example. Supposing due to the failure of our attempts to induce rain or otherwise control the weather, we now turn to the heavens. We are interested in having a variable type for planets, since we are going to record basic information about the solar system. We can define a structure for planets as follows:

```
struct Planet
{
    char Name[80];          /* Normal name */
    double Mass;            /* Relative to Earth = 1 */
    double Year;            /* Time to go round the sun in Earth days */
    float Temperature;      /* Average surface temperature in deg. F */
    int Moons;              /* Number of moons */
    double SunDistance;     /* Average - in millions of miles */
};
```

The keyword **struct** indicates that this is a structure. This statement doesn't define a variable, it just defines a template called **Planet** which can be used to define variables with those data elements appearing between the braces. This amounts to a new type, in this example named **Planet**, but generally called a **structure tag**. The variables within this template are called **members**.

Each variable of type **Planet** will contain its own set of members with the names specified in the definition of the generic structure type. Note that a semi-colon is required after the closing brace in the definition of a structure.

Declaring Variables

We can declare a variable of type **Planet** with the statement:

```
struct Planet Earth;
```

This declares **Earth** as a structure variable of type **Planet**, so the variable **Earth** has the data members **Name[]**, **Mass**, **Year**, **Temperature**, **Moons**, and **SunDistance**. We can also define multiple structure variables in a single declaration:

```
struct Planet Mars, Venus, Pluto;
```

This statement declares the three variables **Mars**, **Venus** and **Pluto**, which are all of type **Planet**.

Declaring Variables and the Structure Together

We could also have declared variables within the initial statement defining the structure:

```
struct Planet
{
   char Name[80];        /* Normal name */
   double Mass;          /* Relative to Earth = 1 */
   double Year;          /* Time to go round the sun in Earth days */
   float Temperature;    /* Average surface temperature in deg. F */
   int Moons;            /* Number of moons */
   double SunDistance;   /* Average - in millions of miles */
} Mercury, Uranus;
```

Here we've defined the structure type, and declared the two variables **Mercury** and **Uranus**. The structure tag name can be omitted from a definition of structure, but obviously since you've no means of referring to the structure type subsequently, all the variables that you want of this structure type must be declared within this original definition.

You can declare structure variables within a block, or as global objects outside of any function. They can also be **static**. The members of a structure can be any kind of variable, including being another structure, although a given structure **MyStruct** cannot contain a structure object member of type **MyStruct**.

Using typedef

We can also use **typedef** when we define a structure. For example we could define the structure **Planet** with the statement:

```
typedef struct Planet
{
   char Name[80];          /* Normal name */
   double Mass;            /* Relative to Earth = 1 */
   double Year;            /* Time to go round the sun in Earth days */
   float Temperature;      /* Average surface temperature in deg. F */
   int Moons;              /* Number of moons */
   double SunDistance;     /* Average - in millions of miles */
} PLANET;
```

Don't confuse this with the previous declaration where we also defined **Mercury** and **Uranus** as instances of the structure **Planet**. Here we've defined the structure **Planet**, and we've also defined **PLANET** as a new name for the type **struct Planet**. We can now use this new name to define instances of the structure **Planet** with a statement such as:

```
PLANET Mercury, Uranus;
```

This declares two variables **Mercury** and **Uranus**, and is equivalent to the statement:

```
struct Planet Mercury, Uranus;
```

When we use **PLANET** we no longer need to insert the keyword **struct**, so using a **typedef** can make your programs easier to read and more succinct.

Initializing Structures

Structure members can be initialized when they're declared in a similar way to arrays. The initializing values are specified between braces, and appear after an equals sign following the variable name, for example:

```
struct Planet Mars = {"Mars", 0.1074, 686.98, 0.0f, 2, 136.79};
```

This declares the structure **Mars**, and initializes it with a variety of data values. The correspondence between the values specified and the members of **Mars** is as follows:

Mars		
char Name [80];	/* Normal name */	"Mars"
double Mass;	/* Relative to Earth = 1 */	0.1074
double Year;	/* Time to go round the sun in Earth days */	686.96
float Temperature;	/* Average surface temperature in deg. F */	0.0f
int Moons;	/* Number of moons */	2
double SunDistance;	/* Average - in millions of miles */	136.79

The initializing values must appear in the order that corresponds to the sequence in the structure type definition.

Using Structures

The ways in which you can use a structure as a whole are actually quite limited. You cannot compare structures, or use one in an arithmetic expression, but you can assign one structure to another of the same type. If we define a structure object like this:

```
struct Planet RedPlanet;
```

then we can write the assignment:

```
RedPlanet = Mars;
```

This will result in member-by-member copying from the object **Mars** to the object **RedPlanet**. So after this statement, the data members of **Mars** and **RedPlanet** will be identical.

The only other operations you can carry out on a structure object are to take its address using the **&** operator, and to pass it to a function as an argument, or to return it as a value from a function. However, this isn't quite so restricting, since we can do just about anything we like with the individual members of a structure - as long as they aren't structure objects themselves, of course.

Using Members

You can refer to individual members of a structure by using the **structure member operator**, which is a period. For example, to set the member **Mass** in the structure **Earth**, you could use the statement:

```
Earth.Mass=1;              /* Set the mass of planet Earth */
```

You can also use a structure member just like a variable of the same type. For example, if we've declared a variable **MassRatio** as a double, we can type:

```
MassRatio = Mars.Mass/Venus.Mass;
```

Naturally, the values of the structure members involved in this statement must have previously obtained values from somewhere, for the calculation to work.

Using Members that are Structures

Where a member of a structure is another structure, we can still access the members of the second structure. Let's take a geometric example, suppose that we define a structure for a screen co-ordinate object as:

```
struct Point
{
   double x;                /* x coordinate */
   double y;                /* y coordinate */
};
```

A **Point** object will contain the pair of co-ordinates **x** and **y**, which are both of type **double**. We could define and initialize two **Point** objects with the statement:

```
struct Point P1={1.0, 1.0}, P2={5.0, 5.0};
```

so **P1** has the coordinates 1.0,1.0, while **P2** takes the coordinates 5.0,5.0. We can now define a structure to represent lines with the definition:

```
struct Line
{
    struct Point P1;
    struct Point P2;
};
```

This defines a **Line** object as a pair of **Point** objects which are also structures themselves. We could now declare and initialize a **Line** object **L1**, with the statement:

```
struct Line L1={Startpt, Endpt};   /* Line defined by two points */
```

Assuming that we've declared another point **P3**, we could assign the value of a member of **L1** to it:

```
P3=L1.P2;
```

This will copy the members **x** and **y** of the structure variable **L1.P2** to the corresponding members of **P3**.

If we now wanted to alter one of the members of the **P1** member of the **Line** structure **L2**, then we just use a second level of the structure member operator:

```
L1.P1.x += 1;
L1.P1.y = L1.P1.x+3;
```

The first statement increments the **x** member of the **P1** member of the **Line** object **L1**. The second statement assigns the **y** member of the member **P1** of **Line** object **L1** to 3 more than the current **x** member. This diagram shows how the **Line L1** and its members are referenced:

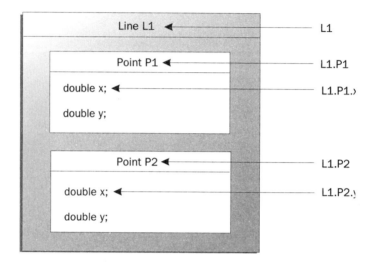

Structures as Function Arguments

Using structures with functions provides a very powerful combination. We can define a function to calculate the length of a line by passing a **Line** object as an argument, and returning the value of the length. The function definition would be:

```
/* Function to calculate the length of a line *

double LineLength( struct Line aLine )
{
   return sqrt( (aLine.P2.x- aLine.P1.x)* (aLine.P2.x- aLine.P1.x) +
               (aLine.P2.y- aLine.P1.y)* (aLine.P2.y- aLine.P1.y) );
}
```

The calculation of line length is illustrated here:

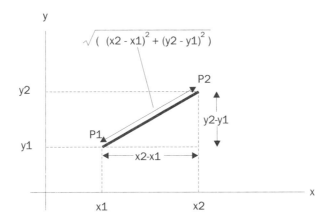

The calculation of the distance between two points uses Pythagoras' Theorem which you'll remember from high school, about the square on the hypotenuse being equal to the sum of the squares of the other two sides. The **sqrt()** function is a standard library function which accepts an argument of type **double**, and returns its square root as a **double** value. You need to include the header **MATH.H** to use it.

Structures as Return Values

Returning a structure from a function isn't a problem either, because you can write a function to create objects of a particular structure type. A function to create a **Point** object from two **double** arguments could take the following form:

```
/* A function to create a point */
struct Point CreatePoint(double x, double y)
{
   struct Point aPoint;        /* Local Point object */
   aPoint.x = x;               /* Set x coordinate */
   aPoint.y = y;               /* Set y coordinate */
   return aPoint;
}
```

The **Point** object is declared local to the function and initialized with the **x** and **y** values passed to it. A copy of this **Point** object is returned from the function. You can use this function to set the value of a **Point** object with the statement:

```
P1 = CreatePoint(1.5,2.5);
```

We could also write a similar function to set up a **Line** object, although in this case we might want to write two functions to take care of the different possible options:

```
/* Creating a line from two points */
struct Line TwoPtLine( struct Point P1, struct Point P2)
{
    struct Line aLine;
    aLine.P1 = P1;
    aLine.P2 = P2;
    return aLine;
}

/* Creating a line from coordinate values */
struct Line CreateLine( double x1, double y1, double x2, double y2)
{
    struct Line aLine;
    return TwoPtLine(CreatePoint(x1,y1), CreatePoint(x2,y1));
}
```

These two functions enable you to create a **Line** object from two points, or from two pairs of co-ordinate values from the two points that define the line. The second function calls the first function as well, just to show that it's possible. You could also implement the second function by using the co-ordinate values to directly set the **x** and **y** values of the **Point** objects contained in a **Line** object.

We shall now see how structures work in practice by trying them out in a complete example. Let's stay with the geometric context for the time being, and look at an example to calculate the intersection of two lines.

An Example

Before we write the program we must look at how we're going to perform the calculation. A line defined by two points **P1** and **P2** with respective co-ordinates **x1,y1** and **x1,y2**, can be represented in the form:

```
P = P1 + (P2-P1)t
```

This is called the 'parametric form' since points on the line are defined by values of the parameter, **t**. When **t** is zero the value of **P** is **P1**, and when **t** is 1 then **P** is the point at the other end of the line **P2**. Intermediate values of **t** between 0 and 1 define points on the line between **P1** and **P2**. Values of **t** less than zero define points on the line extended beyond **P1**, and values greater than 1 define points beyond **P2**. We can define the co-ordinate value for points on the line by this pair of equations:

```
x = x1 + (x2-x1)t
y = y1 + (y2-y1)t
```

The relationship of these equations to the line from **P1** to **P2** is shown here:

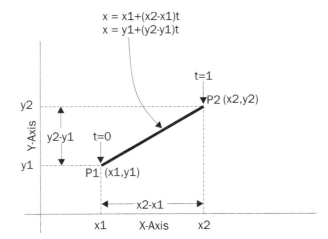

The diagram shows that the horizontal distance between the points **P1** and **P2** is **x2-x1**, and the vertical distance is **y2-y1**. When the parameter **t** is 0, the two equations define the coordinates of the point **P1**, and when **t** is 1 they define the coordinates of **P2**. Points on the line between **P1** and **P2** will be defined by values of **t** between 0 and 1.

Using this representation, it's very easy to obtain the intersection between two lines. Given a line **L1** defined by points **P1** and **P2**, and a second line **L2** defined by points **P3** and **P4**, you just need to solve the equations resulting from equating the **x** and **y** values in the two line definitions:

```
x1 + (x2-x1)t1 = x3 + (x4-x3)t2
y1 + (y2-y1)t1 = y3 + (y4-y3)t2
```

Without going through the gory details of getting there, if you solve these two equations, the value of **t1** defining the position of the intersection point on the first line is determined by:

```
t1=((x4-x3)(y3-y1)-(y4-y3)(x3-x1))/((x4-x3)(y2-y1)-(y4-y3)(x2-x1))
```

This looks a bit messy because the expression for **t1** involves the **x** and **y** co-ordinates of the four points defining the two lines, but it boils down to just one expression - the numerator:

```
((x4-x3)(y3-y1)-(y4-y3)(x3-x1))
```

divided by another - the denominator:

```
((x4-x3)(y2-y1)-(y4-y3)(x2-x1))
```

If the denominator is zero in the expression for **t1**, then the two lines are parallel, otherwise they've got to intersect at some point. In practice, it's better to test whether the magnitude of the denominator is less than some suitably small value, 10^{-10} say, to avoid numerical problems in the geometric calculations. We will do this in the following example:

```
/* EX6-01.C A program to calculate intersection between 2 lines */

#include <stdio.h>        /* For input and output */
#include <math.h>         /* For fabs() function */

/* Structure definitions */
```

```
struct Point                    /* Structure for a point */
{
   double x;                    /* x coordinate */
   double y;                    /* y coordinate */
};

struct Line                     /* Structure for a line */
{
   struct Point P1;             /* Start point for the line */
   struct Point P2;             /* End point for the line */
};

/* Function prototypes */
struct Line GetLine(void);
struct Point GetPoint(void);
int Parallel(struct Line L1, struct Line L2);
struct Point Intersection( struct Line L1, struct Line L2);

int main(void)
{
   struct Point aPoint;         /* Declare a point object */
   struct Line L1, L2;          /* Declare two line objects */

   printf("\nWe need the two points defining the first line.");
   L1 = GetLine();
   printf("\nWe need the two points defining the second line.");
   L2 = GetLine();

   if(Parallel(L1,L2))
      printf("\nLines are parallel - no intersection.");
   else
   {
      aPoint = Intersection(L1,L2);
      printf("\nThe intersection point is %.3f,% .3f", aPoint.x, aPoint.y);
   }
   return 0;
}

/********************************
 * A function to read in a point *
 ********************************/
struct Point GetPoint(void)
{
   struct Point aPoint;         /* Local Point object */
   printf("\n Enter the coordinates of a point:");
   scanf("%lf%lf", &aPoint.x, &aPoint.y);
   return aPoint;
}
```

```
/*******************************
 * A function to input a line *
 ******************************/

struct Line GetLine(void)
{
    struct Line aLine;
    aLine.P1=GetPoint();
    aLine.P2=GetPoint();
    return aLine;
}

/*******************************************************
 * A function to determine if two lines are parallel *
 ******************************************************/
int Parallel(struct Line L1, struct Line L2)
{
    double denom;
    denom=(L2.P2.x- L2.P1.x)*(L1.P2.y- L1.P1.y)-
          (L2.P2.y- L2.P1.y)*( L1.P2.x- L1.P1.x);

    return fabs(denom)< 0.0000000001;
}

/*********************************************************************
 * A function to return the intersection point of two lines *
 ********************************************************************/
struct Point Intersection( struct Line L1, struct Line L2)
{
    struct Point aPoint;  /* Local store for intersection point */
    double t;                /* parameter to define intersection point */

    /* Get parametric value for intersection of L1 and L2 */
    t=(L2.P2.x - L2.P1.x)*(L2.P1.y - L1.P1.y)-
    (L2.P2.y - L2.P1.y)*( L2.P1.x - L1.P1.x);  /* Get numerator and */
    t/=(L2.P2.x - L2.P1.x)*(L1.P2.y - L1.P1.y)-
        (L2.P2.y- L2.P1.y)*( L1.P2.x- L1.P1.x);        /* divide by the
                                                       denominator */

    /* Now get intersection point from the equation for L1 */
    aPoint.x=L1.P1.x+(L1.P2.x- L1.P1.x)*t;
    aPoint.y=L1.P1.y+(L1.P2.y- L1.P1.y)*t;

    return aPoint;                      /* Return the intersection point */
}
```

Program Analysis

The definitions for the structures **Line** and **Point** appear at global scope, so they're accessible throughout the program; any function can declare instances of either of these structures. If a structure were to be defined within a block, then it would only be accessible within that block.

Note that the definition of the **Point** structure must be placed ahead of the definition of the **Line** structure, because the **Line** structure contains objects of type **Point** as members. The definition of a structure must always precede its use. If you reverse the sequence of the definitions then you're guaranteed compiler error messages. The **Point** object names have been changed compared to our previous definition because a couple of the arithmetic statements are rather cumbersome, and we want to keep them as short as possible.

The functions **GetPoint()** and **GetLine()** are used to input data defining a structure object, and to return the object once it has been created. The **GetLine()** function uses **GetPoint()** to construct the **Point** objects, and then returns the **Line** object constructed from the **Point** objects. Creating a function to input values defining a structure is a very useful technique, especially with complicated structure types. You can package all the input processing and data validation into a function, so that reading a structure into your program is more easily managed.

The **Parallel()** function checks whether the two lines are parallel using a direct implementation of the expression we saw earlier. It obtains the absolute value of the denominator by using the standard library function **fabs()** and compares it against 10^{-10}. The function returns 1 if the absolute value of **denom** is less than 10^{-10} indicating that the lines are parallel or almost parallel, and 0 if otherwise.

The function **Intersection()** accepts two **Line** objects as arguments and returns a **Point** object which represents the intersection of the two lines. The **Intersection()** function first checks whether the lines passed as arguments are parallel, since they would cause an error by attempting to divide by zero. If the lines are parallel, a message is displayed and the program is terminated.

> Although a user of this function should verify that the lines aren't parallel before calling the function, we can't be sure that this will always be the case. By putting this check here, there will be an active detection of the error.

The object **aPoint** is local to the function **Intersection()** and is destroyed when you exit from the function, but a copy of it is returned so there's no problem here. Again, the expression for calculating **t** is a direct implementation of the equation we saw earlier. Don't worry if you can't sort out the algebra - it isn't important at the moment.

Note how we can access and use the members of the **Point** members of a **Line** object just like any other variable. What you can do with a structure member is determined by its type. You can use it in the same way as any other variable of the same type.

If you compile and run this example some typical output would be:

```
We need the two points defining the first line.
 Enter the coordinates of a point:1.5 2.5

 Enter the coordinates of a point:6.0 8.0

We need the two points defining the second line.
 Enter the coordinates of a point:3.0 5.0

 Enter the coordinates of a point:4.5 -3.0

 The intersection point is 3.102, 4.458
```

In the case when the lines are parallel, a message is displayed and the function computing the intersection point isn't called.

Arrays of Structures

Once a structure type has been defined, you can also declare arrays of that structure. Given our structure type **Point**, an array of points can be declared with the statement:

```
struct Point MyPoints[10];
```

This declares an array of 10 elements of type **Point** with the name **MyPoints[]**. Referring to members belonging to a particular element of the array is much the same as referring to members of a single structure variable. To increment the member **x** of the third array element, you could write:

```
MyPoints[2].x++;
```

Using an element of an array of structures is governed by exactly the same rules that apply to a single structure object. The only operations you can perform are to assign it to another object of the same type, to take its address, to pass it to a function as an argument, or return it from a function.

Using Pointers with Structures

We saw at the outset that we can obtain the address of a structure variable. We could declare a pointer to a structure of type **Line** with the statement:

```
struct Line *pLine=NULL;    /* Declare a pointer to a Line structure */
```

Now we have the variable **pLine** that can store the address of a **Line** structure object. If we've declared a structure **aLine**, then we can store its address in the pointer in the standard fashion with the statement:

```
pLine=&aLine;                   /* Store address of aLine in pLine */
```

If you dereference a pointer to a structure, ***pLine**, you are referring to the structure at the address contained in the pointer. We can use this to access the members of the structure.

Accessing Structure Members through a Pointer

We can use the member selection operator that we've already seen to refer to the member of a structure through a pointer containing its address:

```
aPoint=(*pLine).P1;      /* Set aPoint to the P1 member of aLine */
```

The parentheses here are essential. Without them you would be attempting to dereference the structure member **P1**, since the dereference operator is of lower precedence than the member selection operator, and the expression would be taken as `*(pLine.P1)`. Because this is a slightly awkward notation, C provides a special operator, the **indirect member selection operator**, which you can use when accessing members of a structure through a pointer. You could use this operator to rewrite the last statement as:

```
aPoint=pLine->P1;        /* Set aPoint to the P1 member of aLine */
```

This has exactly the same effect as the previous statement. As we will soon see, there are compelling reasons for using pointers to structures, so this notation appears quite frequently in C programs.

Structures and Functions

We have seen in the last program that we can pass a structure to a function as an argument, but there is a significant potential overhead in doing this because of the way arguments are passed to functions. As you know, arguments are passed by value in C, so a copy of each argument is produced, and passed on to the function.

We've seen that when you pass an array to a function, the name of the array is converted to a pointer, and a copy of the address of the array is used as the argument.

Structures are handled differently, because in this case a copy of the entire structure is made, and that is passed to the function. The same occurs when you return a structure from a function, so that with a large structure a lot of copying can take place. Even the **Planet** structure which we defined at the beginning of this structure would involve a lot more overhead than an array when passed as an argument to a function.

The answer is to use pointers; we can even construct structures dynamically within a function by allocating memory on the heap.

Creating Structures

We can obtain the size of a structure using the **sizeof** operator. To allocate memory for a **Line** object on the heap, you would write:

```
pLine=(struct Line *)malloc(sizeof (struct Line));
```

The argument to **malloc()** uses **sizeof** to obtain the number of bytes required to store a structure of type **Line**. The pointer to the memory allocated that is returned from **malloc()** will be of type **void *,** so we need to convert this to the type 'pointer to a **Line** structure'. This is done by the cast **(struct Line *)**. The result of this cast is stored in the pointer **pLine**. Needless to say, in practice you must check that you do get a valid pointer back from **malloc()**.

With the memory allocated on the heap, we can use the pointer to initialize the members of the structure:

```
pLine->P1=aPoint;
```

This statement initializes the **P1** member of the new structure with the **Point** object, **aPoint**.

Let's see all this in action with a rewrite of the last example. We can make it work much more efficiently by using pointers, and we can create structures dynamically on the heap.

An Example Using Pointers to Structures

The calculations for determining if the lines are parallel, and to obtain the intersection point are exactly the same as in the previous example, but are now expressed using pointers:

```
/* EX6-02.C Calculating the intersection between two lines */

#include <stdio.h>          /* For input and output */
#include <stdlib.h>         /* For malloc() */

/* Structure definitions */
struct Point                /* Structure for a point */
{
    double x;               /* x coordinate */
    double y;               /* y coordinate */
};

struct Line                 /* Structure for a line */
{
    struct Point *pP1;      /* Pointer to start point for the line */
    struct Point *pP2;      /* Pointer to end point for the line   */
```

```
};

/* Function prototypes */
struct Line *GetLine(void);
struct Point *GetPoint(void);
int Parallel(struct Line *pL1, struct Line *pL2);
struct Point Intersection( struct Line *pL1, struct Line *pL2);
void Delete(struct Line *pLine);

int main(void)
{
   struct Point aPoint;        /* Declare a Point object */
   struct Line *pL1, *pL2;     /* Declare two pointers to line objects */

   printf("\nWe need the two points defining the first line.");
   pL1 = GetLine();
   printf("\nWe need the two points defining the second line.");
   pL2 = GetLine();

   if(Parallel(pL1,pL2))
      printf("\nLines are parallel - no intersection.");
   else
   {
      aPoint = Intersection(pL1,pL2);
      printf("\nThe intersection point is %.3f,%.3f", aPoint.x, aPoint.y);
   }

   /* Release memory back to the heap */
   Delete(pL1);
   Delete(pL2);

   return 0;
}

/********************************
 * A function to read in a point *
 ********************************/
struct Point *GetPoint(void)
{
   struct Point *pPoint;       /* Local Point object pointer */

   /* Get memory for Point object */
   pPoint=(struct Point *)malloc(sizeof(struct Point));
   if(pPoint==NULL)
   {
      printf("\nPoint memory allocation failed. Program terminated");
      exit(1);
   }

   printf("\n Enter the coordinates of a point:");
```

```
      scanf("%lf%lf", &pPoint->x, &pPoint->y);
      return pPoint;
}


/******************************
 * A function to input a line *
 ******************************/

struct Line *GetLine(void)
{
      struct Line *pLine;
      /* Get memory for Line object */
      pLine=(struct Line *)malloc(sizeof(struct Line));
      if(pLine==NULL)
      {
          printf("\nPoint memory allocation failed. Program terminated");
          exit(1);
      }

      pLine->pP1=GetPoint();
      pLine->pP2=GetPoint();
      return pLine;
}

/*******************************************************
 * A function to determine if two lines are parallel *
 *******************************************************/
int Parallel(struct Line *pL1, struct Line *pL2)
{
      double denom;
      denom=(pL2->pP2->x - pL2->pP1->x)*(pL1->pP2->y - pL1->pP1->y)-
            (pL2->pP2->y - pL2->pP1->y)*(pL1->pP2->x - pL1->pP1->x);
      if(denom<0)
          denom = -denom;

    return denom< 0.0000000001;
}

/*************************************************************
 * A function to return the intersection point of two lines *
 *************************************************************/
struct Point Intersection( struct Line *pL1, struct Line *pL2)
{
      struct Point aPoint;   /* Local store for intersection point */
      double t;              /* parameter to define intersection point */

      /* Get parametric value for intersection of L1 and L2 */
      /* First calculate the numerator */
      t=(pL2->pP2->x - pL2->pP1->x)*(pL2->pP1->y - pL1->pP1->y) -
              (pL2->pP2->y - pL2->pP1->y)*(pL2->pP1->x - pL1->pP1->x);
```

201

```
    /*   and then divide the numerator by the denominator */
    t/=(pL2->pP2->x - pL2->pP1->x)*(pL1->pP2->y - pL1->pP1->y) -
       (pL2->pP2->y - pL2->pP1->y)*( pL1->pP2->x - pL1->pP1->x);

    /* Now get the intersection point from the equation for L1 */
    aPoint.x=pL1->pP1->x+(pL1->pP2->x - pL1->pP1->x)*t;
    aPoint.y=pL1->pP1->y+(pL1->pP2->y - pL1->pP1->y)*t;

    return aPoint;                 /* Return the intersection point */
}

/***************************************************************
 * Function to release memory for a Line object back to the heap *
 ***************************************************************/
void Delete(struct Line *pLine)
{
    free(pLine->pP1);         /* Free the memory for P1 member */
    free(pLine->pP2);         /* Free the memory for P1 member */
    free(pLine);     /* Finally free the memory for the Line object */
    return;
}
```

Program Analysis

The structure **Line** now only contains pointers to **Point** objects as members. It assumes that the **Point** objects will be created elsewhere, and that their addresses will be stored in the structure. This reduces the size of the **Line** structure and means that the indirect member selection operator needs to be used to refer to the **x** and **y** members of the points defining the line.

The function **GetPoint()** that reads in the defining data for a **Point** object also allocates memory on the heap for the **Point** object, and returns the address of the memory allocated once the object has been initialized with the data values read. The address returned by **malloc()** is cast to type 'pointer to **Point**' before being stored in the variable **pPoint**. The function **GetLine()** also creates a **Line** object on the heap and returns its address once it has been initialized.

Managing Memory for Dynamic Structures

Where you have objects such as a **Line** object which has members that point to other objects defined on the heap, it's important to manage the release of memory correctly. The function **Delete()** does this in our example. It first releases the memory for the two point objects, and then releases the memory for the **Line** object. If you were to just to release the memory for the **Line** object, then the two **Point** objects defining it would still exist on the heap, and there would be no way of subsequently releasing this memory. In our example it doesn't matter since all memory is returned to the heap at the end of the program, but if you had a program which regularly created and destroyed **Line** objects, then the heap would gradually be occupied by more and more surplus **Point** objects. The effective difference is illustrated here:

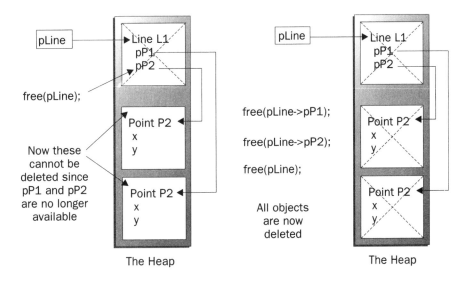

The functions **Parallel()** and **Intersection()** in the example now have their parameters declared as pointers, so just a copy of a pointer to a structure is passed to the function for each argument. The computations in the function use two levels of the indirect member selection operator to get to the co-ordinate values of the **Point** objects defining each **Line** object, but you should have no difficulty in seeing how this relates to the previous version. The expression **pL1->pP1** accesses the pointer **pP1** which is a member of the **Line** object pointed to by **pL1**. Therefore **pL1->pP1->x** refers to the member **x** of the **Point** object pointed to by **pP1** in the **Line** object pointed to by **pL1**.

Data Organization Using Structures

In the last example we saw how the structure type **Line** could have pointers to other structures as members. A structure can also have a pointer to an object of the same type as itself as a member. This provides us with some very powerful techniques for managing data in a program.

Linked Lists

A structure with a member that is a pointer to an object of the same type as itself enables you to daisy chain objects together. This is very useful when you don't know exactly how many objects your program will need to deal with. For example, we could define a structure **Phone** as follows:

```
struct Phone
{
   char *Name;              /* Pointer to a name */
   char *Number;            /* Pointer to telephone number */
   struct Phone *pNext;     /* Pointer to another Phone object */
};
```

This can provide a basis for storing names and associated telephone numbers. Each object of type **Phone** will contain a pointer to a name, a pointer to a telephone number, and a pointer to another **Phone** object. We can construct a chain of objects of this type, as in this diagram:

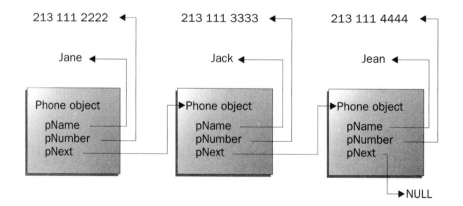

A chain like this, with each object pointing to the next in the chain, is called a **linked list**. As long as you know where the first object in the chain is, you can get to any object in the list by following the chain of **pNext** pointers. The last **pNext** pointer will contain **NULL**, so when you find a **NULL** stored in **pNext**, you know that you've reached the last object in the chain. You can use this technique with any kind of structure; you just need to add a pointer member to a structure to allow objects to be linked together. We can see how this works through an example.

Using a Linked List

This example will read a series of names and associated telephone numbers which it will store in a linked list using the **struct** definition **Phone**. Input will end when you enter a blank line, and the program will then produce a list of the names and numbers you have entered. Before we get into the code, let's think about how this is going to work. We need to perform three separate steps:

- Read the input
- Display the list
- Clean up the heap

Let's now consider each of these in turn.

Reading the Input

The basic unit of input is a name plus a number from which we need to construct an object of type **Phone**. We could implement reading the data for a single object in a function which will create the **Phone** object on the heap, and return the address of the object. If an object isn't created then the function can return **NULL**. The prototype of this function will be:

```
struct Phone *GetPhone(void);
```

We can create the linked list in another function that uses **GetPhone()** to read the data and construct each **Phone** object. The function will only need to worry about linking the **Phone** objects together and returning the address of the first object in the list. The prototype of this function will be:

```
struct Phone *CreateList(void);
```

Displaying the List

The task of displaying the list once it's complete falls naturally into the lap of another function. All it needs to know about is the address of the head of the list, so we can pass that as an argument. No return value is necessary as all we are doing is writing to the screen. We can write the prototype of this function as:

```
void DisplayList(struct Phone *pHead);
```

Cleaning Up the Heap

The last operation we need to perform is cleaning up the heap. This will also fit into a single function very well, and given the address of the head of the list, all it needs to do is walk through the objects in the list, deleting the name and number strings from the free store before deleting each **Phone** object.

Now let's have a look at what the code looks like:

```c
/* EX6-03.C  Using a linked list for phone numbers */
#include <stdio.h>            /* For input and output */
#include <stdlib.h>           /* For malloc() */
#include <string.h>           /* For string functions */

#define MAXLEN 40             /* Maximum input length */

/* Structure definitions */
struct Phone
{
   char *pName;               /* Pointer to a name */
   char *pNumber;             /* Pointer to telephone number */
   struct Phone *pNext;       /* Pointer to another Phone object */
};

/* Function prototypes */
struct Phone *CreateList(void);
void DisplayList(struct Phone *pHead);
void DeleteList(struct Phone *pHead);
struct Phone *GetPhone(void);

int main(void)
{
   struct Phone *pHead;       /* Pointer to head of list */

   printf("\n Enter names and telephone numbers as prompted, each less \n"
          " than 40 characters. Enter an empty line to end input.");
```

```c
   pHead=CreateList();
   DisplayList(pHead);
   DeleteList(pHead);
   return 0;
}

struct Phone *CreateList(void)
{
   struct Phone *pHead=NULL;        /* Pointer to head of the list */
   struct Phone *pCurrent=NULL;     /* Pointer to current object */

   pHead=pCurrent=GetPhone();
   while(pCurrent!=NULL)
   {
      pCurrent->pNext=GetPhone();
      pCurrent=pCurrent->pNext;
   }
   return pHead;     /* Return the pointer to the start of the list */
}

void DisplayList(struct Phone *pList)
{
   while(pList!=NULL)
   {
      printf("\n%-40s\t%s",pList->pName, pList->pNumber);
      pList=pList->pNext;
   }
}

struct Phone *GetPhone(void)
{
   struct Phone *pPhone=NULL;
   char Buffer[MAXLEN];             /* Input buffer */
   size_t Length=0;                 /* Input length */

   printf("\nEnter a name:\n");
   gets(Buffer);                    /* Read the name into Buffer */
   Length=strlen(Buffer);           /* Get name length */
   if(!Length)                      /* Length=0 for empty name */
      return NULL;;                 /* so return NULL */

   /* Create a new Phone object and initialize it */
   pPhone=(struct Phone *)malloc(sizeof(struct Phone));
   if(!pPhone)                      /* Check we got some memory */
   {
      printf("\nError allocating memory for Phone object. Program ended");
      exit(2);
   }

   /* Get enough memory to hold the name and store the address */
   pPhone->pName=(char *)malloc(Length+1);
```

```
    if(!pPhone->pName)                  /* Check we got some memory */
    {
        printf("\nError allocating memory for name. Program ended");
        exit(2);
    }
    strcpy(pPhone->pName, Buffer);      /* Copy the name to the heap */

    /* Now get the telephone number */
    printf("\nEnter the telephone number for %s\n", Buffer);
    gets(Buffer);                       /* Read the number */

    /* Get enough memory to hold the number and store the address */
    pPhone->pNumber=(char *)malloc(strlen(Buffer)+1);
    if(!pPhone->pNumber)                /* Check we got some memory */
    {
        printf("\nError allocating memory for phone number. Program ended");
        exit(2);
    }
    strcpy(pPhone->pNumber, Buffer); /* Copy the Buffer to the heap */

    pPhone->pNext=NULL;                 /* Set next pointer to NULL */
    return pPhone;                      /* Return a pointer to the object */
}

void DeleteList(struct Phone *pHead)
{
    struct Phone *pTemp=NULL;               /* Temporary pointer */
    while(pHead!=NULL)
    {
        free(pHead->pName);                 /* Release the name memory */
        free(pHead->pNumber);               /* Release the number memory */
        pTemp=pHead;        /* Save the address of the current object */
        pHead=pHead->pNext;/* Get the address of the next object */
        free(pTemp);        /* Now release the current object memory */
    }
    return;
}
```

Program Analysis

Because our functions do all of the work, the function **main()** is very simple. All it does is output a prompt and then call the functions to create the list, display the list, and delete the list.

Creating the List

The **CreateList()** function calls **GetPhone()** to obtain the first list object and store the address returned in the pointer variable **pHead**, which is where we keep the head of the list. The address of the first object is also saved in the pointer **pCurrent** which we'll use to store the address of the current object as we extend the list.

CreateList() then calls the function **GetPhone()** in the **while** loop which continues as long as valid addresses are returned for new **Phone** objects. When a new object is received, the first action is to store its address in the **pNext** member of the last object, which has its address saved in the pointer, **pCurrent**. We then make the new object current by storing its address in **pCurrent**. As soon as a **NULL** is returned from the function **GetPhone()**, the list is complete and the loop ends.

Library Functions to Handle Strings

The header file **STRING.H** contains definitions necessary to use string processing functions provided by the standard library. We use two of these in the function **GetPhone()**. One is **strlen()**, which returns the length of the string pointed to by its argument, excluding the `'\0'`. Its prototype is:

```
size_t strlen(char *s);
```

You will remember that **size_t** is the type of value returned by the operator **sizeof**, and is equivalent to **unsigned int**.

The other is **strcpy()** which copies the string pointed to by its second argument, to the **char** array address given by its first argument. Copying continues until `'\0'` is found, which is also copied. The prototype of this function is:

```
char *strcpy(char *pToString, char *pFromString);
```

Reading Phone Objects

The function **GetPhone()** first reads a name string into the array **Buffer[]**. If its length, returned by **strlen()**, is zero, then an empty string must have been entered - so input ends and **NULL** is returned. For a non-zero length name, memory is allocated on the heap to store a **Phone** object.

Note how the address returned from **malloc()** is cast to the required type, before storing it in **pPhone**. Note also how in the call to the function **malloc()** we use the expression **sizeof(struct Phone)** to specify the space required. This is most important with structures, because you cannot rely on adding up the lengths of the members to determine the number of bytes required to store a structure.

On many computers, variables of two bytes or more are subject to boundary alignment, which means that the address in memory of 2-byte variables must be a multiple of 2, the address of a 4-byte variable must be a multiple of 4, and so on. As a result, if a 4-byte variable follows a 2-byte variable, then it may be necessary to leave two bytes unused to ensure correct boundary alignment. This is illustrated here:

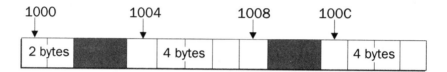

With this sequence of a 2-byte variable, a 4-byte variable, a 1-byte variable, and then another 4-byte variable, a total of 5 bytes can't be used. Thus, a **struct** with these variables as members will require 16 bytes of memory, even though only 11 bytes are used to store data.

Next, the function **GetPhone()** obtains sufficient memory from the heap to exactly accommodate the string, and the name is copied to it using **strcpy()**. The address is then stored in the **pName** member of the new **Phone** object pointed to by **pPhone**. The telephone number is then read, and is processed in the same way as the name. Finally, after setting the **pNext** member of the **Phone** object to **NULL**, the address of the object is returned.

Displaying the List

The **DisplayList()** function shows how easy it is to go through a list. The address of the first element is passed to the function, and this is used to control the **while** loop. The loop only has two actions: display the current object, and then copy the address of the next object to **pList**. As soon as the pointer **pList** is **NULL**, we've processed the last object and the loop ends. Of course, **pList** is a copy of the original address passed to the function, so there's no problem with changing it as we go along.

Deleting the List

The function **DeleteList()** walks through the list deleting objects. Note how before deleting each object, the memory occupied by the strings pointed to by the members of each object is freed first. The address contained in the **pNext** member of each object is obtained before the memory for the object itself is freed.

Doubly Linked Lists

One limitation of the linked list we have just seen, is that you can only go through it one way, from the first to the last. To retrieve any member of the list you must start at the beginning and trawl through the list until you find the one you are looking for, even if you may know that it's near the end. Even if the member you want to retrieve is just ahead of the one you found last, you must still go right back to the beginning of the list to find it. One way of improving the situation is to add an extra pointer to each member that points to the preceding member. If we modify the **Phone** structure to accommodate this, its definition will be:

```
struct Phone
{
    char *pName;               /* Pointer to a name */
    char *pNumber;             /* Pointer to telephone number */
    struct Phone *pNext;       /* Pointer to next Phone object */
    struct Phone *pPrevious;   /* Pointer to previous Phone object */
};
```

A linked list of objects with backward- and forward-pointing pointers is called a **doubly linked list**. It can graphically be represented in this illustration:

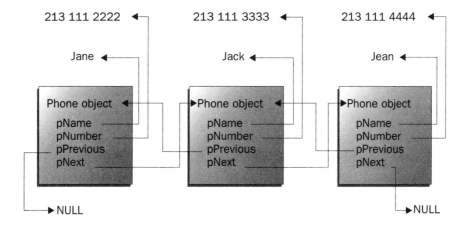

With this arrangement, if you know the address of the last object in the list, you can work backwards through the list using the **pPrevious** pointer members. The object at the head of the list has its **pPrevious** member set to **NULL**. From any position in the list you can move backwards or forwards so that searching objects randomly will be a lot faster that the simple linked list.

We could use a doubly linked list in the previous example but this time we will automatically construct the list in alphabetical order. Apart from updating the structure definition, the only changes necessary are to the functions `GetPhone()` and `CreateList()`.

The new version of `GetPhone()` will look like this:

```
struct Phone *GetPhone(void)
{
    struct Phone *pPhone=NULL;

    /* ...code exactly as before */

    pPhone->pNext=NULL;          /* Set next pointer to NULL */
    pPhone->pPrevious=NULL;      /* Set previous pointer to NULL */
    return pPhone;               /* Return a pointer to the object */
}
```

Well that doesn't look too strenuous, does it? Just one statement added to initialize the **pPrevious** pointer. Let's take a look at the new version of the `CreateList()` function:

```
struct Phone *CreateList(void)
{
    struct Phone *pHead=NULL;        /* Pointer to head of the list */
    struct Phone *pCurrent=NULL;     /* Pointer to current object */
    struct Phone *pInsert=NULL;      /* Pointer to insert position */
    struct Phone *pPrevious=NULL;    /* Pointer to preceding object */

    pHead=pCurrent=GetPhone();           /* Get the first object */

    while((pCurrent=GetPhone())!=NULL)   /* Now get the rest */
    {
        pInsert=pHead;                   /* Start at the beginning */
        while(pInsert!=NULL)
        {
            if(strcmp(pCurrent->pName, pInsert->pName)<0)
            {                            /* Insert current object here */
                pInsert->pPrevious=pCurrent; /* Reset backward pointer */
                pCurrent->pNext=pInsert;     /* Set forward pointer */
                pCurrent->pPrevious=pPrevious; /* Set backward pointer */

                if(pPrevious==NULL)      /* If we added to the beginning */
                    pHead=pCurrent;      /* change the head pointer */
                else
                    pPrevious->pNext=pCurrent;  /* Reset pNext for previous */
                break;                          /* We are done with this one */
            }
```

```
        else
        {
          pPrevious=pInsert;             /* Update pointer to previous */
          pInsert=pInsert->pNext;        /* Move to next object */
        }
    }

    if(pCurrent->pNext==NULL)
    {                                    /* Current was not inserted */
      pCurrent->pPrevious=pPrevious;     /* so add to the end */
      pPrevious->pNext=pCurrent;
    }
  }
  return pHead;          /* Return the pointer to the start of the list */
}
```

We've had to make some quite radical changes here. This is because we need to search the current list every time we add a new **Phone** object to see where it fits. We do this in the inner **while** loop which uses the standard library function **strcmp()** for comparing two strings. Its prototype is:

```
int strcmp(char *pS1, char *pS2);
```

It returns a negative integer if **pS1** is less than **pS2**, a zero if the strings are equal, and a positive integer if **pS1** is greater than **pS2**.

The process of adding an object to the list involves dealing with three situations:

1 Adding to the head of the list.

2 Adding to the middle of the list.

3 Adding to the end of the list.

The first two are handled within the inner **while** loop, and the third after exiting the inner loop. Let's now take a look at each of these possibilities in turn.

Adding to the Head of the List

The first case arises when the name for the new object should come before the name for the first object in the list. This position is illustrated here:

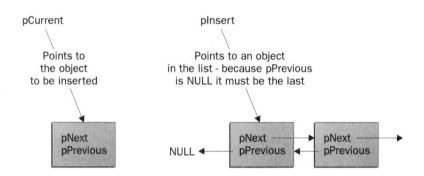

Adding to the Head of the list:

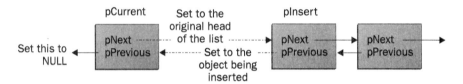

The **pPrevious** pointer holds the address of the object in the list preceding the one indicated by the pointer **pInsert**, so when **pPrevious** for the current object in the list is **NULL**, we're inserting the current **Phone** object at the head of the list, so **pInsert** must contain the address of the first object in the list. To insert the new object pointed to by **pCurrent**, we need to do the following:

- Set the **pNext** pointer member of the new **Phone** object to the address in **pInsert**, since **pInsert** points to the object previously at the head of the list.

- Set the **pPrevious** member of the object pointed to by **pInsert**, which is the old head of the list, to the address of the new object.

- Set the **pPrevious** pointer of the new object to **NULL**.

Adding to the Middle of the List

In the second case, where we're inserting the new object in the middle of the list somewhere, we have to break the chain, as illustrated here:

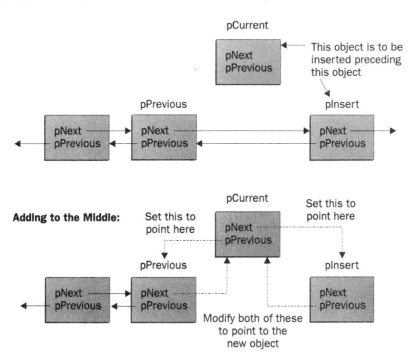

The new object is linked to the object pointed to by **pInsert** in the same way as the previous case. The links to the object pointed to by **pPrevious** also have to be set, so the **pNext** pointer in the **pPrevious** object is set to **pCurrent**, and the **pPrevious** pointer of the new object is set to **pPrevious**.

Adding to the End of the List

The last case arises if we pass completely through the current list without finding two objects between which the current one should be inserted. This situation is illustrated in the diagram over the page:

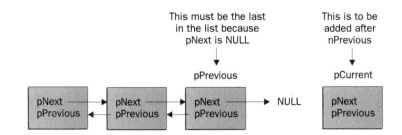

Adding to the Tail:

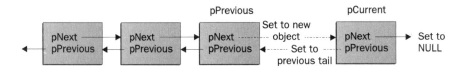

Since the **pNext** member of the new object is set whenever the new object is inserted into the list within the loop, we can detect the occasions when we pass completely through the list without inserting the new object by checking if **pNext** is **NULL**. In this case **pPrevious** will contain the address of the last object in the list, so this is used to link the new object at the end of the list. The **pNext** pointer of the last object in the list is set to the address of the new object stored in **pCurrent**, and the **pNext** pointer for the new object is set to **NULL**. The **pPrevious** pointer for the new object is set to point to what was the last object in the list.

Displaying and Deleting the List

The **DisplayList()** and **DeleteList()** functions work as before. The output will now be in alphabetical order. If you want a bit of practice with a doubly linked list, try rewriting the output function to present the list in reverse order. You can get the address of the tail of the list by passing through it once from the beginning, following the **pNext** pointer members until you find **NULL**.

Trees

The linked list is fine for many applications, particularly as it's so easy to create a sorted list from the outset, but as soon as you need to do any searching, it can be a bit slow. For n objects in a list that you've created in order, you will need n/2 comparisons on average to find a particular object. With a doubly linked list it reduces to n/4, if you can work out in which half of the list the search target is to be found, but it's still proportional to the number of items in the list.

An alternative is to use a structure with two pointers to structures of the same type, where one pointer points to an object that is less than the current object, and the other pointer points to an object that is in some way greater than or equal to the current object. The terms 'less than' and 'greater than' can be defined to suit the objects concerned, and the subject of the comparison is whatever you want for your application.

In the case of strings, 'less than' would usually be interpreted as earlier in alphabetical sequence, or, if one string is the same as the other except for characters appended to it, the shorter string. The library function **strcmp()** for comparing strings uses this meaning, and we'll be using this function a bit later on in this chapter. Objects of this kind of structure can be arranged in a structure called a **binary tree**. We could redefine the **Phone** structure to allow this kind of arrangement:

```
struct Phone
{
    char *pName;            /* Pointer to a name */
    char *pNumber;          /* Pointer to telephone number */
    struct Phone *pLeft;    /* Pointer to Phone object<current */
    struct Phone *pRight;   /* Pointer to Phone object>=current */
};
```

A binary tree of **Phone** objects is illustrated on the following page:

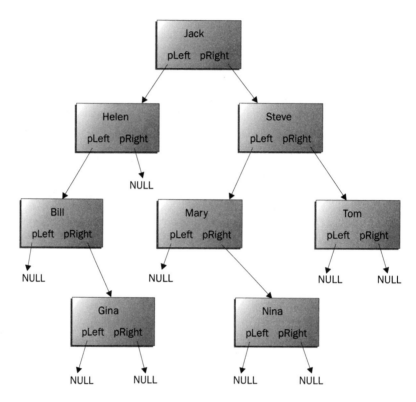

Objects in a tree are usually referred to as **nodes**, and the first node is called the **root**. Other than the root node, each node in a tree is pointed to by one other node called its **parent**. The root node in the tree shown above contains the name Jack. The node pointed to by the pointer `pLeft` has a name less than Jack, Helen, and the node pointed to by `pRight` has the name Steve, which is greater than Jack. The shape of the tree will depend on the sequence in which nodes were added, and the shape will determine how long it takes to search the tree for a particular node. Searching this tree involves a maximum of 4 comparisons, and less than 3 comparisons on average, whereas a linked list with the same objects would require a maximum of 8 comparisons and an average of 4.

Let's rewrite the last example to use a tree instead of a doubly linked list, and add the capability to allow a search for the number of a particular person.

An Example Using a Binary Tree

This is going to be quite a long example so let's build it piecemeal. As with previous examples we will ignore error checking in the interests of being reasonably concise. First we should get the process mapped out for the program in terms of functions. The program is going to perform the following distinct operations:

1 Build the tree from a series of data items entered from the keyboard.

2 Search the tree for a given name and return the corresponding number.

3 Display the complete tree in alphabetical order.

4 Delete the tree.

We can map these directly to these function prototypes:

```
struct Phone *CreateTree(void);
void ShowNumber(char *pName, struct Phone *pRoot);
void DisplayTree(struct Phone *pRoot);
void DeleteTree(struct Phone *pRoot);
```

The function to build the tree returns a pointer to the root node. The function to search the tree accepts two arguments, a pointer to the name to be found, and a pointer to the root node of the tree. The functions to display the complete tree and to delete the tree only require the pointer to the root node to be passed as an argument.

Creating the Tree

Since we need to read the data to create **Phone** objects which we will organize into a tree, we can use a modified version of the **GetPhone** function from the previous example:

```
/* Function to obtain input and create a Phone object */
struct Phone *GetPhone(void)
{
   struct Phone *pPhone=NULL;
   char Buffer[MAXLEN];                  /* Input buffer */
   size_t Length=0;                      /* Input length */

   printf("\nEnter a name:\n");
   gets(Buffer);                         /* Read the name into Buffer */
   Length=strlen(Buffer);                /* Get name length */
   if(!Length)                           /* Length=0 for empty name */
      return NULL;;                      /* so return NULL */

   /* Create a new Phone object and initialize it */
   pPhone=(struct Phone *)malloc(sizeof(struct Phone));

   /* Get enough memory to hold the name and store the address */
   pPhone->pName=(char *)malloc(Length+1);
   strcpy(pPhone->pName, Buffer);      /* Copy the name to the heap */

   /* Now get the telephone number */
   printf("Enter the telephone number for %s\n", Buffer);
   gets(Buffer);                         /* Read the number */

   /* Get enough memory to hold the number and store the address */
   pPhone->pNumber=(char *)malloc(strlen(Buffer)+1);
   strcpy(pPhone->pNumber, Buffer);  /* Copy the Buffer to the heap */

   pPhone->pLeft=NULL;                /* Set left pointer to NULL */
   pPhone->pRight=NULL;               /* Set right pointer to NULL */
   return pPhone;                     /* Return a pointer to the object */
}
```

This is almost identical to the earlier version, the only difference being the
two pointers **pLeft** and **pRight** which are initialized with **NULL**. It returns a
pointer to the new object, or **NULL** if an empty name string was entered. We
can now use this function in the function **CreateTree()**.

We can create the tree in two steps. Since there should be at least one
Phone object, we can read the first one and use it as the root node. We'll
then have a tree with one node. Any other **Phone** objects can be inserted
into the initial tree using a standard approach that we can package in a
function called **InsertNode()**. This will need two parameters, a pointer to
the new **Phone** object to be inserted, and the pointer to the root node of the
existing tree. Its prototype will therefore be:

```
void InsertNode(struct Phone *pNew, struct Phone *pRoot);
```

We need to think about how a node is inserted. With a tree of one node it is simple. If the name member of the new object is less than the name member of the root node then we plug it into the **pLeft** pointer, and if it isn't we plug it into the **pRight** pointer. What if the tree has more than one node?

If the node we would have plugged the new object into isn't **NULL**, then we have another node to check. What we then have to do is see if the new name is less than the name for this node. If it is, then we plug it into the left node, and if it isn't then we plug it into the right node. But this is exactly what we did with the root node. This suggests that a general method for inserting a new node can be implemented as a recursive function. Let's look at the code:

```
/* Function to insert a new node in the tree */
void InsertNode(struct Phone *pNew, struct Phone *pNode)
{
   if(strcmp(pNew->pName,pNode->pName)<0)
   {
      if(pNode->pLeft==NULL)
      {
         pNode->pLeft=pNew;
         return;
      }
      else
         InsertNode(pNew,pNode->pLeft);
   }
   else
   {
      if(pNode->pRight==NULL)
      {
         pNode->pRight=pNew;
         return;
      }
      else
         InsertNode(pNew,pNode->pRight);
   }
   return;
}
```

It turns out to be very simple. The function will be called with a pointer to the new **Phone** object, and a pointer to the root node of the tree as arguments. If the name member of the new object is less than the name field of the current node, then we check whether the pointer **pLeft** is **NULL**. If it is, then we plug in the address of the new object, and we're done. If it isn't then we call the function **InsertNode()** with the new object as the first argument and the node pointed to by **pLeft** as the second. The process if the name isn't less than the name field for the current node is the same. The function will call itself until a suitable **pLeft** or **pRight** pointer is found that's **NULL**, whereupon the new object will be inserted and the whole process will unwind.

To complete the process for creating a tree, all we need is the **CreateTree()** function. This needs to be able to create a tree with one node using the first **Phone** object, and then insert all the additional objects into it:

```
/* Function to create a tree */
struct Phone *CreateTree(void)
{
    struct Phone *pRoot=NULL;          /* Pointer to root of the tree */
    struct Phone *pNew=NULL;           /* Pointer to new entry */

    pRoot=GetPhone();                  /* Create a one node tree */

    while((pNew=GetPhone())!=NULL)     /* Now insert the rest */
        InsertNode(pNew, pRoot);

    return pRoot;      /* Return the pointer to the root of the tree */
}
```

The **while** loop continues as long as the pointer returned by the function **GetPhone()** isn't **NULL**. The only loop action is the call **InsertNode()** for each new object. As soon as a **NULL** is returned by **GetPhone()** the tree is finished.

Searching the Tree

We want to be able to search the tree for a name and get back the telephone number for that name. The function to do this will need the name to be found and the pointer to the root node of the tree as arguments. We can get the function to display the number, so we don't need a return value. The prototype will therefore be:

```
void ShowNumber(char *pName, struct Phone *pRoot);
```

How is the function **ShowNumber()** to find a particular name in the tree? Our experience with constructing the tree is a good indicator of an approach. For any node, if the name equals the name member for the current node, then we've found it so we can display the number and we're done. If the name is less than the name for the current node, we test the node pointed to by **pLeft**, and if not, we test the node pointed to by **pRight**. If we arrive at a **pLeft** or **pRight** pointer that's **NULL**, then the name isn't in the tree. We can implement this as another recursive function:

```
/* Function to find a given name and display the number */
void ShowNumber(char *pName, struct Phone *pNode)
{
   int Test;                           /* Value from string comparison */

   if(pNode==NULL) /* If this node is NULL then */
   {                                   /* is not in the tree */
      printf("The name %s was not found.\n\n", pName);
      return;
   }

   Test=strcmp(pName,pNode->pName);    /* Compare name to current node */

   if(Test<0)                          /* If it is less */
   {                                   /* try the left node */
      ShowNumber(pName,pNode->pLeft);
      return;
   }
   if(Test>0)                          /* If it is greater */
   {                                   /* try the right node */
      ShowNumber(pName,pNode->pRight);
      return;
   }

   /* We have got it-so flaunt it*/
   printf("The number for %s is %s\n\n",pName, pNode->pNumber);
   return;
}
```

The first action in the function is to check whether the second argument is **NULL**. If it is, then we've been passed a **pLeft** or **pRight NULL** pointer so the name isn't in the tree, and we display a message and return. Otherwise we compare the name sought with the name member of the current node using the library function **strcmp()**. If the value returned is negative, then the name is less than the name for the current node, so we call **ShowNumber()** to check the node pointed to by **pLeft**. If the result of the comparison is positive then we search the right node. If the result of the comparison is neither less than nor greater than zero, that leaves only one possibility - it must be equal to zero, so we've found the name and we can display the number.

Displaying the Tree

To display the entire tree in alphabetical order, we can again use a recursive function. For any node in the tree, the node pointed to by **pLeft** must be displayed before the current node because its name field will be less than the name for the current node. We set it up this way. It follows then that for any node we need to display the node pointed to by **pLeft**, then the current node, and then the node pointed to by **pRight**. Of course if **pLeft** or **pRight** are **NULL** then there's nothing to display. We can implement this process as the function **DisplayTree()**:

```
/* Function to display the tree */
void DisplayTree(struct Phone *pNode)
{
    if(pNode==NULL)
        return;
    DisplayTree(pNode->pLeft);
    printf("\n%-40s\t%s",pNode->pName, pNode->pNumber);
    DisplayTree(pNode->pRight);
    return;
}
```

This is remarkably short for a function that is to display a tree of any size and shape. If the passed pointer **pNode** is **NULL**, then there's nothing to be done and the function returns. Otherwise it calls itself with the **pLeft** pointer as the argument, displays the current node, and then calls itself with the **pRight** pointer as an argument. The whole process is kicked off by calling the function with a pointer to the root node as the argument. Easy, isn't it?

Deleting the Tree

With the amazing success of recursion in the other functions, this must be another opportunity to apply it, and indeed it is. Before you can delete any node, we must first delete the left and the right node. All we need is a recursive function that does exactly that:

```
/* A function to delete a tree */
void DeleteTree(struct Phone *pNode)
{
    if(pNode==NULL)                        /* If the pointer passed is NULL */
        return;                            /* then we are done */
```

```
   if(pNode->pLeft!=NULL)              /* If there is a left node */
      DeleteTree(pNode->pLeft);        /* then delete it */

   if(pNode->pRight!=NULL)             /* If there is a right node */
      DeleteTree(pNode->pRight);       /* then delete it */

   free(pNode->pName);                 /* Delete name for this node */
   free(pNode->pNumber);               /* Delete number for this node */
   free(pNode);                        /* Now we can delete this node */
   return;
}
```

If the pointer passed is **NULL** then there's nothing to do, so we return from the function. Otherwise, the function calls itself to delete the left node, and then calls itself again to delete the right node, and finally deletes the current node after first removing its name and number. That's it. All we need now is the function **main()** to tie everything together.

The Rest of the Program

```
/* EX6-04.C  Storing phone number using a binary tree */
#include <stdio.h>                     /* For input and output */
#include <stdlib.h>                    /* For malloc() */
#include <string.h>                    /* For string functions */

#define MAXLEN 40                      /* Maximum input length */

/* Structure definitions */
struct Phone
{
   char *pName;                        /* Pointer to a name */
   char *pNumber;                      /* Pointer to telephone number */
   struct Phone *pLeft;                /* Pointer to Phone object<current */
   struct Phone *pRight;               /* Pointer to Phone object>=current */
};

/* Function prototypes */
struct Phone *CreateTree(void);
void InsertNode(struct Phone *pNew, struct Phone *pRoot);
void DisplayTree(struct Phone *pRoot);
void ShowNumber(char *pName, struct Phone *pRoot);
void DeleteTree(struct Phone *pRoot);
struct Phone *GetPhone(void);

int main(void)
{
```

```
    struct Phone *pRoot;                /* Pointer to root of tree */
    char Name[MAXLEN];

    printf("\n Enter names and telephone numbers as prompted, each less \n"
           " than 40 characters. Enter an empty line to end input.\n");

    pRoot=CreateTree();

    /* Search for entries */
    printf("Enter a name to look up, or blank to end.\n\n");
    while(strlen(gets(Name)))
        ShowNumber(Name,pRoot);

    printf("\nThe complete tree is:\n\n");
    DisplayTree(pRoot);
    DeleteTree(pRoot);
    return 0;
}

/***************************************************************
 * The function definitions we have already seen go here...  *
 ***************************************************************/
```

Program Analysis

The function **main()** is quite straightforward as virtually all the work is done in the other functions. The address of the tree root returned by the function **CreateTree()** is stored in **pRoot**. After a prompt, the **while** loop will search for successive names, and when an empty name is entered the process ceases. The complete tree is then displayed by calling **DisplayTree()** and finally the memory occupied on the heap is freed by calling **DeleteTree()**.

Unions

A union is like a structure, but its members all occupy the same memory area. A union is defined using the keyword **union**, in a statement with syntax similar to that for a structure. To define a template for a union type **Shared**, which can contain a **double** value, a **long** value, and a pointer, you could use the statement:

```
union Shared
{
    double Value;
```

```
    long Number;
    char *pName;
};
```

As with a structure definition, this is a template, and doesn't define any variables. The size of a union is the size of its largest member, so in this case its size will be that of the **double** member, **Value**. We can define a variable of type **Shared** with the statement:

```
union Shared MyData;
```

This declares the variable **MyData** which can contain values for any of the three variables **Value**, **Number** or **pName**, but since they all occupy the same memory area, only one can be active at a single time. Referencing a member of a union is exactly the same as referring to a member of a structure. To set the member **Number** in the union **MyData**, you would use the statement:

```
MyData.Number=99;
```

If you now attempted to use this value as **MyData.pName** or **MyData.Value**, you would obviously be working with garbage values, since you would be interpreting an integer 99 as a pointer, or as part of a floating point number.

A union can also be a member of a structure, and vice versa. You access the members of a union that are members of a structure in the same way that we accessed members of a structure of type **Point** nested in a structure of type **Line**.

Applications of Unions

In the days of very limited memory capacity, unions were often used to save memory space - this is rarely the case today. One thing a union can help you with which is hard to do by any other means, is to treat the same data in two different ways, or to manage a collection of data values of different types as an array of bytes. If you have a data value of type **long** passed to a function, that sometimes contains a single 4-byte **long** value, and at other times contains a pair of 2-byte **int** values, you can define a union:

```
union MyUnion
{
    long iValue;
    int jValue[2];
}MyData;
```

Now you can refer to the same memory as two values of type **int**, **MyData.jValue[0]** and **MyData.jValue[1]**, or as a single long value **MyData.iValue**.

The situation can arise where you have a collection of different kinds of data stored in different variables that you want to handle as a simple array of bytes, to write away to a disk file as a single binary record for example. You can create a mapping between the variables of different kinds and an array of bytes, by aggregating the variables in a structure, and then creating a union with the structure, and a suitably sized array of type **char**, as members.

For example, if we wanted to be able to treat an object of type **Planet**, the first example of a structure we saw, interchangeably as an array of bytes, we could define a union as:

```
union MyUnion
{
    struct Planet aPlanet;
    char Array[sizeof(struct Planet)];
}Mapping;
```

By copying a **Planet** object to the union with a statement such as:

```
Mapping.aPlanet=Mars;
```

we could then move it around as a byte stream using **Mapping.Array[]**.

Summary

We've now covered all of the ways for handling data in C. Structures are a very powerful mechanism for managing data, providing the foundation for a vast variety of techniques. The discussion on trees here barely scratched the surface. Although there are many more possibilities for different kinds of tree structures beyond what we have discussed, you should now have sufficient understanding of the basics to appreciate how the more complicated trees work, and are applied, when you meet them.

The essential points from this chapter are:

- A structure is an aggregate of several variables that can be of different types, grouped under a single name. Members of a structure can be of any type, except the same type as the structure itself, although they can include pointers to structures of the same type.

- The only operations you can perform on a structure as a whole, are to take its address, copy or assign it to a variable of the same structure type, or pass it as an argument to a function.

- A structure member is referenced using the member selection operator by combining the name of the structure variable and the member variable name. A structure member can be used in the same way as any other variable of the same type.

- Structure members can also be accessed through a pointer to a structure by using the indirect member selection operator, ->.

- Structures containing pointers to structures can be used to implement many important data structures, such as linked lists, doubly linked lists, and trees.

- A union is a collection of variables that are stored starting at the same address. Members of a union are referenced using the same mechanisms as those for a structure.

Programming Exercises

1 Write a program using the **Planet** structure that constructs a tree of **Planet** objects, and then provides a search capability for a condition to be met for a given member, for example, to find all the **Planet** objects that have a mass greater than 1.5. (You'll need to provide a means of recording pointers to multiple objects in the tree.)

2 Write a program to read in several lines of text, and then use a tree to store the words occurring in the text in alphabetical order. Record and display the frequency of occurrence of each word. Search the tree for the word with the maximum number of occurrences in the text.

3 Define a structure to include a name, an address and a telephone number. Write a program to construct a binary tree in name order. Sort the structures by telephone number, and by city. (You can construct a new tree for each ordering of the data.)

4 Write a program to calculate the maximum and average search lengths for a binary tree. Use the tree in the previous example as the base for doing this. (You will need to find ever left or right pointer that is **NULL**, and keep track of how many levels it took to reach each one.)

Chapter

Using Libraries

The standard libraries that support applications written in C are defined by an ANSI standard, so you will find the same sets of functions available with any ANSI-compliant C compiler. By the end of this chapter you will understand:

- What groups of functions are provided by the standard library.

- How you can use standard library functions for classifying characters.

- How you can obtain the date and the time in your programs.

- How you can convert numeric values expressed as a character string to their numeric equivalents.

- How to generate pseudo random numbers.

- How to use string handling and searching functions.

- What mathematical functions are available in the standard library.

The Standard Library

The standard library provides functions, type definitions, constant definitions of various kinds, and macros that you can use in your programs (we will discuss what macros are in Chapter 9). The contents of the standard library are sub-divided into 15 groups of facilities. The declarations necessary to use each group are defined in a standard header file, so there are 15 standard headers too:

ASSERT.H	Debugging support
CTYPE.H	Tests for character types
ERRNO.H	Defines symbols corresponding to error codes
FLOAT.H	Parameters for floating point routines
LIMITS.H	Upper and lower limits for integer types.
LOCALE.H	Specific country and language support
MATH.H	Mathematical functions
SETJMP.H	Non-local branching support
SIGNAL.H	Errors and other exception handling
STDARG.H	Variable argument lists
STDDEF.H	Defines standard data types and macros
STDIO.H	Input and output
STDLIB.H	Utility functions including dynamic memory allocation
STRING.H	String processing functions
TIME.H	Date and time functions

Including a Standard Library

In order to use the contents of any particular group of facilities, you must incorporate the appropriate header file into your program using an **#include** command. For example, we've already used this library in all the examples we have seen so far:

```
#include <stdio.h>
```

The **#include** command must appear at global scope, and always prior to using any of the facilities it supports.

It would take a whole book to cover all the functions and facilities provided by the standard library in detail, so we'll have to be selective. The file input/output functions supported by **STDIO.H** will be discussed in

Chapter 8, and the keyboard and screen operations are summarized in Appendix A. We will look in Chapter 9 at the facilities defined in **ASSERT.H**, when we will be looking at debugging and the preprocessor.

Character Classification Functions

You will often need to test a character to see if it's of a particular classification - a digit, or a lower case letter for instance. The **CTYPE.H** header file supports a range of functions that all accept an argument of type **int**, and return a 1 if the argument corresponds to the type of character sought. They return 0 otherwise. The functions provided are as follows:

islower()	Tests for lower case.
isupper()	Tests for upper case.
isdigit()	Tests for a decimal digit, 0 to 9.
isxdigit()	Tests for a hexadecimal digit, 0 to 9, A to F (or a to f).
isalpha()	Tests for a letter, either upper case or lower case.
isalnum()	Tests for an upper case or lower case letter, or a digit.
iscntrl()	Tests for a control character.
isprint()	Tests for a character that prints including space.
isgraph()	Tests for a character that prints excluding space.
ispunct()	Tests for a character that prints excluding space, letters and digits.
isspace()	Tests for a whitespace character.

In addition, two functions are provided to convert the case of letters. The function **tolower()** returns the lower case equivalent of its argument, and **toupper()** returns the upper case equivalent.

Time and Date Functions

Sooner or later you will need to measure time in a program. The standard library includes functions which can enable you to work with the time and the date. They provide output in various forms, generated from the hardware clock or clocks in your computer. To use them you must include the header file **TIME.H** in your program. Let's take a look at a few of them.

Getting Processor Time

Perhaps the simplest function in this area has the prototype:

```
clock_t clock(void);
```

This function returns the processor time (not the elapsed time) that your program has used since it began execution. The processor time is provided as a value of type **clock_t**, which is defined in **TIME.H** and usually equivalent to type **long**. The value is measured in **clock ticks**, units dependent upon your hardware clock. To convert the value returned by the function **clock()** to seconds, you must divide it by the constant **CLOCKS_PER_SEC** also defined in the **TIME.H** library. The function **clock()** returns a value of -1 if an error occurs.

Getting the Time and Date

The function **time()** returns the calendar time from a fixed reference date, and time as a value of type **time_t**, also defined in **TIME.H**, and equivalent to type **long**. The prototype of the function **time()** is:

```
time_t time( time_t *pTime );
```

If the argument isn't **NULL**, then the current calendar time is also stored in the location pointed to by the argument. However, the function is most commonly used with a **NULL** argument. You can convert the value returned to a structure containing day and date information in local time, by using the library function **localtime()**, which has the prototype:

```
struct tm *localtime(const time_t *pTime);
```

This function returns a pointer to a structure containing members with values detailing the time and the date. The structure type **tm** is defined in the **TIME.H** header file as:

```
struct tm
{
    int tm_sec;          /* Number of seconds after the minute */
    int tm_min;          /* Number of minutes after the hour */
    int tm_hour;         /* Number of hours since midnight */
    int tm_mday;         /* Day of the month */
    int tm_mon;          /* Number of months since January */
```

```
    int tm_year;                    /* Number of years since 1900 */
    int tm_wday;                    /* Number of days since Sunday */
    int tm_yday;                    /* Number of days since January 1 */
    int tm_isdst;                   /* Daylight saving time flag */

};
```

So to obtain data on the current time and date, you could use the statements:

```
struct tm *pNow=NULL;              /* Pointer to time structure */
time_t MyTime;                     /* Store for time value */
MyTime=time(NULL);                 /* Get current time in seconds */
pNow=localtime(&MyTime);           /* Convert to a local time structure */
```

This passes the address of **MyTime**, which stores the value returned from the function **time()** as an argument to the function **localtime()**. So with **pNow** pointing to the **tm** structure returned from the **localtime()** function, you can obtain the current time by accessing the members **pNow->tm_hour**, **pNow->tm_min**, and **pNow->tm_sec**.

Formatting the Time and Date

If you want to convert the time and date to a character string for output purposes, the standard library provides a fancy function to do this for you. Its prototype is:

```
size_t strftime(char *pTimeStr, size_t MaxChars,
                const char *pFormatStr, const struct tm *pTime);
```

The first argument, **pTimeStr** points to the string where the output from the function will be stored. The second argument is the maximum number of output characters, usually specified as **sizeof(pTimeStr)**. The **pFormatStr** argument specifies how the output is to appear in **pTimeStr**. This works in a manner similar to that used for the format string to the function **printf()**. Format specifiers are used to indicate which fields from the structure pointed to by the fourth argument, **pTime**, are to appear where. The format specifiers you can use here are:

%a	Abbreviated weekday name
%A	Full weekday name
%b	Abbreviated month name
%B	Full month name

%c	Local date and time representation
%d	Day of the month number (01-31)
%H	Hour in 24-hour format (00-23)
%I	Hour in 12-hour format (01-12)
%j	Day number in the year (001-366)
%m	Month number in the year (01-12)
%M	Minute as a decimal number (00-59)
%p	Local AM or PM indicator for a 12-hour clock
%S	Second as a decimal number (00-59)
%U	Week number, with Sunday as the first day of the week (00-51)
%w	Weekday number (0-6; Sunday is 0)
%W	Week number, with Monday as the first day of the week (00-51)
%x	Local date representation
%X	Local time representation
%y	Year number without the century (00-99)
%Y	Year number with the century
%Z	Time-zone name or abbreviation; no characters if time-zone is unknown
%%	Percentage sign

Displaying the Day and the Date

For example we can use some of these in a program like:

```
/* EX7-01.C  A program to display the day and the date */
#include <stdio.h>              /* For input and output */
#include <time.h>               /* For time functions */

int main(void)
{
   char Buffer[100];            /* Buffer for time and date string */
   struct tm *pNow=NULL;        /* Pointer to time structure */
   time_t MyTime;               /* Store for time value */

   MyTime=time(NULL);           /* Get current time in seconds */
   pNow=localtime(&MyTime);     /* Convert to a local time structure */

   /* Now convert to a string for output */
   strftime(Buffer, sizeof(Buffer),
       "I used the time functions on %A %B %d, %Y  at %I.%M %p", pNow);

   printf("\n%s",Buffer);
   return 0;
}
```

Program Analysis

This example will produce output similar to:

I used the time functions on Tuesday September 15th, 1995 at 11.53 AM

but unless there is something really weird happening, you'll get a different time and date.

The process is very straightforward. We obtain the current time (in seconds) using the function **time()**, and store it in the variable **MyTime**:

```
MyTime=time(NULL);              /* Get current time in seconds */
```

The address of this variable is passed on to the function **localtime()** to obtain a structure containing the time and date data:

```
pNow=localtime(&MyTime);        /* Convert to a local time structure */
```

We pass the pointer to this structure to the function **strftime()**:

```
strftime(Buffer, sizeof(Buffer),
        "I used the time functions on %A %B %d, %Y  at %I.%M %p", pNow);
```

for it to generate formatted output in the array **Buffer[]**. As you see, each format specifier selects a particular member of the structure pointed to by **pNow**, and inserts it in the output.

Calculating Elapsed Time

You can also use the output from the function **time()** to calculate elapsed time. You can get the elapsed time in seconds between two successive **time_t** values returned by **time()**, by using the function **difftime()**, which has the prototype:

```
double difftime( time_t T2, time_t T1 );
```

This function will return the value **T2-T1** expressed in seconds as a value of type **double**.

We could define functions to log the elapsed time and the processor time used between successive calls, and exercise them in the following example:

```
/* EX7-02.C  Timing intervals      */
#include <stdio.h>
#include <time.h>


double CPU_Timer(void);              /* CPU timer function prototype */
long ElapsedTimer(void);             /* Elapsedtimer function prototype */

int main(void)
{

    long i=0L;                       /* Loop counter */
    double CPU=0.0;                  /* Store for CPU time used */
    double x = 0.0;                  /* Result of multiply */

    CPU_Timer();                     /* Initialize processor timing */
    ElapsedTimer();                  /* Initialize elapsed timing */

    for(i=0L;i<10000000L;i++)
       x=3.4567 * 4.5678;            /* Multiply 10m times */

    CPU=CPU_Timer();                 /* Get time after 10m multiplies */

    printf("\nCPU time for ten million multiplies is %.2f seconds", CPU );

    for(i=0L;i<5000000L;i++)
       x = 3.4567 * 4.5678;          /* Multiply another 5m times */

    /* Output total time elapsed */
    printf("\nTotal elapsed time is %d seconds",
                              ElapsedTimer() );
    return 0;
}

/* Timer function */
double CPU_Timer(void)
{
    static clock_t CPU_Last = 0;    /* Holds clock value from last call */
    clock_t CPU_This = 0;
    double CPU_Used=0.0;

    if(CPU_Last)
    {
       CPU_This=clock();            /* Get current processor time */
       CPU_Used=(CPU_This-CPU_Last)/(double)CLOCKS_PER_SEC;
```

```
      CPU_Last=CPU_This;
      return CPU_Used;
   }
   /* Only do this first time through */
   CPU_Last=clock();
   return 0.0;
}

long ElapsedTimer(void)
{
   static time_t El_Last= 0;      /* Holds calendar time from last call */
   time_t El_This = 0;
   long Elapsed=0L;
   if(El_Last)                    /* If its not the first time */
   {
      El_This=time(NULL);         /* Get current time value */
      /* Get elapsed clock time  */
      Elapsed=(long)difftime( El_This, El_Last );

      El_Last=El_This;            /* Save the current clock time */

      return Elapsed;             /* Return the time intervals */
   }

   /* We do this only the first time around */
   El_Last=time(NULL);            /* Initialize clock time */
   return 0L;                     /* Return zero intervals */
}
```

Program Analysis

This example performs the rather trivial activity of doing the same multiplication 10 million times, and then repeats it another 5 million times for good measure. The functions `CPU_Timer()` and `ElapsedTimer()` provide the CPU time used between calls, and the total elapsed time between calls, respectively. We call both functions at the beginning of the `main()` which sets a current value in the `static` variable in each function.

The function `CPU_Timer()` is called after executing the multiply operation in the for loop 10 million times:

```
for(i=0L;i<10000000L;i++)
   x=3.4567 * 4.5678;            /* Multiply 10m times */

   CPU=CPU_Timer();             /* Get time after 10m multiplies */
```

241

You may want to reduce or increase this figure, depending on how much money you've invested in your computer.

After completing the loop, the `CPU_Timer()` function is called again to obtain the total CPU time consumed:

```
CPU=CPU_Timer();                        /* Get time after 10m multiplies */
```

and this is displayed by the `printf()` function:

```
printf("\nCPU time for ten million multiplies is %.2f seconds", CPU );
```

After another 5 million multiply operations in the next **for** loop, we display the total elapsed time. The output from this example on my computer is:

```
CPU time for ten million multiplies is 19.99 seconds
Total elapsed time is 31 seconds
```

Of course the total elapsed time is down to *all* the instructions executed between calls, and not just the multiply operations.

String Handling Functions

The declarations necessary to use the string handling functions in the standard library appear in the header file **STRING.H**. We have already used the functions **strlen()** to get the length of a string, **strcpy()** to copy from one string to another, and **strcmp()** to compare two strings. There are some others in this category which you may find particularly helpful.

Joining Strings

To append one string on to the end of another, you can use the function **strcat()**. This has the prototype:

```
char *strcat(char *pStr, char *pAddStr);
```

The function will copy the string pointed to by the second argument, on to the end of the first string pointed to. The return value is a pointer to the

242

modified string. The original first string must be big enough to hold the extra characters, otherwise you'll be in deep water.

Where you need to copy a specific number of characters from one string to another, you can use the function `strncat()`. This function has the prototype:

```
char *strncat(char *pStr, char *pAddStr, size_t MaxLen);
```

This will copy up to **MaxLen** characters from the string pointed to by **pAddStr** to the string pointed to by **pStr**, excluding the terminating `'\0'`. The resulting string will thus be up to **MaxLen** characters longer that the original string, **pStr**. This function can be very useful if you want to append a particular word from the middle of one string on to the end of another.

Comparing Strings

As well as the compare function that we've already seen, there is another function that can compare a specific number of characters:

```
int strncmp(char *pStr, char *pAddStr, size_t MaxLen);
```

This will compare the string **pAddStr** to, at most, **MaxLen** characters of **pStr**.

Searching a String

We can use the **strncmp** function to search for words in a string, as shown with this example:

```
/* EX7-03.C  Searching a string */
#include <stdio.h>          /* For input and output */
#include <string.h>         /* For string functions */

int main(void)
{
   char String[120];        /* String to be search */
   char FindStr[80];        /* String sought */
   char *pString=String;    /* Pointer to String */
```

```
    char *pFind=FindStr;      /* Pointer to FindStr */
    size_t FindLen=0;         /* Length of string to be found */
    int Count=0;              /* Count of occurrences of FindStr in String */

    printf("\nEnter a string to be searched less than 120 characters:\n");
    gets(String);
    printf("\nEnter a string to be found less than 80 characters:\n");
    gets(FindStr);

    FindLen=strlen(FindStr);                 /* Get length of string sought */

    while(strlen(pString)>=FindLen)          /* Search while there is space */
    {
      if(strncmp(pString,FindStr,FindLen)==0)
      {
        Count++;                             /* Found one - so up the count */
        pString+=FindLen;                    /* Move past the one we found */
      }
      else
        pString++;                           /* Move to next character */
    }
    printf("\nIn the string:\n%s\nthe string \"%s\" was found %d times.",
                       String, FindStr, Count);
    return 0;
}
```

Program Analysis

The program prompts for two strings to be entered, the first is to be searched, and the second contains the string to be found within the first. The pointer to the string to be searched, **pString**, is moved through the string as the string **FindStr** is compared with the characters in **pString**, up to the length of **FindStr**. The loop continues as long as there are enough characters in **pString** for a comparison to be made.

When **FindStr** is found, **Count** is incremented, and the pointer, **pString**, is incremented by the number of characters in **FindStr**. Each time **FindStr** isn't found, **pString** is incremented in order to move to the next position in the string. This mechanism is shown in this illustration for part of the sample input:

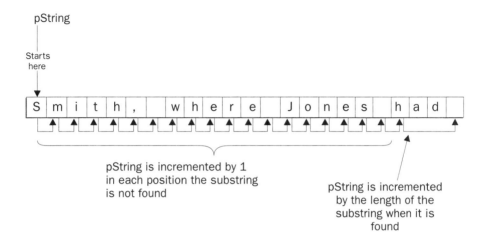

pString

Starts here

| S | m | i | t | h | , | | w | h | e | r | e | | J | o | n | e | s | | h | a | d | |

pString is incremented by 1 in each position the substring is not found

pString is incremented by the length of the substring when it is found

An example of output from the program is:

Enter a string to be searched less than 120 characters:
Smith, where Jones had had "had", had had "had had".

Enter a string to be found less than 80 characters:
had

In the string:
Smith, where Jones had had "had", had had "had had".
the string "had" was found 7 times.

Searching for Characters

You can also search a string to find how much of the string consists entirely of characters from a particular set. For example, you could search the string **"1.2 1.3 coordinates"** for characters from the set **"0123456789."** which is all the digits, a decimal point and a blank space.

The strspn Function

This has the following prototype:

```
size_t strspn(char *pString, char *pCharSet);
```

This will return the number of characters from the beginning of **pString** that consists entirely of characters that are from the set appearing in the string **pCharSet**. This mechanism is illustrated here:

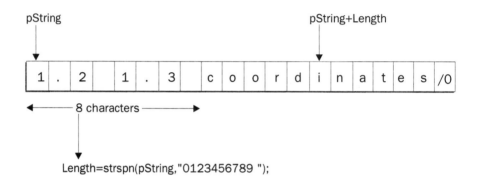

The value returned by the function will be 8, since the first eight characters of the string can be found amongst the characters **"0123456789."**, but the ninth cannot. To find the first non-numeric character, you just need to add the value returned to the address of the first character in the string.

The strcspn Function

On the other hand you might want to ask the question in another way - how much of the string, starting from the beginning, consists entirely of characters that aren't alphabetic? The function to make this search has the prototype:

```
size_t strcspn(char *pString, char *pCharSet);
```

To use this function to perform a search for what length of a string doesn't contain decimal digits, you would write:

```
Length= strcspn(pString, "0123456789");
```

The variable **length** will contain the count of the number of sequential characters from the beginning of **pString**, which aren't decimal digits. Thus the first decimal digit will be at position **pString+Length**. This mechanism is shown here:

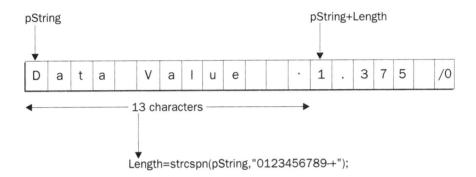

The first 13 characters don't contain any of the characters from the string specified as the second argument to the function **strcspn()**, so this value is returned. This example is spacing over non-numeric data. The first occurrence of any character from the defined set is indicated by **pString+Length**.

The strpbrk Function

Another useful function will directly find the position in a string where the first character from a particular set can be found. It has the prototype:

```
char *strpbrk(char *pString, char *pCharSet);
```

To find the first position in a string that contains a sign, or a decimal digit, you would write:

```
pPos= strpbrk(char *pString, "+-0123456789");
```

the position in the string where the first occurrence is found is stored in **pPos**, which is of type 'pointer to **char**'. If none of the characters specified by the second argument are found, a **NULL** is returned.

Analyzing a String

You will often come across a situation where you want to analyze a string - usually keyboard input, consisting of a number of substrings separated by some given character. Such substrings are usually referred to as **tokens**, and the characters used to separate them are called **delimiters**. The process of separating a string into tokens is referred to as **parsing** the string.

The strtok Function

You don't necessarily know how many numerical substrings there are, or precisely what they contain. All you know is that they're separated by commas, and that the numerical substrings won't contain a comma. You could write your own routine to do the analysis, but there is an easier method; the standard library provides a function to extract tokens from a string separated by given delimiters. It has the prototype:

```
char *strtok( char *pString, const char *pDelimiters);
```

The first parameter is a pointer to the string that you want to analyze, and the second argument is a pointer to a constant string containing the delimiters. The address of a token in the string is returned by the function.

However, it's not quite as straightforward as that, since a string will typically contain several tokens, but this function provides you with a mechanism for getting at all of them. It will be easier to understand how the function works by looking at an example, so let's assume that we want to analyze a string containing numerical values separated by commas. Suppose that we have a string defined as:

```
char String[] = "1.25,37.5,500,212";
```

We can call the function **strtok()** with the statement:

```
pToken = strtok( String, ",");
```

The first argument is the address of the string to be analyzed, and the second is a string containing the delimiter, which is a comma. Although we've only specified a single delimiter, there could be more than one. The variable **pToken** is of type 'pointer to **char**'. The function will search from the beginning of the string for the first occurrence of the delimiter, and will replace it with the string terminating character, `'\0'`. It will finally return the address of the first character of the first token, in this case corresponding to the first character in the string, and this will be stored in **pToken**. We can then process the token however we like.

To get the next token in the string, we call **strtok()** again, but this time with the first argument as **NULL**. We will assume that we can reuse the variable **pToken** to store the address of the next delimiter, so the statement to do this will be:

```
pToken = strtok( NULL, ",");
```

The function will find the next token, and after replacing the next delimiter with '\0', will return its address. By repeatedly calling **strtok()** with the first argument as **NULL**, all the tokens in the original string can be found. When there are no more tokens in the string, the function **strtok()** will return **NULL**, so you can end the process of searching for tokens by testing the returned value. For example, if we wanted to list all the tokens in our sample string on separate lines, we could do this with the statements:

```
pToken = strtok( &String, ",");
printf("\n%s", pToken);
while( (pToken = strtok( NULL, ",")) !=NULL )
   printf("\n%s", pToken);
```

We have used the same delimiter string for each call of **strtok()** in analyzing the string. This is the norm, but the function does allow you to use different delimiter strings on successive calls if you need to. There may be times when you would like to split your parsing into functions, and in these cases you must be very careful not to nest calls to **strtok()**, since this will confuse your compiler.

The 'Mem' Functions

There are a group of functions, defined in **STRING.H**, which are useful for manipulating arrays of bytes, and aren't limited to null-terminated strings. All the names of these routines begin with '**mem**' (for 'memory'), and the most commonly used is **memset()**, which is used to fill an area of memory with a particular value, and which returns a pointer to the newly-filled memory. This function has the prototype:

```
void * memset(void *buff, int n, size_t num);
```

Note the use of **void** pointers. We need to be able to pass any sort of pointer to **memset** and return it. A **void** pointer is the only way we can do this without causing errors.

If, for example, we had a large character array which we wanted to completely fill with dashes, we could:

```
char myString[5000];
memset(myString, '-', 5000);
myString[4999]= '\0';
```

> Two things to watch for - make sure that you specify the correct length, or **memset** will write off the end of the string, and secondly, remember to put a null on the end of the string before you use it!

Two other routines, **memcpy()** and **memmove()**, both copy a number of bytes from one buffer to another, but for **memcpy** the buffers mustn't overlap, while for **memmove** they can.

```
void * memcpy(void *buff1, void *buff2, size_t num);
void * memmove(void *buff1, void *buff2, size_t num);
```

String Conversion Functions

These functions, defined in header file **STDLIB.H**, will convert numbers represented as a character string into their numeric form. The need for this might arise if you read input as a character string, and you want to sort out its contents for yourself. There are two basic functions: **strtol()** which converts a character string to **long**, and **strtod()** which converts a character string to **double**.

Converting a String to an Integer

The prototype of the function to convert a string to an integer is:

```
long strtol(char *pStr, char **pEnd, int Base);
```

This function converts characters from a string to a **long** value until it finds a character that isn't part of the character sequence defining the value. The first parameter defines the string to be converted, whilst the second parameter, **pEnd** is a pointer to a pointer, and will point to the character that stopped the processing of the string. The third parameter specifies the number base used to represent the number in the string. **Base** can have any value between 2 and 36, although you will rarely need to deal with numbers to base 36.

> **Base 36 is the maximum mainly because the digits can be 0 to 9 plus A to Z, so beyond 36 we don't have symbols to represent the digits.**

If **Base** is set to zero, then the first couple of characters in the input string determine the base that is assumed. This works as follows:

First Character	Second Character	Number Base
0	1 to 7	Octal
0	x or X	Hexadecimal
1 to 9		Decimal

The number in the string can be preceded by whitespace characters which are ignored. A plus or minus sign may also be present. For octal numbers the first digit character should be 0, and for hexadecimal numbers the digits characters should start with **0X** or **0x**. So **+1239**, and **–0X3ABC** are valid strings. Of course, you mustn't have more digits than you can actually store as a **long** integer.

If you just want to convert a string to an **int** decimal value, and you don't need to know where it ends in the string, you can use the function **atoi()** which has the prototype:

```
int atoi(const char *pStr);
```

This simply returns the converted decimal value as type **int**. For type **long**, the function **atol()** is also provided.

> Be aware of something that can affect `atoi`, `atol` and `atof` (mentioned in the next section). If the conversion fails for any reason, a value of zero is returned. This horrible design flaw means that it is impossible to differentiate between an error and a valid value of zero using the standard library routines. The only reliable way round this is to write your own versions of these routines, which is harder than it sounds, but a very good exercise!

Converting a String to Floating Point

The general library function to convert a string to a value of type **double** has the prototype:

```
double strtod(const char *pStr, char **pEnd);
```

The parameters here have the same significance as the corresponding parameters for **strtol()**. The value in the string can be preceded by whitespace, and is otherwise represented as a floating point constant or a decimal integer. We can represent the general form as:

```
[+ or -]  [digit string]  [decimal point]  [digit string]
[e or E]  [+ or  -]  [digit string]
```

where the square brackets indicate that the item is optional. The following are all valid floating point values:

234   -1.234   .025E-3   34e10   3.45-2

A simple conversion to **double** without determining where the value ends in the string is provided by the function:

```
double atof(const char *pStr);
```

Exercising Conversions

In order to demonstrate such conversion routines, here is a sample program:

```
/* EX7-04.C a program to exercise conversion routines */
#include <stdio.h>                    /* For input and output */
#include <stdlib.h>                   /* For conversion routines */

int main(void)
{
    char Buffer[100];                 /* Input buffer */
    char *pChar=NULL;                 /* Pointer to position in Buffer */
    long aLong1=0L, aLong2=0L;        /* Long values */
    double aDouble1=0.0, aDouble2=0.0;  /* Double values */

    printf("\nEnter two floating point values, a decimal integer,
            and a hexadecimal value\n");
    gets(Buffer);                            /* Get the input string */
    aDouble1=strtod(Buffer, &pChar);         /* Read double value */
    aDouble2=strtod(pChar, &pChar);          /* Read double value */
    aLong1=strtol(pChar, &pChar,10);         /* Read integer value */
    aLong2=strtol(pChar, &pChar,16);         /* Read hexadecimal value */
    printf("\nThe converted values are %f %f %ld %ld",
                    aDouble1, aDouble2, aLong1, aLong2);

    return 0;
}
```

Program Analysis

The program reads a string into the **Buffer[]** array. The first **double** value is read by calling **strtod()**, with **Buffer** and the address of the pointer **pChar** as arguments. To obtain the second **double** value, the pointer **pChar** is used to specify the start point for conversion, and the address of **pChar** is again used as the second argument to the function.

The function **strtol()** is used to convert the integer and hexadecimal value. In each case the address stored in **pChar** by the previous function call is used to specify the start of the string to be converted. Typical output from this program is:

Enter two floating point values, a decimal integer, and a hexadecimal value
123.4   -3.234E-1   7696   0X3bf

The converted values are 123.400000 -0.323400 7696 959

Try running it with incorrect values to see how the functions cope.

Converting a Number to a String

We've covered how to convert strings to numbers, but what about going in the opposite direction, and converting numbers to strings? You'll find, if you look, that there aren't any library functions to perform this task, and the most common way to do it is to use a cousin of **printf**, called **sprintf**.

Like **printf**, **sprintf** takes a format string and some optional arguments, and formats the arguments according to the instructions. Unlike **printf**, it then saves the output in a string rather than outputting it to the screen. Here's an example of how **sprintf** works:

```
/* declare a character string to hold the result */
char buff[10];
/* declare a value to be converted */
double val = 3.14159;


/* write the value into the string... note that the format */
/* applies to the arguments, not the buffer! */
sprintf(buff, "%.2f", val);


/* print the buffer */
printf("val is %s\n", buff);
```

Mathematical Functions

All the functions in this group return values of type **double**, and are supported by the header file **MATH.H**. The following trigonometric functions are provided:

sin(x)	sine of **x**	**asin(x)**	inverse sine of **x**
cos(x)	cosine of **x**	**acos(x)**	inverse cosine of **x**
tan(x)	tangent of **x**	**atan(x)**	inverse tangent of **x**

`sinh(x)`	hyperbolic sine of **x**	`atan2(y,x)`	inverse tangent of **y/x**
`cosh(x)`	hyperbolic cosine of **x**	`tanh(x)`	hyperbolic tangent of **x**

All angles as arguments or return values are in radians.

We've already used the functions `fabs()` (for obtaining the absolute value of its argument), and `sqrt()` which calculates a square root. You can calculate a logarithm to base 10 with the function `log10()` and a natural logarithm with the function `log()`, and to evaluate e^x, the function `exp()` is available. The other functions provided through `MATH.H` are:

`frexp(x, int *exp)`	Converts **x** to a value $m2^n$, returning 'm' and storing 'n' in `*exp`. The value returned will be fractional but not less than 0.5.
`modf(x, double *ipart)`	Stores the integral part of **x** in `*ipart`, and returns the fractional part of **x**.
`ldexp(x,n)`	Returns **x** multiplied by 2^n.
`ceil(x)`	Returns the smallest floating point integer that isn't less than **x**.
`floor(x)`	Returns the largest floating point integer that isn't greater than **x**.
`pow(x,y)`	Returns x^y.
`fmodf(x,y)`	Return the floating point remainder when **x** is divided by **y**.

If you use values as arguments to mathematical functions outside the range permitted for the function, you'll get a **domain error**. This is recorded by storing a value in a standard variable `errno` of type `int`, which is defined in `ERRNO.H`. It will be set to the value defined by the standard symbol `EDOM` when a domain error occurs. This is also defined in `ERRNO.H`. With some functions, `tan()` or `pow()` for example, it is possible that results can exceed the maximum that can be stored in a double variable. In this case `errno` will be set to the value defined by the standard symbol, `ERANGE`. If you want to be sure your results are correct, you should check `errno` after using such functions.

Random Number Generation

Another requirement you will run up against sooner or later is the need to generate pseudo-random numbers. For example, if you want to write a game, then a random number generation capability is usually necessary. The standard library includes two functions in header file **STDLIB.H** which are related to pseudo-random number generation, namely **rand()** and **srand()**.

> A pseudo-random number is a number generated by computer in a deterministic manner. They appear to be truly random but are repeated over a certain period.

The srand Function

The function **srand()** initializes the process of random number generation. Its prototype is:

```
void   srand(unsigned int Seed);
```

The value of **Seed** is used to start the process off. A given value for the parameter **Seed** will always produce the same sequence of pseudo-random numbers. If you want to get a different sequence each time, then you can initialize the process using the value returned by the library function **time()**. For example:

```
srand((unsigned int)time(NULL));
```

> This is a typical way of generating a pretty random number - seeding the generator with the current time (in seconds). Another popular seed value is the use of elapsed time before a keypress, although such times are hard to determine on different platforms.

The rand Function

The pseudo-random numbers are actually produced by the **rand()** function. The prototype for the function **rand()** is:

```
int rand(void);
```

This will return an integer value from zero to **RAND_MAX**. The value of **RAND_MAX** is implementation dependent, but it will be at least 32,767.

A Random Program

To demonstrate how we can use such functions, here is a suitable program:

```
/* EX7-05.C  Using pseudo-random numbers */
#include <stdio.h>              /* For input and output */
#include <stdlib.h>             /* For random number generation */
#include <time.h>               /* For the time() function */

int main(void)
{
   char *pPrize[]=
     {"first prize- a gift certificate for an Edsel service.",
      "second prize - a first edition of `The Paper Clip Users Guide'.",
      "third prize - an inflatable watch.",
      "fourth prize - a self teach guide to sword swallowing.",
      "fifth prize - free entry to the world's strongest man competition.",
      "sixth prize - a waterproof ink eraser.";

   srand((unsigned)time(NULL));

   printf("\nYou have won %s",
            pPrize[rand()%(sizeof pPrize/sizeof pPrize[0])]);

   return 0;
}
```

Program Analysis

This program should produce random output from the set of available messages. Since there are only two statements that do anything, this will not take long to explain. The array of pointer **pPrize[]** point to the set of initializing strings. The call to **srand()** initializes the random number generator using the current value returned from the library function **time()**. One of the strings pointed to by **pPrize[]** is selected by the index value based on the value returned from the function **rand()**. The remainder after dividing the value returned by **rand()** by the number of elements in the array **pPrize[]** is used as the index. This value will be between 0 and the maximum legal index for the array. You can add further initializing strings and the program will adapt automatically.

Summary

We have only just penetrated the surface of the standard library here. There are many more functions available, so you will be well repaid if you spend a little time looking into what there is on your system. Of course, in this chapter we have only been discussing those defined in the ANSI standard. Just about any C compiler system will contain others which are not within the standard. These will certainly provide a broader range of capabilities, and in some instances will provide functions which overlap with those in the standard library, but which are superior or easier to use.

The libraries are an essential element in C programming. Once you have mastered the language, you need to take some time to familiarize yourself with all the functions that seem relevant to your interests. Remember, if you are likely to be moving your program between different systems, it is important to limit yourself to the functions in the standard library to avoid unnecessary difficulties in porting your program from one machine to another.

Programming Exercises

1 Write a program to convert an input string containing mixed integer and floating point values in an arbitrary sequence. Display the values found.

> (Hint: you will need to find out where each number starts and ends, and then search for the occurrence of the distinguishing characters or a floating point value. A floating point should contain a decimal point, or an E or an e, or both.)

2 Write a program that is the equivalent of `printf()` for integers and floating point values corresponding to `%d` and `%f`.

> **(Hint: You will need to support a variable number of arguments determined from the format specifiers in the format string. You can use the string search functions to find the format specifiers. Look for %, then look at what follows to decide what type the argument is.)**

3 Write a program to simulate a fruit machine. Display each row of symbols as words. Keep track of winnings and losses. The payout is up to you.

4 Write and test a function to deal a hand of n cards at random. Display the hand as characters, for example: Club A, Diamond Q, Spade A, Spade 10, Spade J.

Chapter

File Operations

This chapter is all about reading and writing data to files in your program, which are usually hard disk files. By the end of this chapter you will have learnt:

- What a stream is.
- What the purpose of opening a file is, and how you do it.
- How you can read and write to a file one character at a time.
- What file buffering is, and how it works.
- How formatted input and output for a file works.
- How to read and write binary files.
- How to randomly access a file.
- What error processing functions are available for file operations.

The Concept of a File

You're probably familiar with the basic mechanics of how the hard disk on your computer works. If not, it would be a good idea to look into it as this can help you to recognize when a particular approach to file usage will be efficient, and when it may not be. There is nothing in the concept of file processing in C that depends on knowledge of any physical storage device. All the functions provided by the standard library are device independent.

However, a disk drive in a particular operating system environment will have particular operating characteristics that can affect the performance of your programs, and the efficiency with which you use the available disk space. Therefore a knowledge of the characteristics of the disk storage on your computer will help you to avoid inefficient approaches.

A file in C is visualized as a serial sequence of bytes:

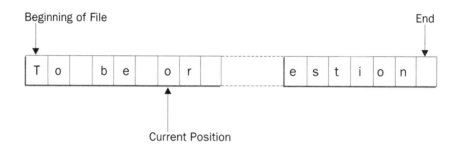

It has a beginning, an end, and a current position, the latter being typically defined as a particular number of bytes from the beginning.

The current position is where any file action, a read or write, will take place. You can move the current position to any other point in the file. A new current position can be specified as a positive offset from the beginning of the file, a negative offset from the end of the file, or in some circumstances, as a positive or negative offset from the current position.

In C a file is referred to as a **stream**, a flow of data between your main computer memory and an external device. The data flow can be to or from memory and can be related to almost any external device including the keyboard and the screen.

Processing Files

When you write a program to process a file, you need a mechanism to associate the file operations that go on in your program, with the name of a particular physical file on the disk. This will allow your program to operate with different files at different times.

Opening a File

Before you can use any file it must be opened. This is true even of the standard streams **stdin**, **stdout**, and **stderr**, but these are automatically opened for you when your program is executed.

The fopen Function

You open a file using the function **fopen()** from the standard library, which returns a pointer to a structure of type **FILE** containing the data needed for a specific file. When you declare a pointer of this type, you don't need to use the **struct** keyword because **FILE** has already been defined using a **typedef** in the header file **STDIO.H**.

Declaring fopen

The function **fopen()** is also declared in the header file **STDIO.H** along with all the other functions for operations with files. It has the prototype:

```
FILE *fopen(const char *pName, const char* pMode);
```

The first argument to the function **fopen()** is a pointer to a string containing the name of the file that you want to process.

The second argument to the function `fopen()` is a character string which specifies what you want to do with the file. This is called the **file mode**. As we shall soon see this spans a whole range of possibilities, but for the moment we shall just look at three, which nonetheless comprise the basic set of file operations:

"w"   open a file for write operations
"a"   open a file for append operations
"r"   open a file for read operations

Note that these mode specifiers are character strings defined between double quotes, not single characters defined between single quotes.

Calling fopen

Assuming that the call to `fopen()` is successful, a pointer is returned that you can now use to reference the file in other input and output operations. As we saw earlier, the structure associated with a file pointer will contain information about the file that the functions supporting file operations need. This information includes the name of the file, the specified mode, and a pointer to the current position in the file.

However, you don't need to worry about the precise contents of this structure in practice, since it's all taken care of by the input and output functions. Obviously, if you want to work with several files at once, they must each have their own file pointer variable declared, and they each need to be opened with a separate call to the function `fopen()`.

Using fopen to Create Files

If we suppose that we wanted to write to an existing file with the name **MYFILE**, we would use the statements:

```
FILE *pFile=NULL;                    /* Declaration of file pointer */
pFile=fopen("MYFILE", "w");          /* Open file MYFILE */
```

The first statement is a declaration for our file pointer, which we've initialized to **NULL** to be on the safe side. The second statement opens the file and associates the physical file called **MYFILE** with our internal pointer **pFile**. Because we have specified the mode as "**w**", we can only write to the file - we can't read from it. The file position will be set at the beginning of the file, so subsequent write operations will overwrite the file's existing contents.

If the file name **MYFILE** doesn't already exist, then the **fopen()** function will create it. When you just want to create a new file, simply call **fopen()** in mode "**w**", with the first argument specifying the name that you want to call the file.

Using fopen to Append to a File

If you want to add to an existing file rather than overwriting it, you can specify the mode as "**a**", which is the append mode of operation. Opening the file in this mode positions the file at the end of the last piece of data. If the file specified doesn't exist, then a new file will be created as it was in the case of mode "**w**", and since the new file is empty, write operations will start at the beginning of the file.

Using fopen to Read From a File

If we want to read a file, once we have declared our file pointer we would open it using the statement:

```
pfile=fopen("MYFILE", "r");
```

Clearly, if we're going to read the file, it must already exist.

If you inadvertently try to open a file for reading that doesn't exist, **fopen()** will return **NULL**. You should always check the return value to be sure that the file open command succeeded. As with the write mode, opening a file for reading sets the file position at the beginning of the data in the file.

Writing Characters to a File

Once we have opened a file for writing we can write to it at any time from anywhere in our program, provided that we have access to the file pointer which has been set up by the function **fopen()**. So if you want to be able to access a file anywhere in a program containing multiple functions, you can declare the file pointer at global scope. As you will recall, this is achieved by placing the declaration outside all of the functions, usually at the beginning of the program code.

The fputc Function

The simplest write operation is provided by the function **fputc()**, which writes a single character to a file. It has the prototype:

```
int fputc(int c, FILE *pFile);
```

The first argument specifies the character to be written to the file as type **int**, and the second is the file pointer. The character is converted to type **unsigned char** and then written to the file as a single byte.

If the write is successful, then it returns the character written. Otherwise it returns **EOF**, a special character called the **end of file** character which is defined in **STDIO.H**. The **EOF** character is guaranteed to be different from all the other standard ASCII characters, which is one reason why the first argument and the values returned are of type **int** rather than **char**.

The standard library function **putc()** performs the same operation as **fputc()**, but is usually implemented as a macro.

Buffering

In practice, characters aren't written to the physical file one by one - this would be very inefficient. Hidden from your program and managed by the output routine, output characters are written to an area of memory called a **buffer**, until it's full, and they're written to the file all in one go. The buffer size is usually based on the minimum block of data that can be written to the storage device:

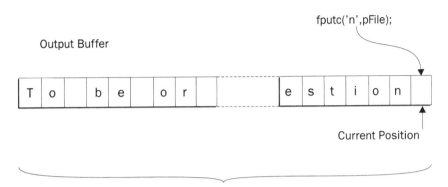

Buffer is written to disk when full
or when the file position is moved.

File buffering is provided automatically, although operations with **stdout** aren't buffered. If you redirect a general file to the screen, buffering is usually inhibited.

Reading Characters from a File

Once a file has been created, we can read from it at any time from anywhere in our program, provided that we have access to the pointer for the file which has been set up by the function **fopen()**.

The fgetc Function

The function `fgetc()` is complementary to the function `fputc()` and reads a character from a file which has previously been opened for reading, the file being specified by the file pointer passed as an argument. The character is read as a single byte of type **unsigned char** and is returned from the function as a value of type **int** if the read is successful. If the operation isn't successful then it returns **EOF**. Typical use of `fgetc()` can be illustrated by the statement:

```
MyChar=fgetc(pFile);                /* Reads a character into MyChar */
```

The variable **MyChar** is assumed to have been declared as type **int**. If you want to store the character read as **char**, you can cast the return value to that type, but the check for **EOF** must be with the original type **int** value.

Behind the scenes, the actual mechanism for reading a file is the inverse of writing to a file. A whole block of characters is read into a buffer. The characters are then handed over to your program one at a time as you request them until the buffer is empty, whereupon another block is read. This makes the process relatively fast, since most `fgetc()` operations won't involve reading the disk, but simply move a character from the buffer in main memory to the place where you want to store it, although you do have the overhead of calling a function for each character you want to read.

> Remember that each file you create is a text file, and can be treated as you would any other text file. Viewing any files you create in a text editor or word processor is an excellent technique, if you're not convinced that you are reading the data files you created back in correctly.

Pushing a Character Back

The library function `ungetc()` enables you to return a character back to the stream, in effect 'unread' it:

```
int ungetc(int ch, FILE *pFile);
```

The character supplied as the first argument, **ch**, will be returned to the buffer, and will be available to be read again on the next read operation. The character put back into the buffer will be returned from the function and if the operation fails, **EOF** is returned. The **EOF** character can't be returned to the buffer.

> **Don't try to push more than one character back onto the stream.**

The function **ungetc()** is very helpful when you're processing a variable stream of input, such as a character string of unknown length, immediately followed by some numeric data. You could read the input until you find a digit with a loop such as:

```
while( (Input=getc(stdin)) != EOF && (!isdigit(Input)) )
     /* Process the string here */
```

When the loop ends, the last character read is either **EOF** or a digit. If it isn't an **EOF** character, then you may want to put the character back into the input stream in order to enable the numeric value to be processed as a separate and complete entity. You could use the **ungetc()** function to do this, as follows:

```
if(Input != EOF)
   ungetc(Input, stdin)
```

Closing a File

When we've finished with a file, we need to tell the operating system so that the file can be released for other purposes, and our file pointer can be freed up too. This is referred to as **closing** a file. We do this through the function **fclose()** from the standard library, which accepts a file pointer as an argument. The function returns an **int** value which is set to **EOF** if an error occurs, and 0 if otherwise. Typical usage would be:

```
fclose(pFile);              /* Close the file associated with pFile */
```

After execution of this statement, the connection between the pointer **pFile** and the physical file name is broken, so **pFile** can no longer be used to access the physical file it represented. If the file was being written, then the contents of the output buffer are written to the file before it's closed, ensuring that data isn't lost.

Why Files Should be Closed

It's good programming practice to close a file as soon as you've finished with it. If your program crashed, and you hadn't closed your files properly then you could lose the contents of the output buffer. Another reason for closing files as soon as you've finished with them, is that the operating system may limit the number of files that you can have open at one time. The header file **STDIO.H** defines the symbol **FOPEN_MAX** as the maximum number of files you can have open at once.

A Read/Write Example

We now have enough knowledge of the file input and output capabilities of C to write a simple program to write and use a file. So let's do just that:

```
/* EX8-01.C  Writing a file one character at a time */
#include <stdio.h>                    /* For input and output */
#include <string.h>                   /* For string functions */

int main(void)
{
    char MyStr[80];                   /* Input string */
    int i=0;                          /* Loop counter */
    int lstr=0;                       /* Length of input string */
    int MyChar=0;                     /* Character for output */
    FILE *pFile=NULL;                 /* File pointer */

    printf("\nEnter an interesting string of less than 80 characters.\n");
    gets(MyStr);                      /* Read in a string */

    pFile=fopen("MYFILE", "w");       /* Create a new file we can write */
    if(pFile==NULL)                   /* Check for a valid file pointer */
    {
        printf("\nOpen to create a new file failed.");
        return 1;
    }

    lstr=strlen(MyStr);               /* Get the length of the string */
    for(i=lstr-1 ; i>=0 ; i--)
        fputc(MyStr[i], pFile);       /* Write string to file backwards */
```

```
    fclose(pFile);                      /* Close the file */

    pFile=fopen("MYFILE", "r");         /* Open the file for reading */
    if(pFile==NULL)                     /* Check for a valid file pointer */
    {
        printf("\nOpen to read the file failed.");
        return 1;
    }

    /* Now read the file back and output it to the screen */
    while((MyChar=fgetc(pFile))!=EOF)
        putchar(MyChar);                /* Output character from the file */

    fclose(pFile);                      /* Finally close the file */
    remove("MYFILE");                   /* and delete the physical file */
    return 0;
}
```

Program Analysis

This program provides an illustration of how you can write a file character by character. Before running this program, or indeed any of the examples working with files, make sure that you use a unique file name, in order to avoid overwriting an existing (and perhaps important) file. An example of the output is:

Enter an interesting string of less than 80 characters.
a man a plan a canal Panama
amanaP lanac a nalp a nam a

The call to **fopen()** creates a new file with the name **MYFILE** in the current directory, and opens it for writing. If you don't wish to create the file in the current directory, then you can specify a full drive and path name, such as **C:\TMP\MYFILE**.

The **if** statement checks that we got a valid file pointer back from **fopen()**, and if the file couldn't be opened, then the program terminates:

```
    if(pFile==NULL)                     /* Check for a valid file pointer */
```

The loop which writes the string to the file counts backwards from the last character in the string to the first, and so the **putc()** function call within the loop writes the string to the new file character by character, and in reverse order.

271

Once the file has been written, it is closed and then reopened, this time in read mode, which sets the file position to the first character in the file. Again, we check to make sure that the open operation worked.

We then read the file character by character in the **while** loop, the read operation actually taking place within the loop continuation condition and displaying each character as read:

```
while((MyChar=fgetc(pFile))!=EOF)
```

The process stops when **EOF** is returned by the function **getc()**, which will occur when we reach the end of the file.

The last two statements in the program provide the necessary final tidying up now we have finished with the file. After closing the file, the program calls a new function from the standard library, **remove()**. This will delete the file with the name that is passed as the argument to the function. Deleting the file here will avoid cluttering up your disk with stray files.

Writing a String to a File

Analogous to the function **puts()** which we've used previously for writing a string to **stdout**, we have the function **fputs()** for writing a string to a file. Its prototype is:

```
int fputs(char *pStr, FILE *pFile );
```

This accepts as arguments, a pointer to the character string to be output, and the file pointer. The function continues to write the string to the file until it reaches a '\0' character, which it doesn't write to the file. For example, the statement:

```
fputs("Many hands make light work by pressing the switch", pFile);
```

will output the string appearing as the first argument, to the file pointed to by **pFile**.

Reading a String from a File

Complementing the function **fputs()** is the function **fgets()**, which reads a string from a file. It has the prototype:

```
char *fgets(char *pStr, int nChars, FILE *pFile );
```

This function differs from **fputs()** in that it has three parameters. The function will read a string from the file specified by **pFile** into the buffer pointed to by **pStr**, which can hold at least **nChars** characters. Characters are read from the file until a newline character, '**\n**', is read, or a maximum of **nChars-1** characters have been read from the file. If a newline character is read, then it's retained in the string, and '**\0**' is appended in memory. If there is no error then the function will return the pointer **pStr**, otherwise **NULL** is returned.

An Example

We could exercise the functions to transfer strings to and from a file in an example which uses the append mode:

```
/* EX8-02.C   As the saying goes...it comes back! */
#include <stdio.h>                    /* For input and output */
#define MAXLEN 80                     /* Maximum string length */

int main(void)
{
    char *pProverbs[]=
    {
        "Many a mickle makes a muckle.\n",
        "Too many cooks spoil the broth.\n",
        "He who laughs last didn't get the joke in the first place.\n"
    };
    char More[MAXLEN]="A nod is a good as a wink to a blind horse.\n";
    FILE *pFile;                      /* File pointer */
    int i=0;                          /* Loop counter */

    /* Create a new file if MYFILE does not exist */
    pFile=fopen("MYFILE", "w");
```

```
    if(pFile==NULL)                        /* Check for a valid file pointer */
    {
        printf("\nOpen to create a new file failed.");
        return 1;
    }

    /* Write our first three sayings */
    for(i=0 ; i<sizeof(pProverbs)/sizeof(pProverbs[0]) ; i++)
        fputs(pProverbs[i], pFile);
    fclose(pFile);                         /* Close the file */

    pFile = fopen("MYFILE", "a" );         /* Open it again to append data */
    if(pFile==NULL)                        /* Check for a valid file pointer */
    {
        printf("\nOpen to append to the file failed.");
        return 1;
    }

    fputs(More, pFile );                   /* Write another proverb */
    fclose(pFile);                         /* then close the file */

    pFile=fopen("MYFILE", "r" );           /* Open the file to read it */
    if(pFile==NULL)                        /* Check for a valid file pointer */
    {
        printf("\nOpen to read the file failed.");
        return 1;
    }

    /* Now read and display the complete file */
    while(fgets(More, MAXLEN, pFile)!=NULL)
        printf("\n%s", More);

    fclose(pFile);                         /* Close the file */
    remove("MYFILE");                      /* and delete it */
    return 0;
}
```

Program Analysis

In this example, the array of pointers **pProverbs[]** is initialized using three string constants, leaving the compiler to work out the array dimension. Each string has '\n' as the last character so that the function **fgets()** will be able to recognize the end of each string. Of course, if they were of fixed length, then we could just use the length of the string to control how many characters were read.

After creating and opening the file **MYFILE** for writing, each of the proverbs in the **pProverbs[]** array is written to the file using the function **fputs()**, in a **for** loop:

```
for(i=0 ; i<sizeof(pProverbs)/sizeof(pProverbs[0]) ; i++)
   fputs(pProverbs[i], pFile);
```

This function is extremely easy to use, just requiring a pointer to the string as the first argument, and a pointer to the file as the second. The number of iterations is calculated using:

```
sizeof(pProverbs)/sizeof(pProverbs[0])
```

which will give us the number of elements in the pointer array. We could have manually counted how many initializing strings we supplied, but doing it this way means that the correct number of iterations is determined automatically.

Once the first set of proverbs has been written, the file is closed, and then reopened in append mode, which causes the current position for reading and writing to be set to the end of the data in the file.

With the file now open in append mode, we write the additional proverb to the file in the array **More[]**, using **fputs()**. Since we are in append mode, the new proverb will be added after the existing data in the file. Having written the file, we close it once again and then reopen it for reading by using the mode specifier **"r"**, and then read the strings successively into the array **More[]**. Finally the file is closed, and then deleted.

Formatted File Input and Output

Writing files one character at a time isn't adequate for many purposes though. Even the ability added by the function **fputs()** to output a string doesn't solve the problem of us wanting to store away large chunks of data at a time.

You're also likely to want to write data to a file as formatted text, derived from the numerical values in your program. With this sort of capability you'll be able to readily transfer information to other environments, such as your word processor for instance. The mechanism for doing this is provided by the standard library functions for formatted file input and output.

275

Formatted Output to a File

The standard library function for formatted output to a file is `fprintf()`. It's almost the same as the `printf()` function, with one extra parameter and a slight name change. Its prototype is:

```
int fprintf(FILE *pFile,const char *pFormat,...);
```

The first parameter is a file pointer, and the remaining parameters are the same as those for `printf()` - a format string, followed by the variables to be written. The function returns a count of the number of characters written to the file, or a negative value if an error occurs.

An fprintf Example

The use of the function `fprintf()` is typified in the statement:

```
fprintf(pFile, "%12d%12d%14f", Num1, Num2, Fnum);
```

The file pointer, `pFile`, must point to a file which has previously been opened in write or append mode. The values of the three variables `Num1`, `Num2`, and `Fnum`, are written to the file, under the control of the format string specified as the second argument. Thus the first two variables are of type `int` and are to be output with a field width of 12, whilst the third variable is of type `float`, and is to be written to the file with a field width of 14.

Formatted Input from a File

Formatted input from a file is accomplished using the function `fscanf()`. To read three variable values from a file pointed to by the pointer `pFile` you would write:

```
i = fscanf(pFile, "%12d%12d%14f", &Num1, &Num2, &Fnum);
```

This function works in exactly the same way as `scanf()` does with `stdin`, except that here we're obtaining input from a file specified by the first argument, `pFile`. The rules that govern the specification of the format string and the operation of the function are the same as those that apply to `scanf()`. If an error occurs, such as no input is read, then the function returns **EOF**, otherwise it returns an **int** value specifying the number of values read.

> It's probably fairly obvious to you by now, but you need to be aware that a formatted write doesn't necessarily capture the precise value of a variable that is written. For example, if you write the value 1.23 with the format **%.1f**, you actually write 1.2 to the file (ignoring any leading blanks), losing the possibly very important .03.
>
> There's also a potential problem when you read a file. A file is simply a string of characters. How these characters are interpreted is determined entirely by the format string used to read them, and has no connection with the original values that were written.

Should mistakes such as these be made, then it can be quite difficult to locate the source and solve the problem.

An Example of Formatting Input and Output

We could exercise the formatted input and output functions with an example which will also demonstrate how the data is subject to interpretation in these operations:

```
/* EX8-04.C  Formatted writing and reading of a file */
#include <stdio.h>                      /* For input and output */
int main(void)
{
   long Num1=234567L, Num2=345123L, Num3=789234L;        /* Input values */
   long Num4=0L, Num5=0L, Num6 = 0L;    /* Values read from the file */
   float Fnum=0.0f;                     /* Value read from the file */
   int iVal[6]={ 0 };                   /* Values read from the file */
   int i = 0;                           /* Loop counter */
   FILE *pFile = NULL;                  /* File pointer */

   pFile = fopen("MYFILE", "w" );       /* Create file to be written */
   if(pFile==NULL)                      /* Check for valid file pointer */
   {
      printf("\nOpen to create a new file failed.");
      return 1;
   }
```

```
/* Write the file */
fprintf( pFile, "%61d%61d%61d", Num1, Num2, Num3 );
fclose(pFile);                              /* Close the file */

/* Display the values written */
printf("\n %61d %61d %61d", Num1, Num2, Num3 );

pFile = fopen("MYFILE", "r" );       /* Open file to read it */

/* Read back the file and display what we got */
fscanf( pFile, "%61d%61d%61d", &Num4, &Num5 ,&Num6);
printf("\n%61d %61d %61d", Num4, Num5, Num6);

/* Go to the beginning of the file and read the stuff again */
rewind( pFile );
fscanf( pFile, "%2d%3d%3d%3d%2d%2d%3f",
        &iVal[0], &iVal[1], &iVal[2],
        &iVal[3], &iVal[4], &iVal[5], &Fnum);


fclose(pFile);                      /* Close the file and */
remove("MYFILE");                   /* delete it.*/

/* Now display what we got the second time */
printf( "\n\n");
for( i = 0 ; i < 6 ; i++ )
    printf( "%siVal[%d] = %d", i == 4 ? "\n\t" : "\t", i, iVal[i]);
printf( "\nFnum = %f", Fnum);
return 0;
}
```

Program Analysis

If you compile and run this program you should get the following output:

```
234567 345123 789234
234567 345123 789234

        iVal[0] = 23    iVal[1] = 456   iVal[2] = 734   iVal[3] = 512
        iVal[4] = 37    iVal[5] = 89
Fnum = 234.000000
```

This example writes the values of **Num1**, **Num2**, and **Num3**, to the file **MYFILE**. The file is closed and re-opened for reading, and the values are read from the file in the same format as they were written. The first two lines of the output demonstrate that the original data, and that read from the file, are the same.

We then call the standard library function **rewind()** which simply moves the current position back to the beginning of the file so that we can read it again:

```
rewind( pFile );
```

We could have achieved the same thing by closing the file then re-opening it again, but **rewind()** is more efficient.

Having repositioned the file, we read the file again with another call to **fscanf()**:

```
fscanf( pFile, "%2d%3d%3d%3d%2d%2d%3f",
        &iVal[0], &iVal[1], &iVal[2],
        &iVal[3], &iVal[4], &iVal[5], &Fnum);
```

this time reading the data into the array **iVal[]** and the variable **Fnum**. This reads the same data as before, but with different formats from those used for writing the file.

You can see in the program output, that the file consists of just a string of characters once it has been written, exactly the same as the output to the screen from **printf()**. You can also see that the values you get back from the file when you read it will depend on both the format string that you use, and the variable list you specify in **fscanf()**.

Finally we leave everything clean, neat, and tidy by closing the file, and using the function **remove()** to delete it.

Further File Operation Modes

Thus far we've only processed files in **text mode**, where information is written as strings of ASCII characters. Text mode is generally the default mode of operation, but you can specify explicitly that file operations are in to be in text mode if you wish by adding a **'t'** at the end of the existing file mode specifiers.

This gives us the mode specifiers of **"wt"**, **"rt"**, and **"at"**. In some environments certain characters will be changed in text mode. Under MS-DOS for example on IBM compatible PCs, writing a newline character to

279

a file, causes two characters to be written, a carriage return character (**CR**), and a line feed character (**LF**). On reading the same file, the two characters will be recombined into a single character once more. This can cause problems with file position operations which we'll be looking at later in this chapter.

Updating a File

We can also open a file for update, which means that you can read and write to the file. For this mode you use the **"r+"** specifier. You can also specify update mode as **"w+"**. If you wanted the mode to be specified explicitly as a text operation, you add a 't' to the mode specifier, so update mode would become **"r+t"** or **"rt+"**. Either is perfectly acceptable. You could also use **"wt+"** or **"w+t"**.

As we have said, in update mode you can both read and write to the file, but not one operation immediately following the other. The reason for this is because of the nature of the buffer used by functions. If you write to the file, then you're changing the contents of the buffer, not the physical disk. A subsequent read would transfer information from the physical disk into the buffer overwriting the change you have just made.

To do a read followed by a write, or vice versa, you must make sure that the buffer is cleared to the physical disk. You can do this by performing a file position change such as **rewind()** or doing a **fflush()** on the file. The only exception to this rule is if an EOF was returned by the initial operation.

Similarly, the first read from a file will fill a buffer area in memory, and subsequent reads will transfer data from the buffer until it's empty, whereupon another file read to fill the buffer will be initiated. So for a switch from read to write something must be performed to sort the buffer out from the previous operation.

Flushing an Output Buffer

As well as repositioning within the file, there's a library function **fflush()**, which causes the contents of a write buffer to be written to the file or **flushed**. It has the prototype:

```
int fflush(File *pFile);
```

The single argument specifies the file to be flushed. If the argument is **NULL**, then all buffered output files are flushed. If the function **fflush()** is applied to an input file, then the effect is undefined.

Unformatted File Input/Output

The alternative to text mode operations is called **binary mode**, where there's no need for a format string to control input or output, making it much simpler than text mode. The binary data as it appears in memory is transferred directly to the file. Characters such as `'\n'` and `'\0'` which have specific significance in text mode are of no consequence in binary mode. As there is no data transformation, binary mode is somewhat faster than text mode.

Specifying Binary Mode

Binary mode is specified by appending a `'b'` to the basic mode specifiers, giving us the additional specifiers **"wb"** to write to a binary file, **"rb"** to read from a binary file, **"ab"** to append data to the end of a binary file, and **"rb+"** to enable the reading and writing of a binary file.

Since binary mode involves handling the data to be transferred to and from the file in a different way from the text mode, we have a new set of functions to perform input and output.

Writing to a Binary File

To write a binary file, you use the **fwrite()** function, best explained with an example. Assuming that we open the file to be written with the statement:

```
pFile=fopen("MYFILE", "wb");
```

then we could write to the file with:

```
wCount=fwrite(pData, Size, NumItems, pFile);
```

This operates by writing a specified number of objects to a file, where each object is a given number of bytes long. The first argument, **pData**, is a pointer containing the starting memory address of the data objects to be written. The second argument, **Size**, specifies the size of each object to be written, whilst the third argument, **NumItems**, defines a count of the number of objects to be written to the file. The file is identified by the last argument, **pFile**, which is the file pointer. The function **fwrite()** returns the count of the number of items actually written. If the operation was unsuccessful, then this value will be less than **NumItems**.

The return value, and the arguments **Size** and **NumItems**, are all of the same type as that returned by the **sizeof** operator defined as **size_t**, which is an unsigned integer.

Let's assume that we want to write objects stored in an array **Data[]**. Without knowing anything about the type of the array, we can write the entire array to a file with the statement:

```
wCount=fwrite(Data, sizeof(Data[0]), sizeof(Data)/sizeof(Data[0]), pFile);
```

The **sizeof** operator is used to specify the size in bytes of the objects to be transferred, as well as determining how many objects there are in the array. Using **sizeof** is the best way to define the size of an object to be written to a file, particularly when the object is a structure where it isn't always obvious how many bytes are involved. Of course, in a real context we should also check the return value in **wCount**, to be sure that the write was successful.

Thus our function for binary writes to a file is geared to writing a number of objects of any length. You can write in units of your own structures as easily as you can write **int**s, **double**s, or bytes.

Reading from a Binary File

To read a binary file once it has been opened in read mode, you use the function **fread()**. Using the same variables that we used in our example of writing a binary file, to read the file we would use a statement such as:

```
wCount=fread(Data, sizeof(Data[0]), sizeof(Data)/sizeof(Data[0]), pFile);
```

This operates as the exact inverse of the write operation. This function reads the number of objects determined by the expression `sizeof(Data)/sizeof(Data[0])`, each of size `sizeof(Data[0])` bytes, into memory starting at the address of `Data`, and returning a count of the number of objects read. If there's insufficient data in the file, or if an error occurs, then the count will be less than the number of objects requested.

A Binary File Example

We could apply binary file operations to the program that we saw in Chapter 4 that calculated prime numbers. This time we'll use a disk file as a buffer to enable the program to calculate a larger number of primes. As this program consists of several functions, let's first take a look at `main()`:

```c
/* EX8-04.C  A prime example using binary files */
#include <stdio.h>                  /* For input and output */
#include <math.h >                  /* For square root function */

#define ROW_SIZE 5                  /* Number of primes output per line */
#define MEM_PRIMES 100              /* Count of number of primes in memory */

/* Function prototypes */
int TestPrime(unsigned long Trial);                 /* Test for primeness */
void PutBuffer(unsigned long *Primes, int Index); /*Write primes to file*/
int Check(unsigned long *Primes, int index, unsigned long Trial);

char *MyFile="MYFILE";             /* Physical file name */
FILE *pFile;                       /* File pointer */
unsigned long Primes[MEM_PRIMES]={ 2UL,3UL,5UL,0L };
int index=3;                       /* Index of free location in memory */
int nRec=0;                        /* Number of file records */

int main(void)
{
   unsigned long Trial=5UL;        /* First prime candidate */
   long NumPrimes=3L;
   long Total=0L;                  /* Prime count, total required */

   printf("How many primes would you like?  ");
   scanf("%ld", &Total);           /* Read how many */

   /* Prime finding and storing loop    */
   while(NumPrimes<Total)          /* Loop until we get total required */
   {
      Trial+=2UL;                  /* Next value for checking */
```

```
    if(TestPrime(Trial))          /* Check if trial value is prime */
    {                             /* We have got one */
       Primes[index++]=Trial;     /* so store it */
       NumPrimes++;               /* Increment total number of primes */

       if(index==MEM_PRIMES)      /* Check if memory is full */
       {                                /* It is so */
          PutBuffer(Primes, index);      /* Display the current block */
          pFile=fopen(MyFile, "ab");      /* and write them away */
          fwrite(Primes, sizeof(long), MEM_PRIMES, pFile);
          fclose(pFile);                 /* Now close the file */
          index=0;                 /* Reset count of primes in memory */
          nRec++;                  /* Increment file record count */
       }
    }
  }

  PutBuffer(Primes, index);       /* Display any primes in memory */
  remove(MyFile);                 /* Get rid of the file */
  return 0;
}
```

Program Analysis

After the **#include** statements, we have the definition of **ROW_SIZE** for the number of primes to be output on a line, and **MEM_PRIMES** which is the maximum number of primes to be held in memory. Ideally, **MEM_PRIMES** should be an integer multiple of **ROW_SIZE**, otherwise the output won't be quite so neat.

Once the program has computed a **MEM_PRIMES** number of primes, the primes in memory will be written to a disk file automatically. This will free up the array used to store them in memory so that it can be used to store the succeeding primes. If you request a number of primes less than **MEM_PRIMES** then none will be written to disk.

We have included the file pointer **pFile** and the pointer **MyFile** as global variables to allow input and output operations from anywhere in the program.

The task of checking for a prime is performed by the function **TestPrime()** which is called within the loop, and returns 1 if the value passed to it is prime, or 0 if otherwise. If a prime is found then we store it in the next available element in the **Primes[]** array, and increment the variable **index** to point to the next element. We keep track of how many primes we have in total with the variable **NumPrimes**.

Each time that we find a new prime and add it to the **Primes[]** array, we need to check whether the array is full. If it is, then we need to display the primes in the array and write the array to the file. This is achieved with the statements:

```
if(index==MEM_PRIMES)              /* Check if memory is full */
  {                                /* It is so */
      PutBuffer(Primes, index);    /* Display the current block */
      pFile=fopen(MyFile, "ab");   /* and write them away */
      fwrite(Primes, sizeof(long), MEM_PRIMES, pFile);
      fclose(pFile);               /* Now close the file */
      index=0;                     /* Reset count of primes in memory */
      nRec++;                      /* Increment file record count */
  }
```

The primes are displayed by the function **PutBuffer()**. You may wonder why we need to keep opening and closing the file here, rather than opening it once and then writing to it whenever the need arises. Remember that once we have primes in the file, they will need to be read back for use as divisors in testing for a new prime. The easiest way to handle this is to open the file for writing here and then close it, opening it again for reading when we're testing a value, and closing it again when we're done. After writing the primes to the file, the variable **index** is reset to zero, and **nRec**, which counts the number of blocks of primes in the file, is incremented by 1.

When sufficient primes have been found, the function **PutBuffer()** is called once more to display any still remaining in memory that weren't written to the file.

Validating a Prime

The function to check whether a value is prime is as follows:

```
/*********************************************************************
 * Function to test for primeness using primes in memory and on file *
 * Returns a positive value for a prime found, zero otherwise        *
 *********************************************************************/
int TestPrime(unsigned long N)
{
   unsigned long Buffer[MEM_PRIMES];    /* local buffer for file data */
   int i=0;                             /* Loop counter */
   int k=0;                             /* Return value from Check() */

   if(nRec>0)
```

285

```
   {                               /* If we have some records written */
       pFile=fopen(MyFile, "rb");      /* open the file. */
       for(i=0; i<nRec ; i++)
       {                               /* Check against primes on file first */
           fread(Buffer, sizeof(long), MEM_PRIMES, pFile);
           if((k=Check(Buffer, MEM_PRIMES, N))>=0)       /* Check primes in
                                                                Buffer*/
           {
               fclose(pFile);         /* For zero or +ive return close the */
               return k;              /* file and return the value k */
           }
       }
       fclose(pFile);
   }

   return Check(Primes, index, N); /* Check against primes in memory */
}
```

Function Analysis

The function **TestPrime()** accepts a candidate value as an argument, and returns 1 if it's prime, and 0 if it isn't. It uses the function **Check()** to test for exact division of the candidate by a block of primes passed to it as an argument.

If the function **Check()** finds an exact division then it returns 0 indicating that the candidate isn't prime. The function **Check()** also determines whether a prime used as a divisor of the candidate exceeds the square root of the value being tested. If it does, then the value must be prime and 1 is returned. The function **Check()** returns -1 if all the primes passed to it have been used as divisors without an exact division, but the largest of them is less than the square root of the candidate. This means that more checking is necessary against larger primes.

As you may remember, a prime is a number with no factors other than 1 and itself. It is sufficient to check whether a number is divisible by any of the primes less than the square root of the number.

If we've written anything to the file, then this will be indicated by a positive value of **nRec**. The primes in the file need to be used as divisors first, because they're lower than those in memory since we compute the primes in sequence.

If **nRec** is positive, then we read one block of primes from the file into the array **Buffer()** using the function **fread()**:

```
fread(Buffer, sizeof(long), MEM_PRIMES, pFile);
```

The count of the number of objects will always be **MEM_PRIMES** since we always write the whole array to the file each time.

If the contents of the file have been exhausted, the function **Check()** is called with the array of primes in memory being passed as an argument. If a prime is found then the function **Check()** will return 1, otherwise zero will be returned.

Checking for a Divisor

The code for the function **Check()** is as follows:

```
/*******************************************************************
 * Function to check for division by an array of primes           *
 * Returns 1 if a prime found, zero if not a prime, -1 for more checks *
 *******************************************************************/

int Check( unsigned long *pBuffer, int Count, unsigned long N )
{
   unsigned long *pEnd=&pBuffer[Count-1];
   unsigned long RootN=0UL;

   RootN=( unsigned long)(1.0+sqrt((double)N));    /* Upper limit for
                                                          checking */

   while(pBuffer++!=pEnd)
   {
      if(N%(*(pBuffer))==0UL)                  /* Check for exact division */
         return 0;                             /* If so not a prime...*/

      if(*pBuffer>RootN)     /* Check whether divisor exceeds square root */
         return 1;                             /* if so it must be a prime */
   }
   return -1;                                  /* More checks necessary... */
}
```

Function Analysis

This function checks whether any of the primes contained in the area pointed to by **pBuffer**, divide exactly into the test value supplied as the second argument. Because the computation will be carried out using pointers, the function defines a pointer **pEnd** of type pointer to **long**, which points to the last prime in the block passed as a parameter.

The integer variable **RootN** will hold the square root of the value to be tested for primeness, representing the upper limit for divisors to be checked against the trial value. Only divisors less than the square root of the test value **N** are tried.

On each iteration, the pointer **pBuffer** is incremented to point to the next prime. This occurs on the first iteration too, so we automatically avoid making the unnecessary check with the first prime which is 2. When **pBuffer** contains the same address as **pEnd** the loop is terminated, since all the primes in the current block have been used as test divisors.

Checking for exact division is done by dividing the current contents of the address pointed to by **pBuffer** into **N**. If the result is zero then **N** isn't prime, and zero is returned. If the test division isn't exact, then the current divisor is checked to see whether it's greater than the square root of **N**, and if it is then we have a prime and we're done, so 1 is returned. Otherwise testing continues with the next prime.

Outputting Primes

The last function in our program transfers those primes stored in the buffer pointed to by the first argument, to the display screen in lines of five. The number of primes to be displayed is specified by the second argument. The code for the function is as follows:

```
/***********************************************
 * Function to display an array pointed to    *
 * by pBuffer containing K primes. They are    *
 * displayed with ROW_SIZE primes to a row     *
 ***********************************************/
void PutBuffer( unsigned long *pBuffer, int K )
{
   int i=0;                                 /* Loop counter */

   /* Display ROW_SIZE primes to a line */
   for(i=0;i<K;i++)
   {
      if(i%ROW_SIZE==0)                      /* Every ROW_SIZE values */
         printf("\n");                       /* go to a new line */

      printf ("%12lu",*(pBuffer+i));
   }
   return;
}
```

Each time the loop index **i** can be divided by **ROW_SIZE** without a remainder, we write a newline character. This ensures that we get **ROW_SIZE** values on each line. The format specifier is for **unsigned long** integers in a field width of 12, so that they line up.

Collating The Parts

To run the program you need to enter all the functions we've described into a single text file, compile and link it. Assuming that you've keyed it all in correctly you should be able to get as many primes as your computer and your patience will permit.

Moving Around in a File

For many applications you'll need to be able to access data in a file in a seemingly random order. You can always find some information stored in the middle of a file by reading from the beginning, and continuing in sequence until you find what you want. But if you have written a few million items to the file and you have a few thousand access operations, then this may take some time.

Of course, to access data in a random sequence necessitates that you have some means of knowing where the data you would like to retrieve is actually stored in the file. Arranging this is a complicated topic, and there are many different ways of constructing pointers or indexes to make direct access to file data faster and easier. The basic idea is similar to that of an index in a book, where you have a table of keys that identify the contents of each record in the file that you might want, and where each key has an associated position in the file defined where the data is stored.

We will only cover the basic tools in the library necessary to enable you to understand file input/output, and leave further research as a follow-on project for you once you get to the end of the book, and achieve the status of an accomplished C programmer.

File Positioning Operations

There are two aspects to file positioning, finding out where you are at a given point in a file, and moving to a given point in a file. The former is a pre-requisite for the latter. If you never know where you are, you can never decide where you want to go.

Accessing a random point in a file can be done regardless of whether the file concerned was written in binary or text mode. However, working with text mode files gets rather complicated if the system you're using records a newline as two characters. This results from the fact that the number of characters recorded in the file can effectively be greater than the number you actually wrote.

The problem arises when you think that a point in the file is 100 bytes from the beginning. If you subsequently write different data which is the same length in memory, it will only be the same length in the file if it contains the same number of '**\n**' characters. For this reason we shall sidestep the complications of moving about in text files and concentrate on the much more useful - and easier - context of binary files.

Finding Out Where You Are

We have two functions to tell us where we are, which are both very similar in what they do, but not identical. They each complement a different positioning function. The first is **ftell()** which has the following prototype:

```
long ftell(FILE *pFile);
```

This function accepts as an argument a file pointer, and returns a **long** integer value specifying the current position in the file. This would be used with the file referenced by a pointer such as **pFile** which we've used previously, as in the statement:

```
fPos=ftell(pFile);
```

The **long** variable **fPos** now holds the current position in the file, and as we shall see, we can use this in a function call to return to this position at any subsequent time. For a binary file the value is actually the offset in bytes from the beginning of the file.

The second function providing information on the current file position, is a little more complicated. The prototype of the function is:

```
int fgetpos( FILE *pFile, fpos_t *pPos);
```

The first parameter is our old friend the file pointer, while the second is a pointer to a type pre-defined in **STDIO.H**, with the type name **fpos_t**. You can look at how the type name is defined in **STDIO.H** if you want to know exactly what it is, but you really don't need to worry about it. This function is designed to be used with the positioning function **fsetpos()** which we will come to very shortly. The function **fgetpos()** will store the current position in the file in ***pPos**. It returns zero if the operation is successful, and a non-zero integer value if otherwise.

Setting a Position in a File

As a complement to **ftell()** we have the function **fseek()** with the prototype:

```
int fseek(FILE *pFile, long OffSet, int RefPt);
```

The first parameter is a pointer to the file we're repositioning. The second and third parameters define where we want to go to, with the second being an offset from a reference point specified by the third parameter. The reference point can be one of three values which are specified by the pre-defined names **SEEK_SET**, which defines the beginning of the file, **SEEK_CUR**, which defines the current position in the file, and **SEEK_END** which, as you might guess, defines the end of the file. For a text mode file, the second argument must be a value returned by **ftell()** if you are to avoid getting lost. The third argument for text mode files must be **SEEK_SET**.

Thus for text mode files, all operations with **fseek()** are performed with reference to the beginning of the file. For binary files you can do what you like, as long as you know what you are doing - or even if you don't if you like living dangerously. The offset argument in binary files is simply a relative byte count. Thus you can supply positive or negative values for the offset when the reference point is specified as **SEEK_CUR**.

To go with `fgetpos()`, as we said, we have `fsetpos()`. This has the prototype:

```
int fsetpos(FILE *pFile, fpos_t *pPos);
```

The first parameter is a pointer to the file set up with `fopen()`, and the second is a file position pointer of the same type used in `fgetpos()`. You can't go far wrong with this one really. As with `fgetpos()`, a non-zero value is returned on error.

The verb **seek** is used to refer to operations of moving the read/write heads of a disk drive directly to a specific position in the file. This is how the function `fseek()` gets its name. With a file that you have opened for update, by specifying the mode as **"rb+"** or **"wb+"** for example, either a read or a write may be safely carried out on the file after executing either of the file positioning functions, `fsetpos()` or `fseek()`, regardless of what the previous operation on the file was.

A Random File Access Example

To exercise our new found file handling skills we could write a simple example which will write a series of names and addresses to a binary file, and then retrieve them in alphabetic sequence by using the names and associated file positions which we record in memory.

We will be making some simplifying assumptions to keep the number of lines of code down. First of all we won't be worrying about errors, but you know by now that it's important to check for them in your programs. Secondly we will accept any single string for a name, an address line, or a phone number. In practice you would need to handle first names or initials as well as surnames, and you would probably want to validate the phone number. Of course a real application would also have much more data in a record, but at least we will see how randomly accessing a file works.

Designing the Program

Let's start by deciding how it will work as a whole. We can read all the records for people, write them to a file, and then construct an alphabetical index, using a linked list. The records can then be displayed in the sequence determined by the index. First though, we will need a structure to store the personal data.

```
typedef struct person          /* Person structure type definition */
{
    char Name[40];             /* Name of person */
    char Address[5][40];       /* Address up to five lines */
    char Phone[20];            /* Phone number as string */
}Person;
```

This shows how we can define a structure type, **person**, and the type **Person** as equivalent to **struct person**. This will allow us to define variables of type **Person** without using the keyword **struct**. Therefore the declaration:

```
Person aPerson;
```

is equivalent to the statement:

```
struct person aPerson;
```

We can also define a structure and a type for members of the linked list containing the index to the file in a similar way:

```
typedef struct index           /* Linked list element for the index */
{
    char Name[40];             /* Name of person */
    struct index *Next;        /* Pointer to next index entry */
    long fPos;                 /* Position in the file */
}Index;
```

Here we have defined the structure **index**, and the type **Index** which is equivalent to **struct index**. Note that you cannot use the type **Index** in the definition of the member **Next** in the structure **index**, because **Index** is not defined at that point.

Let's assume that all the input processing will be done by a function **ReadPeople()**, and that function will use **Insert()** to construct the linked list which will be the index. We can also assume a function **Display()** to write the details of a **Person** object to the screen. Based on these assumptions we can write the function **main()**:

```
/* EX8-05.C  Accessing a file randomly */
#include <stdio.h>
#include <stdlib.h>                      /* For exit() and dynamic memory */
#include <string.h>                      /* For string functions */

#define FILENAME "MYFILE"                /* Physical file name */

/* Person structure type definition */
typedef struct person
{
   char Name[40];
   char Address[5][40];
   char Phone[20];
}Person;

/* Linked list element for the index */
typedef struct index
{
   char Name[40];
   struct index *Next;                   /* Pointer to next index entry */
   long fPos;                            /* Position in the file */
}Index;

/* Function prototypes */
Index *ReadPeople(void);                         /* Read all the people data */
Index *Insert(Index *pIndex, Index *pHead); /* Insert in the list */
void Display(Person *pPerson);                   /* Output a person */

int main(void)
{
   Index *pHead=NULL;              /* Pointer to 1st index list element */
   Person aPerson;                 /* Working person structure */
   FILE *pFile;                    /* File pointer to person file */

   pHead=ReadPeople();             /* Read person records and create file */

   pFile=fopen(FILENAME,"rb");    /* Now open the file to read it */

   /* Display the file content in index order */
   while(pHead!=NULL)
   {
      fseek(pFile, pHead->fPos, SEEK_SET);        /* Position the file */
      fread(&aPerson, sizeof(aPerson), 1, pFile); /* Read the person */
      Display(&aPerson);
      pHead=pHead->Next;                          /* Go to next in list */
   }
   fclose(pFile);
   remove(FILENAME);
   return 0;
}
```

We first have the necessary include statements, a definition for a symbol **FILENAME** for the name of the file to be used, the structure definitions and the function prototypes. You should change the definition of **FILENAME** if necessary in your environment. The function **ReadPeople()** will return a pointer to the first element in the index to the file. The function **Insert()** will accept a pointer to the new index entry, and a pointer to the first element in the list.

The function **main()** declares a pointer to the first element in the index, **pHead**, a **Person** object, **aPerson**, and a file pointer **pFile**. The first action in **main()** is to call the function **ReadPeople()**. This does almost all the work. Once this function has been executed, the file will have been written, the index will have been created and a pointer to the index is returned. The file is then opened in read mode as a binary file.

The file is read in the **while** loop, and within the loop, the **fPos** member of each entry in the index list is used to position the file using the function **fseek()**. Each **Person** record that is retrieved is output using our function **Display()**. When the **Next** pointer for an entry in the linked list is **NULL**, we have processed all the entries so the loop ends. The file is then closed and deleted from the disk.

Processing the Input

All the input processing, including writing the file and generating the index is managed by the function **ReadPeople()**:

```
/**********************************************
 * Function to read a person's details, construct *
 * a Person object and write it to a file, and    *
 * construct an index to the file.                *
 **********************************************/
Index *ReadPeople(void)
{
    Person aPerson;              /* To store a person */
    Index *pIndex=NULL;          /* Pointer to an index entry */
    Index *pHead=NULL;           /* Pointer to the first list element */
    FILE *pFile;                 /* File pointer to person file */
    int i=0;                     /* Loop counter */

    pFile=fopen(FILENAME,"wb");  /* Open or create a file in write mode */

    for(;;)                      /* Read data until a blank name */
```

```
{
    printf("\nEnter a name:");
    gets(aPerson.Name);
    if(!strlen(aPerson.Name))
        break;                        /* An empty name so we are done */

    /* Create an index entry */
    pIndex=(Index *)malloc(sizeof(Index))
    if(pIndex==NULL)                  /* Check for valid pointer */
    {
        printf("\nMemory allocation failed. Exiting program.");
        exit(1);
    }
    pIndex->Next=NULL;                          /* Set Next pointer to NULL */
    strcpy(pIndex->Name, aPerson.Name);
    if(pHead==NULL)                             /* If pHead is NULL then */
        pHead=pIndex;                           /* this is the first element */
    else
        pHead=Insert(pIndex, pHead);       /* Insert the new index entry */

    /* Get the address */
    printf("\nEnter the address up to 5 lines of 40 characters.\n"
            "Enter an empty line after the last line"
            " if there are less than 5 lines.\n");

    for(i=0;i<5;i++)                      /* Get up to 5 lines */
    {
        gets(aPerson.Address[i]);
        if(strlen(aPerson.Address[i])==0) /* Empty address line to end */
            break;
    }

    /* Get the phone number */
    printf("\nEnter the phone number for %s: ",aPerson.Name);
    gets(aPerson.Phone);

    pIndex->fPos=ftell(pFile);                  /* Store file position */
    fwrite(&aPerson,sizeof(aPerson),1,pFile); /* Write the file */
}

fclose(pFile);                              /* Close the file */
return pHead;                               /* Return the list head */
}
```

The call to **fopen()** will open an existing file at the beginning, so if you have a file of the same name you need to change the **FILENAME** symbol definition if you don't want to overwrite it. All input processing is done in the infinite **for** loop. Within the loop, the name of a person is first read directly into the structure member **aPerson.Name**. We leave the loop using a **break** statement if an empty name string is entered.

An index entry is created on the heap, and the **Next** member is set to **NULL**. If the pointer **pHead** is still **NULL** then the linked list for the index must still be empty, so we assign the address of the index entry which is stored in **pIndex**, to **pHead**, so that it becomes the head of the list. If the list isn't empty, we insert the new element pointed to by **pIndex** in the list by calling our function **Insert()**. Because each element will be inserted in alphabetical sequence, the new element could be added at the head of the list, so the function **Insert()** returns a pointer to the head of the list once the new entry has been inserted.

The function **ReadPeople()** then reads up to five lines of address, and the phone number, each being stored in the **Person** object. Having read all the data for a person, we are ready to write it to the file, but first we need to obtain the current file position by calling the library function **ftell()**, and storing it in the index member **fPos**. After writing the **Person** object to the file, we repeat the process for the next person.

When all data has been read, the file is closed, and the pointer **pHead** is returned to **main()**.

Inserting into the Linked List

The function **Insert()**, places a new structure of type **index** into the linked list in alphabetical sequence. The code for the function is:

```
/*************************************************
 * Function to insert a new element in a list *
 * in alphabetical sequence                   *
 *************************************************/
Index *Insert(Index *pIndex, Index *pHead)
{
   Index *pNext;                         /* Pointer to next list element */

   /* Check to see if the new member should go at the front */
   if(strcmp(pIndex->Name, pHead->Name)<=0)
   {
      pIndex->Next=pHead;                /* Set the current head as next */
      return pIndex;                     /* Return the new head */
   }

   pNext=pHead;                          /* Start pNext at the beginning */
   while(pNext->Next!=NULL)              /* Stop if the next is NULL */
   {
      /* Check for insertion in front of the next one */
      if(strcmp(pIndex->Name,pNext->Next->Name)<=0)
```

```
     {
         pIndex->Next=pNext->Next;    /* The next is after the new one */
         pNext->Next=pIndex;          /* The current precedes the new one */
         return pHead;                /* Return the head unchanged */
     }
     pNext=pNext->Next;               /* Move to the next in the list */
   }
   pNext->Next=pIndex;                /* Add the new one to the end */
   return pHead;                      /* Return the head unchanged */
}
```

Inserting a new index entry at the beginning is quite straightforward. We just set the **Next** member of the new entry pointed to by **pIndex**, to point to the existing head of the list, **pHead**, and return the address of the new entry as the new head of the linked list.

Inserting the new entry in the middle might seem a bit confusing, but the diagram below should help to make clear how it is done.

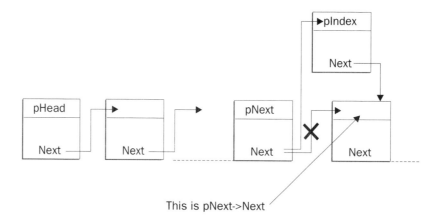

This is pNext->Next

The boxes in the diagram are members of the linked list, and they are labeled with the pointers that contain their respective addresses. If the **Name[]** member of **pIndex** is greater that that of **pNext**, which is the current list element, and less than or equal to that of the next element, which is pointed to by the **Next** member of **pNext**, then **pIndex** is inserted between the two. The **Next** pointer member of **pIndex** is set to the address of the list element following **pNext**. This address is contained in **pNext->Next**. The **Next** member of **pNext** is then reset to point to **pIndex**. Finally, the original head of the list is returned.

Display Details of a Person

This is a very simple function to output the name, phone number and address members of a Person object.

```
/*********************************
 * Function to display a Person *
 * on the screen                *
 *********************************/
void Display(Person *pPerson)
{
    int i=0;                              /* Index to the Address array */

    /* Output the name and phone number */
    printf("\n\n%s\t%s\n", pPerson->Name, pPerson->Phone);

    /* Output up to 5 non-empty lines of address */
    while((i<5)&&strlen(pPerson->Address[i]))
      puts("%s\n", pPerson->Address[i++]);
    return;
}
```

The name and phone number are displayed by the **printf()** function. The lines of the address are displayed by the **puts()** function that is called in the **while** loop. The loop continues as long as the line count is less than five, and the current line is not empty.

Program Analysis

If you want to compile and run this example, you just need to assemble the functions we have described, and the block of code that includes **main()**, into a single file. The program will prompt for input. When you have added all the personal records you want, just press return. The program will read back the records from the file in ascending alphabetical sequence and display them.

Using Temporary Work Files

Very often you'll need a work file just for the duration of a program, which will only be used to store intermediate results and can be thrown away when the program is finished. Our program for calculating primes that we wrote earlier in this chapter is a good example, because we really only needed the file during the calculation.

We have a choice of two functions to help with temporary file usage, and each has its advantages and disadvantages.

Creating a Temporary Work File

The first function will create a temporary file automatically. Its prototype is:

```
FILE *tmpfile(void);
```

It takes no arguments and returns a pointer to the temporary file. If the disk is full for example, and the file can't be created then the function will return **NULL**. The file is created and opened for update (**"wb+"** mode), so that it can be both written and read, but obviously you need to do it in that order. The file is automatically deleted on exit from your program, so there's no need to worry about any messy excess files being left behind. You'll never know what the file is called, and since it doesn't continue to exist after, it doesn't really matter.

The disadvantage of this function is that the file will be deleted as soon as you close it, effectively meaning that you can't close the file, having written it in one part of the program, and then reopening it in another part of the program to read the data. You must keep the file open for as long as you need to access the data. A practical illustration of creating a temporary file is provided by the statements:

```
FILE *pFile;                    /* Declare a file pointer */
pFile tmpfile();                /* Get a temporary file */
```

Creating a Unique File Name

The second possibility is to use a function that provides you with a unique file name. Whether this ends up as a temporary file or not is up to you. The prototype for this function is:

```
char *tmpnam(char *pFileName);
```

If the argument to the function is **NULL**, then the file name is generated in an internal static array of type **char**, and a pointer to it is returned.

If you want the name stored in a **char** array that you declare yourself, you must pass a pointer to the array as an argument to the function. Your array must be at least **L_tmpnam** characters long, where **L_tmpnam** is a predefined constant in **STDIO.H**. In this case, the file name is stored in the array that you specify as an argument. A pointer to your array is also returned.

A Unique File Creation Example

So if we take the first possibility then we can create a unique file with the statements:

```
FILE *pFile=NULL;                              /* Declare a file pointer */
char *pFileName=NULL;                          /* Pointer to a name */
pFile=fopen(pFileName=tmpnam(NULL),"wb+");     /* Create the file */
```

Here we've declared our file pointer **pFile**, and our pointer, **pFileName**, which will contain the address of the temporary file name. We have combined the call to **tmpnam()** with the call to open the file by putting the assignment as the first argument to **fopen()**. Because the argument to **tmpnam()** is **NULL**, the file name will be generated as an internal static object whose address will be placed in our pointer **pFileName**.

Don't be tempted to write:

```
pFile=fopen(tmpnam(NULL), "rb+");
```

If you do then you'll no longer have access to the file name, so you won't be able to use **remove()** to delete the file.

If you want to create the array to hold the file name yourself, you could write:

```
FILE *pFile=NULL;
char FileName[L_tmpnam];
pFile=fopen(tmpnam(FileName), "rb+");
```

Remember that the assistance we've obtained from the library function **tmpnam()** is just to provide a unique name. It's your responsibility to delete any files created, and you should also note that you'll be limited to a maximum of **TMP_MAX** unique names from this function in your program. The symbol **TMP_MAX** is defined in **STDIO.H**, and is usually 65535, which is more file names than most people will ever need in one program.

File Error Functions

In addition to the error return values that we've seen for many of the file input and output functions, there are four functions provided in the standard library for detecting when error flags are set, and for resetting them.

The feof Function

The first of these, function **feof**, has the prototype;

```
int feof(FILE *pFile);
```

This function returns a non-zero value if the end of file indicator for the file pointed to by **pFile**, is set. This indicates that the file position is at the end of the file. The function returns 0 if the end of file indicator isn't set.

The ferror Function

To detect if an error has occurred with a previous file operation, you can use the function **ferror()** with the prototype:

```
int ferror(FILE *pFile);
```

This function returns a non-zero value if an error has occurred, and 0 if otherwise.

Error Numbers

An integer value, **errno**, which is defined in **ERRNO.H**, provides a number by which to identify a particular error. A message corresponding to a particular value for **errno** can be retrieved by using the function **strerror()** which is declared in the header file **STRING.H**. This function has the prototype:

```
char *strerror(int ErrorNumber);
```

The function returns a pointer to a string containing an implementation-dependent error message corresponding to the error number passed as an argument. You can also pass **errno** directly to the function if you wish.

Printing an Error Message

If you just want to output an error message, then the standard library provides the function **perror()**, which has the prototype:

```
void perror(const char *pMyMessage);
```

This will output to **stderr** the string pointed to by **pMyMessage** followed by the implementation-dependent error message corresponding to the current error. So you could write:

```
char *pMessage="Abandon hope. "
if(ferror(pFile))
   perror(pMessage);
```

to output "Abandon hope." followed by whatever error message corresponds to the current file error.

The Clearerr Function

Finally, to clear any outstanding error indicators you can use the library function `clearerr()` which has the prototype:

```
void clearerr(FILE *pFile);
```

This will clear any error indicators set for the file, as well as the end of file indicator too. Executing a `rewind()` operation for a file will also clear the error indicators.

Summary

In this chapter we have covered the device-independent file operations provided by the standard library. These functions are available to support file operations in any ANSI-standard compliant implementation of C. The major points arising in this chapter are:

- Before you can use a file, it must be opened by calling the function `fopen()`. This establishes a link between a file pointer in your program, and the physical file on your storage device.

- The file mode is established when a file is opened. A file can be opened in write mode, append mode, read mode, or update mode, and can be a binary file or a text file.

- The most elementary file operations provided by the standard library enable you to read and write one character at a time using the functions `fgetc()` and `fputc()`.

- You can return a character that's just been read using `fgetc()`, back to the buffer. You can do this by using the function `ungetc()`. The character `EOF` cannot be returned.

- Files other than those associated with the keyboard and screen are automatically buffered in memory.

- Formatted read and write operations are provided by the functions `fscanf()` and `fprintf()`.

- Binary read and write operations are provided by the `fread()` and `fwrite()` functions.

- You can randomly access records in a file. A file position is recorded by the function `ftell()` relative to the beginning of the file and can be recovered by the function `fseek()`.

You can also position a file using the function `fseek()` by specifying an offset relative to the current position, or to the end of the file. You can also use the function `fgetpos()` to record a file position and subsequently restore it with the function `fsetpos()`.

The current position, the end of a file and the beginning of a file are all defined by the standard symbols `SEEK_CUR`, `SEEK_END`, and `SEEK_SET`.

You will find there are alternatives to the standard library functions for input and output in some environments. This is most notable under the UNIX operating system where access to input and output operations (and to other services, including those provided by the standard library functions) can be gained through **system calls**. You will often be able to gain some improvement in performance in your programs by using UNIX system calls directly, but at the expense of limiting your programs portability.

Programming Exercises

1 Write a program to store proverbs or sayings in a file, and then retrieve all those containing a given word or sequence of words.

2 Extend the program from Exercise 1, providing add and delete operations too.

3 Write a program to scan a C program file to count the number of times a set of given keywords has been used.

4 Write a program to scan a C program identifying symbols in `#define` commands, then generate a new program file with substitutions for the symbols and with the `#define` commands deleted.

The Pre-processor and Debugging

In this chapter we'll explore what facilities the pre-processor provides and how they are used. We will also be looking at how the standard facilities in C can help you to debug your programs. By the end of this chapter you will have learnt:

- How the **#include** command operates.
- How the **#define** directive is used.
- What a macro is.
- How to define and use macros with parameters.
- What logical pre-processor directives are available.
- How to use pre-processor directives to avoid accidentally duplicating code in your program.
- What assertions are and how you can use then to help debug your programs.
- What the common causes of bugs in your programs are.

The Pre-processor

The pre-processor is a program which is executed prior to the compilation of your C program source code, providing a means for you to manipulate, modify, and augment your C source code. The pre-processor is controlled by means of commands, or **pre-processor directives**, inserted in your source code, all of which must have a hash (**#**) character as the first non-whitespace character on the line. We've already used two of these quite extensively, the **#include** directive which inserts the contents of a file into your source code, and the **#define** directive which defines a string to replace a symbol used in your program.

You need to keep in mind that all pre-processor operations occur before your program is compiled. They modify the set of statements that constitute your program. None of the pre-processor directives in your program remain after pre-processing is complete, so they're not involved in the execution of your program at all.

Including Files in your Program

You have already used this particular directive several times, but let's go through it from the beginning so that we're crystal clear as to what's happening. The **#include** directive will insert the specified text file into your program at the point where it appears.

Including Standard Header Files

This is most frequently used to add the contents of standard header files to your program, providing a whole host of declarations and definitions to enable you to use standard library functions. By now, you'll be completely familiar with statements such as:

```
#include <stdio.h>
```

which fetches into your program the header file supporting input and output functions from the standard library. This version of the **#include** directive searches for the file that has the name specified between the angled brackets, and inserts its contents into your program source file in place of the **#include** directive.

Most compilers will use a specific directory to store their include files, and you may need to specify this in compiler commands, as an environment variable, or by using a dialog box if you're using a compiler with a graphical development environment.

Including Your Own Files

There is another form of the `#include` directive that is used to add the contents of one of your own files to a program. This uses double quotes instead of the angled brackets. For example:

```
#include "MYFILE.H"
```

The difference between this form and that using angled brackets lies in which directories are searched for the required file. This form of `#include` directive will first search the directory containing your source file, and if the file isn't found in the source directory, then it behaves the same as the form using angled brackets.

Including Strategies

Although `include` files are frequently given names with the extension `.H`, you can call them whatever you like. You can use the `#include` mechanism for dividing your program into several files, which makes a large program much easier to manage. Files containing global definitions such as function prototypes, global variables, and symbol definitions are usually given names with the extension `.H`. Files containing function definitions are commonly given the extension `.C`.

By putting all your symbol definitions into a single file you can make sure that the same symbols are used throughout the program, and same applies to definitions of structures that you want to be global. With one definition used by all program files you ensure consistency, minimize errors, and have the ability to make modifications easily. Another use for a header file is to group together all the standard library `#include` directives, so that they can all be included into any source file by using a single `#include` directive.

You need to avoid duplicating information when you include more than one file in your program, though. A file that you include in your program can also contain an `#include` directive for another file, as is illustrated here:

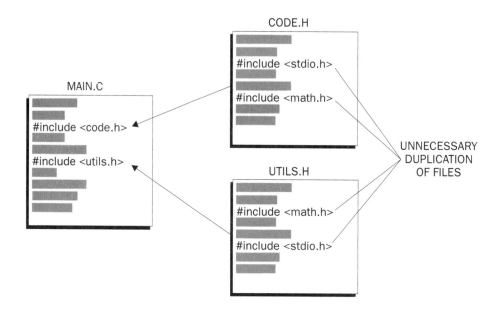

With large programs, the file structure defining the complete program can become quite complicated, and there's considerable potential for introducing a file more than once. Both the duplicated standard header files are included in both of the subsidiary **.H** files, so **MAIN.C** can potentially contain two copies of each of the **.H** files.

Duplicate code will usually cause compilation errors so it's essential to prevent this from happening. We shall see later in this chapter how the pre-processor provides some facilities for ensuring that any given block of code will appear only once in your program, even if you inadvertently include it several times.

Substitutions in your Program

Pre-processor directives that make substitutions in your source code are called **macros**. The simplest kind of substitution or macro that you can specify is one that we've already seen, that of defining a string to replace a symbol. For example, the pre-processor directive to substitute the actual numeric value for the character string **PI**, is as follows:

```
#define PI 3.14159265
```

Other than **PI** actually looking like a variable, it has nothing whatsoever to do with variables. Here the identifier **PI** is a token used to represent the sequence of digits appearing in its definition. The token, **PI**, is used as a marker for where the sequence of digits is to appear in your program, and will be exchanged for the specified sequence of digits.

The pre-processor searches your program for all occurrences of '**PI**', and replaces each with the text **3.14159265**. When your program is ready to be compiled after pre-processing has been completed, the symbol **PI** will no longer appear, having been replaced in every case by the numeric value. As you've already seen, this has the advantage that you can modify the value for all occurrences of **PI** in a program, just by altering its definition in the **#define** directive.

Range Restrictions

The pre-processor, however, won't search strings between quotes. If you have a statement such as:

```
printf("PI=%f", PI);
```

then the **PI** appearing in the string between double quotes won't be changed by the pre-processor, so the statement will become:

```
printf("PI=%f", 3.14159265);
```

It will also fail to change strings embedded in identifiers or keywords, so a variable with the name **PINnumber** wouldn't be affected by our definition for **PI**.

The const Alternative

Although you can use the **#define** directive for numeric constants such as Pi, it's preferable to use **const** variables to do this. You can achieve the same result with a **global** statement such as:

```
const double Pi = 3.14159265;
```

This leaves no doubt as to the type of constant being used, reducing the possibility of the value being misinterpreted by the compiler.

The #define Directive

The general form of the **#define** pre-processor directive is:

```
#define identifier sequence_of_characters
```

Here the **identifier** conforms to the usual definition of a C identifier that we discussed back in Chapter 2. The **sequence_of_characters** is optional, and is used to define a token which has a value, as opposed to just defining the existence of a token.

It's a convention amongst C programmers that identifiers created using **#define** are given names in capitals, so that they stand out. This is especially useful where identifiers look like functions, which we'll look at a little later on.

Using #define

A very common use of the **#define** directive which again we've already seen, is to define array dimensions. When this is done, only one directive needs to be modified, both to alter the dimensions of the array, and the behavior of statements, such as loops, which use the array dimension as a control.

Nesting Substitutions

Substitutions can also use symbols that have been defined by other substitutions. In Chapter 8 we wrote a program to produce an arbitrary number of primes. We defined **ROW_SIZE** for the number of primes to appear in an output line, and **MEM_PRIMES** as the dimension of the array to hold primes in memory. We said at the time that ideally **MEM_PRIMES** should be a multiple of **ROW_SIZE** to ensure a tidy output. We could have enforced this with the directives:

```
#define ROW_SIZE 5              /* Number of primes output per line */
#define MEM_PRIMES (20*ROW_SIZE) /* Count of number of primes in memory */
```

Now **MEM_PRIMES** will definitely be a multiple of **ROW_SIZE**. The parentheses in the substitution string **(20*ROW_SIZE)** are a safety precaution against side effects.

Disregarding Context

The pre-processor is making string substitutions without regard for context, and the context can sometimes produce something different from what you want. This is usually caused by operator precedence.

This is easier to see if we use a slightly different example. Suppose we define **VALUE** with the directive:

```
#define VALUE 10+15
```

Later in the program we will have an expression, **2*VALUE** which we would expect to give the result 50. In fact, it produces 35 because the expression will end up as 2*10+15, which when you see it is clearly 35. If we insert parentheses around the substitution string:

```
#define VALUE (10+15)
```

we would have obtained what we were wanting. It's a good idea to always use parentheses around any substitution string other than a constant.

Macro Substitutions

We can define a **macro** using the **#define** directive, which will accept arguments rather like a function. This allows different arguments to be specified in various instances of using the macro, and these arguments will replace the corresponding tokens in the macro's substitution string.

A Simple Example

We will be able to better understand this by looking at an example:

```
#define PRINT(INTVALUE) printf("%d", INTVALUE)
```

This directive provides for two levels of substitution. There is the substitution for **PRINT(INTVALUE)** by the string immediately following it in the **#define** statement, and there's also the substitution of alternatives for the parameter **INTVALUE**. For example, you could write the statement:

```
PRINT(iVal);
```

This will be converted by the pre-processor to:

```
printf( "%d", iVal);
```

You could use this directive to create a **printf()** statement for any variable or constant of type **int** at various points in your program.

Macros with Multiple Arguments

The most general form of the **#define** directive that accepts an argument can be represented as:

```
#define identifier(list_of_identifiers) substitution_string
```

The **list_of_identifiers** represents one or more parameters separated by commas. This shows that in the general case multiple parameters are permitted, so we're able to define more complex substitutions.

> Note that you mustn't leave a space between the first identifier and the left parenthesis, because the identifier is terminated by the first space.

An Example

To illustrate how you use this sort of definition, we can define a macro for producing the maximum of two values with:

```
#define MAX(x, y) x>y?x:y
```

This has two parameters **x** and **y**, which will be replaced in the substitution string for the macro by whatever arguments are specified when it's used. Therefore, we could use the macro with the statement:

```
Result=MAX(MyValue, 99);
```

This will be expanded by the pre-processor into the statement:

```
Result=MyValue>99?MyValue:99;
```

This will calculate the maximum of the two values specified as arguments to the macro, as we expect. This is a very useful macro, as it's not type-dependent. As long as the arguments are of the same type, this will work with any type of arguments. To implement this as a function we would need a separate function with a different function name for each type of argument we wanted to handle.

Pitfalls with Macros

There is a trap hidden in the last macro. It's important to be conscious of the substitution that's taking place, and not to assume that this is a function. Otherwise you can get some really strange results, particularly if your substitution identifiers include an explicit or implicit assignment. For example, the following modest extension of our last example can produce an erroneous result:

```
Result=MAX(MyValue++, 99);
```

The substitution process will generate the statement:

```
Result=MyValue++>99?MyValue++:99;
```

What happens as a result of this statement now depends on whether the variable **MyValue** is greater than **99** or not.

If the value of **MyValue** is less than or equal to **99**, then the variable **Result** will be assigned the value **99**, and **MyValue** will be incremented. If **MyValue** is greater than **99**, then the variable **Result** will be assigned the value stored in the variable **MyValue**, but in this case **MyValue** will be incremented twice. There is no way to protect against this other than to always use capital letters for your macro names, to provide a visual clue that they aren't real functions.

> You must just remember not to use the increment or decrement operators, or any other expressions that modify variables, as arguments to a macro which may cause the expression to be evaluated more than once.

Precedence Rules

You need to be aware that precedence rules can also catch you out with macros accepting arguments, in much the same way as they did with simple substitutions. We can demonstrate how this can occur with an example. Suppose we write a macro to calculate the product of two arguments:

```
#define PRODUCT(m, n) m*n
```

We then use this macro with the statement:

```
Result=PRODUCT(x, y+1)
```

Of course everything works fine but we don't get the result we want, since the macro expands to:

```
Result=x*y+1
```

It could take a long time to discover that we aren't getting the product of the two parameters, as there's no external indication of what's going on. There is just a more or less erroneous value propagating through our program.

Using Parentheses

The solution is very simple. If you use macros to generate expressions, put parentheses around everything, especially the individual parameters. For our example to work properly every time we need to rewrite our example as:

```
#define PRODUCT(m, n) ((m)*(n))
```

The inclusion of the outer parentheses here may seem excessive, but since you don't know the context in which the macro expansion will be placed, it's always better to include them, and it doesn't cost anything. Our previous macro for the maximum of two arguments would be much better written as:

```
#define MAX(x,y) ((x)>(y)?(x):(y))
```

Now a statement such as:

```
Result=MAX(a+2,b+3);
```

will work as we want, whereas it wouldn't have worked with the previous version.

Verbose Macro Expansion

You also need to be aware that expansion of macros can result in large amounts of ugly code, which can be horrible to debug. For instance, using the definition of **MAX(x,y)** from a couple of lines ago, the expression:

```
Result=MAX(MAX(1,2), MAX(3,4));
```

would expand into the rather horrendous:

```
Result=
((((1)>(2)?(1):(2)))>(((3)>(4)?(3):(4)))?(((1)>(2)?(1):(2))):(((3)>(4)?(3):(4)))));
```

So be very careful!

Macros as Shorthand

If you have an expression of some complexity that you use quite frequently, you can sometimes use a macro in order to reduce the amount of typing. It can also simplify your code and make it more readable in some instances. For example, as we saw in Chapter 8, the standard library function **fgets()** has the merit that it will read a string from an input stream, but the input is limited to the number of characters specified by its second argument. You will recall that it has the prototype:

```
char *fgets(char *pStr, int nChars, FILE *pFile );
```

This function is often used to read a string from **stdin**, because it can ensure that the number of characters read doesn't exceed the length of the array receiving the input. It returns **NULL** if an end-of-file occurs, and **pStr** if otherwise. It can be more conveniently used in a macro such as:

```
#define GetLine(pStr,N) ((fgets(pStr,N,stdin)==NULL)?EOF:strlen(pStr))
```

The macro **GetLine()** will now read a maximum of **N** characters from **stdin** into the array pointed to by **pStr**. It will also generate a value which is either the length of the string if the operation is completed without error, or **EOF** if an end-of-file condition is recognized.

319

You may find other circumstances where you can usefully package other standard library functions inside a macro.

Strings as Macro Arguments

String constants are a potential source of confusion when used with macros, so let's start with the most elementary case, and work our way up. The simplest string substitution is a single level definition such as:

```
#define MYSTRING "This string"
```

If you now write the statement:

```
printf("%s", MYSTRING);
```

then this will be converted by the pre-processor into the statement:

```
printf("%s", "This string");
```

which should be what you're expecting. You couldn't use the **#define** statement without the quotes in the substitution sequence, and expect to be able to put the quotes in your program text instead. For example, if you write:

```
#define MYSTRING This string
...
printf("%s", "MYSTRING");
```

there will be no substitution for **MYSTRING** in the **printf()** function. Anything in quotes in your program is assumed to be a literal string, and as we saw early on in this chapter, the pre-processor won't modify it.

Using Double Quotes

A special technique is provided for indicating that the substitution for a macro argument is to appear between a pair of double quotes to form a string. For example, you could specify a macro to display a string using the function **printf()** as:

```
#define PrintStr(STRING) printf("%s", #STRING)
```

The **#** character preceding the appearance of the parameter, **STRING**, indicates that the argument is to be surrounded by double quotes when the substitution is generated. Therefore if you write the statement in your program:

```
PrintStr(Output);
```

this will be converted by the pre-processor to:

```
printf("%s", "Output");
```

This mechanism ensures that the substitution of the argument always results in a string between quotes. It also provides the possibility of substituting the argument with and without quotes. For example, if we wanted to display the value of a variable, and show its name in the output, we could write the macro:

```
#define PrintInt(IntValue) printf("\n%s=%d",#IntValue,IntValue);
```

Now if you use the statement:

```
PrintInt(nData);
```

the pre-processor will convert this into the statement:

```
printf("\n%s=%d", "nData", nData);
```

Which will output the name and value of the variable **nData**.

Using **#** in a macro substitution string also enables you to generate a substitution producing a string that includes double quotes. If you write the statement:

```
PrintStr("Output");
```

it will be pre-processed into the statement:

```
printf("%s", "\"Output\"");
```

This is possible because the pre-processor is clever enough to recognize the need to put **\"** at each end in order to get a string including double quotes displayed correctly.

Joining Two Results of a Macro Expansion

The pre-processor will allow you to generate two results in a macro and join them together without spaces between them. To join two macro arguments into a single sequence of characters, you can specify the macro as:

```
#define join(a, b) a##b
```

The two characters, ##, work as an operator to separate the parameters, and they indicate to the pre-processor that the results of the two substitutions are to be joined. For example, writing the statement:

```
strlen(join(var, 123 ));
```

will result in:

```
strlen(var123);
```

This might be applied to synthesizing a variable name, building up a fully qualified path name from file and directory names, or generating a format control string from two or more macro parameters.

Pre-processor Directives on Multiple Lines

A pre-processor directive must be a single logical line, but a logical line can be extended to multiple physical lines by using the statement continuation character, \. We could write:

```
#define min(x, y) \
            ((x)<(y)?(x):(y))
```

Here, the backslash indicates that the directive continues on the second line with the first non-blank character found, so you can position the text on the second line wherever you feel it effects the nicest arrangement. You can spread a directive over as many continuation lines as you wish by using the backslash repeatedly. You can use the backslash with C language statements, too, although it generally isn't necessary.

Logical Pre-processor Directives

The last example we looked at appears to be of limited value, since it's hard to envisage when you would want to simply join **var** to **123** - you could always use just one parameter, and write **var123** as the argument. One aspect of pre-processing facilities that adds considerably more potential to such tasks, is the possibility for multiple macro substitution, where the arguments for one macro are derived from substitutions defined in another. In our last example, both arguments to the **join()** macro could have been generated by other **#define** substitutions or macros.

The pre-processor also supports directives which provide a logical **if** capability, enabling you to make decisions about which directives are executed, or whether a block of code is to be included as part of your program. This vastly expands the scope of what you can do with the pre-processor.

Conditional Pre-processing

The pre-processor supports a conditional directive **#if**, which tests a constant integer expression, and if the expression that is tested is zero, subsequent lines of the program up to the point where an **#endif** directive is found are skipped, and therefore not included in the program. If the expression is non-zero, then the following program code is included and processed normally. There are various ways in which the **#if** pre-processor directive can be used, so let's look at them in turn.

Conditional Compilation

The first version of the **#if** directive we shall discuss allows you to test whether an identifier exists as a result of having been created in a previous **#define** statement. The general form of this test is:

```
#if defined identifier
```

This can also be written as:

```
#ifdef identifier
```

Which is exactly the same as the previous version. If the specified **identifier** hasn't been defined, then all the statements following the **#if** are excluded from the program, until we reach the statement:

```
#endif
```

If the **identifier** has been defined, then all the following statements will be included in the program. This is the same logical process that we've used in C programming, except that here it results in the inclusion or exclusion of program statements.

Testing for Identifier Existence

You can also test for the existence (or absence) of an identifier. The general form of this directive is:

```
#if !defined identifier
```

This can also be written in an abbreviated version:

```
#ifndef identifier
```

Here the statements following the **#if** down to the **#endif** will be included in the program, if the identifier hasn't previously been defined. This provides you with a general method to avoid including functions, or other blocks of code and directives, in your programs more than once.

Protecting Include Files

When you have a program consisting of multiple files, you may end up with several **#include** statements referring to the same file, and you need to ensure that the file is only compiled once. A common way to do this is to use a sequence of directives as follows:

```
#ifndef block1
#define block1
   /* Block of code you don't */
   /* want to be repeated.    */
#endif
```

The first time the file containing these directives is included in a program, the identifier **block1** won't been defined. Therefore the block following the **#if** will be processed and **block1** will then be defined. The following block of code down to the **#endif** will also be included in your program. For any subsequent inclusion of the same file in a program, **block1** will already be defined. As a result, all the statements in the file down to the **#endif** won't be included. Of course, any directives or statements following the **#endif** will be processed in the normal way.

It's a good idea to get into the habit of automatically protecting code in your own files in this fashion. Once you have collected a few files containing your own functions, you will be surprised how easy it is to end up duplicating blocks of code accidentally if you don't, and using the conditional directive to protect against this costs absolutely nothing.

Omitting Code using #ifdef

You can also use the **#ifdef** directive to temporarily comment out blocks of code in your program, as follows:

```
#ifdef 0
/* All code here will be omitted from the program */
#endif
```

To include the code you just need to remove the two directives. Of course, you could also use an identifier to control whether the code is included or not, in a similar way to that used to avoid code duplication.

Note that even if part of your program is 'turned off' using **#ifdef**, all the text in the block needs to be valid C, or else you'll get compiler errors. You need to be especially careful of things like unterminated comments and strings, and newlines within comments.

Using Multiple Tests

You aren't limited to testing just one value with the pre-processor **#if** directive. You can use logical operators to test whether multiple identifiers have been defined (or not defined). For example, the statement:

```
#if defined block1 && defined block2
```

will evaluate to True if both **block1** and **block2** have previously been defined, and so the following code won't be included unless this is the case.

Rescinding a Definition

A further extension of the flexibility in applying the pre-processor conditional directives, is the ability to undefine an identifier you've previously defined. This is achieved using a directive:

```
#undef block1
```

Now if **block1** had previously been defined, after this directive it's no longer defined. One use of this directive is to ensure that a function is used for an operation rather than a macro. For example, the directive:

```
#undef max
```

would ensure that the macro we defined earlier wouldn't be used subsequent to this directive. Of course, if you use **max()** after this point, and you haven't provided a function **max()**, then your compiler will generate an error message.

Testing for Specific Values

As we said at the beginning of this section, you can also use a form of the **#if** directive to test the value of a constant expression. If the value of the constant expression is non-zero, then the following statements down to the next **#endif** are included in the program. If the constant expression evaluates to zero, the following statements down to the next **#endif** will be skipped. The general form of the **#if** directive is:

```
#if constant_expression
```

This is most frequently applied to test for a specific value being assigned to an identifier by a previous pre-processor directive, but you can also compare values, or indeed any constant expression, although you mustn't use the **sizeof** operator, and no type casts are allowed. We might have the following sequence of statements:

```
#if PRINTLINE==132
/* Code for wide printer */
#endif
```

The statements between the **#if** and **#endif** statements will only be included in the program here if the identifier **PRINTLINE** has been defined with the value 132 in a previous **#define** directive.

Creating Error Messages

If you detect a condition during pre-processing that warrants an error message being generated, you can use the pre-processor directive **#error** to generate a message. For example, the directive:

```
#error We are in deep trouble
```

will cause a diagnostic message to be generated which will include the file name and the line number, and will include the string of characters appearing in the **#error** directive.

The **#error** directive is usually used with the **#if** directive to ensure that some essential condition is met. An example of this is:

```
#if (PRINTLINE!=80) && (PRINTLINE != 132)
#error PRINTLINE must be set to either 80 or 132
#endif
```

This condition will generate the message if **PRINTLINE** hasn't been set to one value or the other.

Multiple Choice Selections

To complement the **#if** directives, we have the **#else** directive too. This works in exactly the same way as the **else** statement in that it identifies a group of directives or statements to be included in the program if the **#if** condition fails. For instance, the previous example would probably be better written as:

```
#if PRINTLINE==132
/* Code for wide printer */
#else
/* Code for narrow printer */
#endif
```

In this case, the code for a wide printer will be included if **PRINTLINE** has the value 132, otherwise the code for a narrow printer will be included.

The elif Directive

The pre-processor also supports a special form of the `#if` for multiple choice selections, where only one of several choices of statements for inclusion in the program is required. This is the `#elif` directive, which has the general form:

```
#elif constant_expression
```

This is equivalent to an `#else` followed by an `#if`. Here's an example:

```
#if PRINTLINE==132
/* Code for wide printer */
#elif PRINTER==HPLASER
/* Code for laser printer */
#else
/* Code for narrow printer */
#endif
```

This provides for three possible options. If `PRINTLINE` is 132 then the code for a wide printer is included. If it isn't, then if `PRINTER` has been defined as `HPLASER` then the code for a laser printer is included, otherwise code for a narrow printer is used.

For multiple choices you can use several successive `#elif`s to select one choice from a wide range of possibilities.

Standard Pre-processor Macros

There are five standard macros defined by the pre-processor which you can use in your source program statements or in pre-processor directives. They each provide a specific item of information.

Obtaining Date and Time Information

The macro `__DATE__` will be replaced by a string representation of the current date when it's processed in your program. This will be in the form `"Mmm dd yyyy"`. Here `Mmm` is the month in characters, such as `Jan`, `Feb`, and so on. The pair of characters `dd` is the day in the month with values from 1 to 31. Single digit days are preceded by a blank. Finally `yyyy` is the year as four digits, 1995 for example.

A similar macro, __TIME__, provides a string containing the value of the time when it's processed, in the form `"hh:mm:ss"`. The string contains pairs of digits for hours, minutes and seconds, separated by colons.

You could use this to record when your program was last compiled with a statement such as:

```
printf("\nProgram last compiled at %s on %s", __TIME__, __DATE__);
```

Once the program has been compiled, the values output by the `printf()` statement are fixed until you compile it again. Therefore on subsequent executions of the program the time and date will be progressively incorrect.

> Don't confuse these macros with the time and date functions which we saw in Chapter 7. The standard library functions will give you the correct time and date each time the program is executed. The pre-processor macros provide the correct value when the program is compiled, and these values will be used each time the program is executed, until it is recompiled at some point.

Accessing the Filename

You can obtain the name of the source file being compiled as a string literal by using the macro __FILE__. This can be useful if you're working with a large program consisting of many files, some of which may exist in different versions at any one time. Recording the name of the file being compiled can help keep track of which versions of files are being used.

You can also use the __FILE__ macro for error messages in your program. This is particularly helpful when your program consists of more than one file because the error message can pinpoint the file in which the error originated.

Accessing Line Numbers

The __LINE__ macro generates the current line number. This can relate errors which may arise when the program is executed to a particular line of source code. Where the same error can occur at different points in a program, you could provide tracking information with statements such as:

```
if(ferror(pFile))
   printf("\nError in file %s at line %s\n%s",
                      __FILE__, __LINE__, strerror(errno));
```

These statements will output the file name and the line number in the source file when an error occurs, followed by the error message corresponding to the error. With this information you know exactly where the problem was detected.

Verifying ANSI Standard C

The last macro is __STDC__ which will be defined as 1 if the compiler is an ANSI-standard compiler. As well as ensuring that you use the correct compiler for ANSI-standard code, it also offers protection against incorrect options being selected in compilers which may support several different definitions of the C language. To make sure that the ANSI option is set, you just need to put a suitable directive in your program:

```
#if !__STDC__
#error This program requires ANSI C option to be set.
#endif
```

Debugging Your Programs

You are about as likely to produce a bug free version of a realistic program first time out as you are to find hairs on a frog. Thus getting the bugs out of your program is going to occupy a great deal of your time. The process of testing and debugging a program is normally rather more time consuming than the writing of the code in the first place.

> Many programmers who over-estimate their own abilities to write error-free applications find that the proportion of development time spent debugging to the time spent designing the program increases exponentially. It is extremely important to spend a little extra time in the design stage to iron out any potential problems, because if they persist through to the latter stages of development then debugging can become very difficult indeed.

Debugging is a big topic. It is most important that you are familiar with the debug tools provided with your compiler, since they will provide you with the most powerful means of finding and eliminating bugs. The standard library and the pre-processor do provide some tools which are helpful in this context, which we will look at now.

The assert Macro

The **assert** macro enables you to generate diagnostic messages when errors occur, and it's defined in the header file **ASSERT.H**. The macro is invoked by a statement such as:

```
assert(expression);
```

Statements of this kind are called **assertions**, because you assert that the value of **expression** is True. The argument, **expression**, must result in a value of type **int**. If the result of evaluating expression is zero (representing False), then a message will be output to **stderr** with the form:

Assertion failed: expression, file __FILE__, line __LINE__

The argument **expression** is output as it appears in the original assertion, not as its value, which you know must be zero if you see the message. The output therefore provides you with a record of what the expression was that indicated there was an error, the source file that contains the code where the error was detected, and the line number within the source file. After outputting the message, the standard library function **abort()** is called, which writes the message "Abnormal program termination." on **stderr** and calls the standard library function **exit()** with exit code 3.

You can use any kind of expression in an **assert()** macro as long as the result is integer, but comparisons are the most common. You could check that an index to an array falls within the array bounds with statements such as:

```
double MyArray[MAX_SIZE];
...
assert((n>=0)&&(n<MAX_SIZE));
MyArray[n]=999.0;
```

This will generate an error message if the index value **n** is outside the limits of the array.

Pointer Problems

A common source of problems is due to a pointer not being set correctly. You could check that a pointer in a function has a value that isn't **NULL** with statements such as:

```
Index *Insert(Index *pNew, Index *pHead)
{
    assert(pNew);
    /* Code to insert the new item */
}
```

You may be wondering at this point why you need this. After all, you could program this using regular C statements anyway. This is true, of course, but a major advantage of using **assert()** is that you can control whether or not the code is included in the program as well.

Removing Diagnostic Statements

Once your program is fully tested, you don't want the program to be cluttered up with all these diagnostic statements, making the program much larger than it needs to be for one thing, and it may very well make it slower too. On the other hand, you don't want to have to go through and laboriously delete them all, which is what you'd need to do if you simply include output statements executed as a result of an **if** in your program. Equally, if you find you want to alter or extend the program, you may want all your diagnostics back in again. To omit the **assert()** macro diagnostics from your program, all you have to do is add the directive:

```
#define NDEBUG
```

to the beginning of the source file. Now none of the **assert()** statements will be included when your program is compiled. Note that **NDEBUG** doesn't need to have a value. It is sufficient if it appears in a **#define** directive without a value.

Creating your own Error Messages

In some situations, the fact that the **assert()** macro terminates the program can be a nuisance. You may want to apply some local fix if you detect an error, and then let the program stagger on. The most obvious way to do this is to use pre-processor directives to control whether or not the code is included. For example, instead of `assert()` in the last example, we could have written:

```
Index *Insert(Index *pNew, Index *pHead)
{
#ifdef DEBUG
    if(pNew==NULL)
    {
        /* code to display a message and fix up the situation */
    }
#endif
    /* Code to insert the new item */
}
```

Here the fix might be to just do nothing after displaying an error message, and just returning from the function. The diagnostic code will only be included in the program if there's a definition directive for the identifier `DEBUG`, such as:

```
#define DEBUG
```

There is nothing to stop you having several different groups of diagnostic statements, each controlled by their own identifier. You could then switch each group on independently.

Defining Your Own Assert() Macro

You could also define your own macro for assertions - perhaps `Assert()` with a capital A that just displays the message without exiting from the program:

```
#ifdef DEBUG
#define Assert(exp)\
  ((exp)?(void)0:fprintf(stderr,"\nAssertion failed: %s, file %s, line %d",\
                 #exp, __FILE__, __LINE__))
#else
#define Assert(exp)                    /* Define as empty */
#endif
```

We have had to use two continuation lines for the definition of the `Assert()` macro here because it's rather long. If `DEBUG` isn't defined, `Assert(exp)` is in turn defined as an empty statement. If `DEBUG` *is* defined then this macro defines `Assert(exp)` as a statement that does nothing if

exp is positive. If **exp** is zero then a call **fprintf()** is generated to output the asserting expression, the file name and the current source line number to **stderr**.

Common Causes of Errors

Most errors are due to incorrectly keying in a program and will be picked up by the compiler, as they almost always introduce inconsistencies into the code. Mistakes are more of a problem when they are occasional rather than habitual, since if they're habitual you're likely to immediately identify them as a possible source of error.

There are a vast number of ways in which you can cause errors in your programs. There is a small subset though that accounts for a large proportion of the errors, many of which are a consequence of misusing pointers. Here is a list of choice candidates for execution-time bugs in your program. They are in no particular order:

- Omitting the required **&** when specifying address arguments to functions, particularly with **scanf()** or **fscanf()**.
- Using **=** in a condition where you meant **==**.
- Using incorrect format specifiers in a format string, especially on input.
- Using a pointer that contains an address of a variable that is out of scope.
- Returning the address of a local variable from a function.
- Using a pointer that hasn't been initialized so it contains garbage values.
- Using a variable that contains garbage values in an expression.
- Calculating an expression as an integer causing rounding down, when you wanted a floating point result.
- Indexing an array outside of its boundaries.
- Forgetting to divide by the size of an element in an array when calculating the number of elements - a loop count for instance.

Forgetting the **break** statement in **case**s for a **switch** statement.

Failing to check for error conditions with file operations.

Failing to check for memory allocation errors.

Omitting braces round statements to be executed when an **if** condition is True.

Associating an **else** with the wrong **if** in an **if-else** sequence.

Letting the precedence rules fool you by not using parentheses.

Confusing rows and columns in a two-dimensional array.

Exceeding the maximum value that can be stored in an integer variable.

Writing the expression in a loop condition the wrong way round - for example, putting **>** when you mean **<**.

Exceeding the capacity of a **char** array, particularly on input.

Summary

The pre-processor provides powerful augmentation to your C programs. The pre-processor is a fundamental supporting mechanism, particularly where programs defined in several files are concerned. The important points we've covered in this chapter are:

The pre-processor allows you to define symbolic constants that you can use in your program. This enables global changes such as modifying array dimensions to be easily managed.

Logical pre-processor directives **#if**, **#else**, **#elif**, **#ifdef**, **#ifndef** and **#endif** enable you to conditionally execute other pre-processor directives.

Logical pre-processor directives enable you to control whether blocks of code are included or excluded from your program. You can use logical pre-processor directives to ensure that the contents of files that you include into your program can't be included more than once.

335

⬤ You can use the **#define** directive to write macros which accept arguments.

⬤ Macro parameters should be parenthesized in the definition string for a macro, to avoid unwanted effects due to operator precedence.

⬤ Expressions which modify variables should be avoided in macro arguments because of the risk of unwanted side effects. The increment and decrement operators are a particular source of such side effects.

⬤ The **assert()** macro allows you to include conditional diagnostic output in your program. It can be omitted from your program by defining **NDEBUG**.

Programming Exercises

1 Write a macro **Quad(a,b,c,x)** to evaluate ax^2+bx+c.

2 Write a macro to generate the absolute value of any numeric argument (that is, if it's negative, make it positive).

3 Write a macro **min(a,b,c)** to produce the minimum of **a**, **b**, and **c**. All arguments are of the same type.

4 Write a macro **ToUpper(c)** to produce the upper case equivalent of an ASCII character **c** passed as an argument. The macro should do nothing if the character **c** isn't a lower case letter.

5 Write a macro **Bit(x,n)** which will result in 1 if the **n**th bit of the integer argument, **x**, is 1, and zero if the **n**th bit of **x** is zero.

Chapter

Portability and Maintainability

In this chapter we're going to take a look at what aspects of programming in C can restrict the porting of your programs from one machine environment to another. We will also explore what basic things you need to do in order to ease the process of extending your programs, or fixing any problems that might arise. By the end of this chapter, you will have an understanding of:

- What constraints there are to C program portability.
- What you need to consider to produce reasonably portable code.
- How you should structure your programs to make maintenance easier.
- How to approach documenting a program.
- Which programming approaches you can use to ease program testing and maintenance.

Writing Portable Programs

You need to put the need for portability in a proper perspective. Always writing programs conforming to all the rules that apply to maximize portability can be an unacceptable burden. In many situations it may not be practical, and if you don't expect your program will have to run on any other computer, it can involve you in a lot of unnecessary work. On the other hand you don't want to completely ignore it. After all, portability is one of the major advantages of C, and so, within reasonable limits you should endeavor to make your programs as portable as is practical. This need not be difficult or an encumbrance. It's mainly a question of adopting programming techniques which avoid dependencies on the machine and compiler you're using.

There are essentially two aspects to making a program portable:

- Your program needs to be written to conform to a language standard that is available across the range of computing platforms on which you might want to run your application, in this case ANSI C.

- You must also write your code to avoid any dependencies on any one particular machine architecture, or specific hardware facility.

The Minimum ANSI Compiler

The ANSI standard for C provides you with a standard definition of the C language, and definitions of the minimum requirements that such a compiler must meet. If your program conforms to the recommendations for portability defined in the ANSI-standard C, then your program should compile successfully on any system with an ANSI-conforming C compiler. Just in case you need them, here are the upper limits applicable to the code in your program if it's to be processed by any ANSI C compiler:

- 6 characters in an external identifier.
- 8 levels of nested **#if** or **#define** directives.
- 12 (), [], or * in the declaration of a single identifier.
- 15 levels of nested control structures.

- 31 characters in an internal identifier.
- 31 nested parentheses in a single expression.
- 31 nested parentheses in a single declaration.
- 31 arguments in a macro or function call.
- 127 local identifiers in a single block.
- 127 nested expressions.
- 127 members in a single structure or union.
- 127 constants in a single enumeration.
- 255 case labels in a single switch statement.
- 509 characters in a single statement.
- 511 external identifiers in a single source file.
- 1024 macros in a single source file.
- 32,767 bytes in a single array or structure.

Most of these constraints are unlikely to trouble you. After all, how often do you have more than 31 levels of parentheses nesting in an expression? If it's just once, there's likely to be a readability problem with your program. There is one constraint you might need to take note of though: the minimum conforming compiler need only support 6 characters in an external identifier. This limit is low because of linker constraints in some environments, so if you happen to be using a linker that just conforms to the minimum necessary to meet the ANSI standard, it can be very inconvenient.

Portability Constraints

Perhaps the most serious constraint to program portability is the user interface. Most programs these days need to have some kind of graphical interface, but you may have noticed that this book is totally devoid of graphics programming. This is because the ANSI standard for C only provides the ability to interface to a user through the standard library, and this is limited to text.

Generally, since there's no supported graphics standard, implementing an application with a graphical user interface that will run on a UNIX workstation, on a PC under MS-DOS, and with Microsoft Windows is likely to be a very challenging task. It can be eased, however, by using one of the cross-platform graphical user interface tools that are available, and some of these have reached an acceptable level of maturity. Success will depend on the level of graphics your application requires, and the degree to which you need to use advanced graphics hardware facilities will tend to differ from one machine to another.

If you are implementing a graphical application that needs to run on several different platforms, your options on strategy for program development are limited. Designing the program so that the user interface is as separate and independent as possible from the computational and data management parts of the program is fundamental. You must also determine at the outset the range of computers that it's essential for you to support, and select the cross-platform support tool to suit that set.

Dependencies that arise from the way a particular processor works, can be avoided by ensuring you write your program with portability in mind. Let's take a look at what kind of things you need to watch out for.

General Considerations

A general requirement for a C program to be portable is that it should conform to ANSI-standard C. This may seem to be self-evident but it does imply some significant restraint on what you can use in the typical C development environment. It means that you can only use the ANSI-standard library functions, and that all the extra goodies that come with even the lowest priced commercial development environment for C must be avoided.

If you have library functions in C source code form, you can then incorporate them into your program as source code, so that they're fully integrated, removing the dependency on an external library. This presumes that the license agreement for the library functions allows you to use it in this way.

Of course, if you have a program that uses some non-standard functions and you don't have source code for them, you can always try to produce a version of your own, although this may involve a significant amount of work, and if the functions support specific hardware operations, this may not be very easy.

Standard Header Files

The standard ANSI-C header files contain a lot of definitions for common programming constants, such as values for **EOF** and **NULL**. This is to allow the implementation of C in different environments to provide a common interface to such values, and you should always, therefore, use the identifiers defined in the standard header files for standard constants. If you use **EOF** for end-of-file, and **NULL** for setting a pointer to a value that doesn't point to anything, you can be sure that you'll be using values that are correct for any environment.

The same applies to the data types defined in standard headers. The operator **sizeof** produces a result with a value of type **size_t**. In most cases using an **int** will work, but there will also be cases where it won't. It's no hardship at all to use type **size_t** to declare variables concerned with values returned by **sizeof**, and if you do so, you have the security that it will always work as intended.

Avoiding Computer Architecture Dependencies

We can look at programming for portability by considering which aspects of the architecture of a computer have the potential to cause problems depending on how your code is written. It goes without saying that if you write graphics code which directly addresses processor registers, or uses hard-coded addresses for specific operating system data, then your program will definitely be nailed down to whatever machine you are using. However, there are some hardware dependencies that can creep in without you being aware that it's happening, so we're going to be taking a specific look at these:

- The representation and processing of characters
- The representation of numerical values
- The upper and lower limits for numerical values
- Variations in word sizes

Avoiding Character Code Dependencies

You need to avoid making assumptions about what the codes are that represent particular characters, and about what the relationships between various codes are. A rather obvious example of code that reduces portability is:

```
char answer='Y'
...
if(ch==78)            /* Test for N */
/* Do something */
```

The condition in the **if** is dependent on the code being ASCII. This code wouldn't work correctly on any machine that used a code with a different numeric value for **N**. The correct approach is to use the symbol rather than the character code:

```
char answer='Y'
...
if(ch=='N')           /* Test for N */
/* Do something */
```

You also need to avoid constructions that presume character codes for letters are assigned contiguously. An evident mechanism to be avoided is the incrementation of a letter to generate the next in sequence. A slightly less obvious construction that needs to be avoided, is the use of expressions to index an array with a built in assumption that letters are represented by contiguous codes. An example of this sort of thing is:

```
char Letters[26]={0};
char *pStr="An example of a string";
...
for(;*pStr!='\0';pStr++)          /* Loop to count incidence of Letters */
if(isalpha(*pStr)
++Letters[toupper(*pStr)-'A'];
```

This fragment is intended to create a count of how often each letter appears in the string pointed to by **pStr**. This will work fine as long as the codes for upper-case letters are contiguous, like they are in the case of ASCII. If they aren't, then the index expression can produce values outside the bounds of the array. An easy way to achieve the required result without this dependency, is to use a **switch** statement:

```
char Letters[26]={0};
char *pStr="An example of a string";
...
for(;*pStr!='\0';pStr++)              /* Loop to count incidence of Letters */
   switch(toupper(*pStr))
   {
       case 'A':
           ++Letters[0];
           break;
       case 'B':
           ++Letters[1];
           break;
       ...
       case 'Z':
           ++Letters[25];
           break;
   }
```

This version will work with any code representation for letters, regardless of whether they're a contiguous set of codes or not. If you use the standard library functions as far as possible for converting and testing characters rather than writing your own versions, you will minimize the risk of writing code that is dependent on a particular character set for correct operation.

> Of course in this day and age, nearly all computers will use the same representation, so whether you act on this guideline is up to you. For your program to be truly portable, you will have to think long and hard about using it.

You need to be a little careful about converting characters stored as type **char** to other integer types. For characters with codes greater than the decimal value 127 the sign bit will be set. What happens when the character is converted to **int** or **long** is implementation-dependent. In some environments the conversion will treat the **char** value as **signed**, and extend the sign bit so that the senior bits in the word will be set to 1. To avoid this you need to cast the character value to **unsigned**, before the conversion occurs.

345

Avoiding Dependencies on Number Representation

You need to take care to avoid making assumptions about how numbers are represented, especially negative integers. There are two forms for representing negative integers that you may come across.

The first form simply reserves the leading bit in an integer value as a sign bit. For positive values the sign bit is 0 and for negative values the sign bit is 1. The data bits for a number of a given magnitude are the same, the sign bit determining whether a number is positive or negative.

The second form for representing negative integers we have already looked at - the **two's complement** form - and this is rather more common because it simplifies the hardware for integer arithmetic. The two's complement of an integer value is produced by flipping all the bits - a 1 bit is replaced by 0, and a 0 bit is replaced by 1 - and adding 1 to the result. For example, the value +8 as a 16 bit binary number is:

0000 0000 0000 1000

To obtain the two's complement representation for -8, we just flip the bits producing:

1111 1111 1111 0111

and then we add 1, giving the final result:

1111 1111 1111 1000

You can verify that this is indeed -8, by adding the binary representation of +12, which is:

0000 0000 0000 1100

If you try it you will get the binary equivalent of 4.

When a negative integer value in two's complement form is shifted right, the sign bit is propagated, so shifting -8 two positions to the right produces:

1111 1111 1111 1110

This is -2 in decimal form, so propagating the sign in a right shift produces a result equivalent to dividing by 2 for each position shifted. In our example, we shifted right by two bits so we effectively divided -8 by 4, giving the result -2.

While many machines use the two's complement representation for negative integers, this isn't universal, so you need to avoid relying on the behavior of **signed** integers when shifted right. You can't assume a right shift produces the equivalent of a divide operation, and you should only use the right shift operator when it's protected from the effects inherent in two's complement representation.

You can avoid two's complement dependency by ensuring that shift operations are only applied to **unsigned** integer values. One way to do this is to always cast the value to be shifted to an **unsigned** type. For example:

```
NewMask= (unsigned long)Mask >> 4;
```

The cast of the variable **Mask** to **unsigned long** ensures that the sign isn't propagated in the shift operation.

If your code is going to run in a mainframe environment, you must be aware that on some machines floating point numbers are stored with a hexadecimal base. As a consequence, a single precision floating point value with a normalized 24-bit mantissa can have three leading zeros, since the normalization only requires that the leading *hexadecimal* digit is non-zero. This can be a problem with some numerical calculations where you're dependent on full 24-bit accuracy. The solution in such an instance is to change the type from **float** to **double**.

Avoiding Range Dependencies

There can be significant variations in the range of values supported by the different types of variables in C. The ANSI C standard does provide the following specification for the ranges guaranteed to be supported in a conforming compiler:

char	0 to 127
unsigned char	0 to 255
int	-32,767 to +32,767
unsigned int	0 to 65,535

`long`	-2,147,483,647 to +2,147,483,647
`unsigned long`	0 to 4,294,967,295
`float exponent`	-38 to +38
`float mantissa`	6 decimal digits

Note the lower limits for variables of type `long` and `int`. Most machines use two's complement arithmetic which will allow negative numbers that are one less than the lower limits shown here. However, not all machines use the two's complement representation for negative numbers - hence the higher values for the lower limits of these ranges.

The range guaranteed for values of type `float` will be from .999999E-38 to .999999E+38, either positive or negative.

If you can write your program such that values for various types don't fall outside these ranges, then values in your program won't cause you a problem. Of course, the range of numbers you need is usually application-dependent, particularly when it comes to floating point values, and you may not be able to limit yourself to the above ranges. However, most systems will provide ranges of floating point values that comfortably exceed those shown.

Actual Limits for Numeric Values

It's possible that you may want to set a variable to the maximum or minimum possible for whatever type it happens to be. The standard header file **LIMITS.H** defines identifiers which represent the upper and lower limits for each integer type on your particular machine and compiler. The definitions in **LIMITS.H** include:

`SCHAR_MIN`	Minimum value for type `signed char`
`SCHAR_MAX`	Maximum value for type `signed char`
`CHAR_MIN`	Minimum value for type `char`
`CHAR_MAX`	Maximum value for type `char`
`UCHAR_MAX`	Maximum value for type `unsigned char`
`INT_MIN`	Minimum value for type `int`
`INT_MAX`	Maximum value for type `int`
`UINT_MAX`	Maximum value for type `unsigned int`
`LONG_MIN`	Minimum value for type `long`

| LONG_MAX | Maximum value for type **long** |
| ULONG_MAX | Maximum value for type **unsigned long** |

The header file **FLOAT.H** defines values relating to floating point operations. Many of these are rather specialized, but you may have need of:

FLT_MIN	Minimum value of type **float**
FLT_MAX	Maximum value of type **float**
DBL_MIN	Minimum value of type **double**
DBL_MAX	Maximum value of type **double**

By using these definitions for limits rather than explicit numeric values, your values will be trapped if they fall outside the limits specified by the machine and compiler in use.

Variations in Word Sizes

Variations in word sizes are responsible for the variations in the ranges of values that the various types in C can deal with. They also affect memory addressing. A variable of type **int** must be at least two bytes, but it can be more, so if you want to maximize portability, you mustn't write programs that make any assumptions about how much memory your variables occupy. This means always using the operator **sizeof** when you need to know how much memory a particular object in your program requires.

You can use **typedef** to give yourself some flexibility when you expect to be moving your program between different computers. You can redefine the basic types in C with statements at global scope such as:

```
typedef int INT;
typedef unsigned int UINT;
typedef long LONG;
typedef unsigned long ULONG;
...
```

and then write your program in terms of your own type definitions. If you are then constrained by a specific machine environment, you have the possibility to change the definition of a type on a global basis. This technique is usually used to choose between the integer types available in a particular environment, but it can also be used for floating point types.

The size of a pointer shouldn't normally create problems, but there is a potential problem associated with taking the difference between two pointers. The difference is usually of type **int**, but on some machines which allow you to create very large arrays or structures it can be **long**. You can avoid such complications by using a variable of type **ptrdiff_t** to store the difference between two pointers. This type is defined in the standard header file **STDDEF.H**, and will automatically accommodate whatever result you get in any machine environment.

Storage Alignment

We saw in our discussion on structures that some processors require variables to be stored at an address that is a multiple of their size, and that this can cause a structure to occupy more memory than the minimum necessary to hold the members of the structure. This alignment is primarily needed so that data can be moved efficiently between the main memory of a machine and the processor registers, and is usually determined by the width of the data bus. The following diagram shows how the same structure can occupy a different amount of memory as a result of a different boundary alignment for variables:

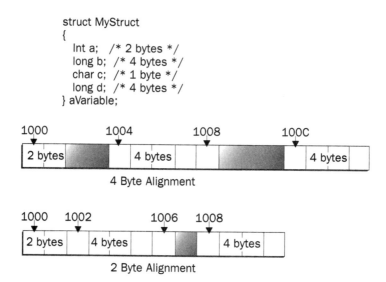

```
struct MyStruct
{
    Int a;   /* 2 bytes */
    long b;  /* 4 bytes */
    char c;  /* 1 byte */
    long d;  /* 4 bytes */
} aVariable;
```

This demonstrates quite clearly why you must always use the **sizeof** operator to determine how much memory is required for a particular object

- not only can the memory for a structure be greater than the sum of the memory required for its individual members, but it can also vary from one machine to another.

Avoiding System Environment Dependencies

The operating system environment can create barriers to portability, and although these can be serious in some environments, if you must write code for these you will just have to live with it. Microsoft Windows, for example, assumes control of all communications with the user, and this has a profound effect on program structure as well as code for handling the user interface. In such cases, it's virtually impossible to avoid built-in barriers to portability, and the best you can do is to try to isolate some parts of your code in order to allow their reuse in a different context. However, in other contexts there are a couple of things which can cause problems but which are avoidable.

UNIX low-level file input and output functions are often used with C, largely on the grounds of efficiency, but if you want your program to be portable you'll need to avoid these, because they're not available on non-UNIX systems, and often vary between versions of UNIX from different suppliers. You should be able to do what you want with files using the standard library functions for file I/O.

Another avoidable dependency is the third parameter to **main()** for passing details of environment variables. This isn't part of the C standard and isn't supported on some systems, so if you must have portability, avoid this. It's usually supported under UNIX, and some compilers also support it for IBM compatible PCs.

Linker Problems

Although it may not be immediately obvious, the linker for object modules generated by a C compiler can seriously restrict some aspects of your source programs. We've already seen that the linker may restrict external names to six characters, and in addition, some other linkers are unable to differentiate between upper- and lower- case text. This means that if your program must be portable to such environments, then you can't rely solely on differences in case to differentiate your external identifiers. You must differentiate them by ensuring that each is composed of a unique sequence of characters.

This effectively removes case sensitivity so far as external identifiers are concerned. While this is often stated as a requirement for portable C, it tends to undermine the fact that C provides case sensitivity. For this reason, it's best to ignore it unless there is a clear need to port to a machine with such an unfortunate disability.

Easing Program Maintenance

The need for program maintenance arises either because a bug in the program needs to be fixed, or because an extension to the program is required. In either case, being able to readily understand the logic and structure of the program is essential for effective and efficient program maintenance. This will be determined by how well the program is documented, and by how clearly written and well structured the program is. It also depends on whether the program has been modified previously, and how well that was done.

Good documentation, and a well-structured program become particularly important when the person undertaking the program maintenance isn't the original author of the program. Items that contribute to making program maintenance a predictable activity come under the heading of programming standards in professional programming circles. This is a large topic for which you will find a number of excellent books available, so here we'll be looking at just a few of the elementary considerations.

Programming Style

A good clear programming style is fundamental to making program maintenance easy, and it also helps you to write good code by enforcing a discipline. There's a lot of debate about which style of code presentation is the best, but if you adopt a clear style, and apply it consistently, you can't go far wrong. Perhaps the aspect of C-programming style which has the most immediate impact is how the code is indented, providing visual cues to the logic of a program. There are three primary approaches to this that we can illustrate with a fragment of code from an example in Chapter 8:

● Aligned braces and indented text

```
if(nRec>0)
{                                       /* If we have some records written */
    pFile=fopen(MyFile, "rb");          /*    open the file.               */
    for(i=0; i<nRec ; i++)
    {
        /* Check against primes on file first */
        fread(Buffer, sizeof(long), MEM_PRIMES, pFile);
        if((k=Check(Buffer, MEM_PRIMES, N))>=0) /* Check primes in Buffer */
        {
            fclose(pFile);              /* For zero or +ive return, close the */
            return k;                   /* file and return the value k        */
        }
    }
    fclose(pFile);
}
```

● Indented and aligned braces and text

```
if(nRec>0)
 {                                      /* If we have some records written */
   pFile=fopen(MyFile, "rb");           /*    open the file.               */
   for(i=0; i<nRec ; i++)
    {
        /* Check against primes on file first */
        fread(Buffer, sizeof(long), MEM_PRIMES, pFile);
        if((k=Check(Buffer, MEM_PRIMES, N))>=0) /* Check primes in Buffer */
         {
            fclose(pFile);              /* For zero or +ive return, close the */
            return k;                   /* file and return the value k        */
         }
    }
   fclose(pFile);
 }
```

● Non-aligned braces with indented text

```
if(nRec>0)
 {                                      /* If we have some records written */
   pFile=fopen(MyFile, "rb");           /*    open the file.               */
   for(i=0; i<nRec ; i++)
    {
        /* Check against primes on file first */
        fread(Buffer, sizeof(long), MEM_PRIMES, pFile);
        if((k=Check(Buffer, MEM_PRIMES, N))>=0) {/* Check primes in Buffer*/
         {
            fclose(pFile);              /* For zero or +ive return, close  */
            return k;                   /* the file and return the value k */
         }
    }
   fclose(pFile);
 }
```

All of these are in common use and which you prefer is purely a matter of taste. The third version is the most compact, but the first version is perhaps the best because the block structure seems easier to see, and there appears to be less chance of accidentally omitting a brace somewhere. The most important consideration is that you choose one style and stick to it throughout your programs.

Program Documentation

You should create program documentation as part of the process of developing a program. There are two distinct and complementary styles of documenting your program, and you must get into the habit of using *both*.

Commenting

This can be a difficult discipline to get into, but the very least you should do is ensure that your program is comprehensively explained with comments once it seems to be working. This needs to be done at two levels. You need to document statements within each function as to their meaning, intended use, and operation, and you also need to provide comments at the beginning of every function that explain its use, the significance of the parameters, and any other important features of its operation. You should also standardize the appearance of the comments at a function level as far as you can.

Let's look at a typical approach to documenting a function:

```
/*************************************************************************
 * Function to check for division by an array of primes                  *
 * Returns 1 if a prime found, zero if not a prime, -1 for more checks    *
 *                                                                        *
 *    pBuffer: a pointer to an array containing primes to be used as      *
 *             divisors                                                   *
 *    Count  : the number of primes in the array                         *
 *    N      : the value to be tested for primeness                       *
 *                                                                        *
 * The function will continue to try division by primes up to the        *
 * square root of N. If none of the primes in the array divide into N     *
 * exactly, and they are all less that the square root of N, -1 is        *
 * returned. If an exact division is found, 0 is returned. If no exact    *
 * division occurs with primes up to the square root of N, then 0 is      *
 * returned to indicate N is prime.                                       *
 *************************************************************************/
```

```
int Check( unsigned long *pBuffer, int Count, unsigned long N )
{
    unsigned long *pEnd=&pBuffer[Count-1];     /* Pointer to end of array */
    unsigned long RootN=0UL;                   /* Store for root of N     */

    RootN=( unsigned long)(1.0+sqrt((double)N));          /* Upper limit for
                                                                  checking */

    while(pBuffer++!=pEnd)
    {
        if(N%(*(pBuffer))==0UL)                /* Check for exact division */
            return 0;                          /* If so not a prime...     */

        if(*pBuffer>RootN)    /* Check whether divisor exceeds square root*/
            return 1;         /* if so it must be a prime                 */
    }
    return -1;                                 /* More checks necessary... */
}
```

As with the indenting of statements, the precise form of comments in your program is relatively unimportant, as long as they're clear and consistent. A uniform and easily understood presentation is the objective. Within the comments documenting each function, you should at least explain the purpose, the return value, and each of the specified arguments.

External Documents

For a program of any size beyond the trivial, you can't assume that the program is self-documenting, no matter how good the comments are. You need to have external documentation providing an overview of the program structure, the functions that go to make up the program, special techniques used in the program, working descriptions of the functions in the program, external libraries used, and so on. Generally, the amount of additional program documentation that is necessary, increases at least in proportion to the size of the program.

Program Structure

A program with a well thought out structure, organized into sensibly-sized file units, is very much easier to maintain than one that isn't. There are two sides to structuring a program: the segmentation of the code into functions, and the packaging of the program into files. There are some rough guides to sizing that you can apply here.

355

Splitting Functions

Functions in C should be small units of code with a well-defined purpose. If you find that you're writing functions with more that 40 to 50 lines of code, then in most instances you should be able to subdivide them into smaller and simpler units. Of course, there are no absolutes here, and there is always the exception to the rule. You can typically identify three kinds of functions used in your programs:

- Standard library functions
- General purpose functions that you use in multiple applications
- Application-specific functions

Creating your Own Libraries

General purpose functions can conveniently be packaged in separate files incorporating all the definitions required by those functions. They become essentially your own extensions to the standard library.

Protecting Program and Header Files

We saw how to use **pre-processor directives** to protect against duplication of functions or definitions in a program, and it's generally good practice always to protect program and header files in this way, even when it may not be necessary in a particular application context. You need to keep your program and header files within size limits that you find comfortable to work with, and usually the functions that make up your program will fall into suitable groups. Most people are happy working with files containing up to four or five hundred lines of code, but naturally they can be much smaller, or even larger, if the structure of the application dictates.

Segmenting Files

A good segmentation of a program into files will give you several advantages. In most environments, you only need to recompile those files that you've altered at any point, which can save a lot of compilation time when you're developing a large program. Editing a file of a modest size is

relatively easy, since you can keep in mind what it contains, and maintain a
feel for where various functions appear in the file. If the files represented
fairly self-contained groups of functions, you will minimize the need for
fiddling with two or more files when making changes to the program.

Defensive Programming

As we have gone through the various aspects of the language, we've seen a
number of things that provide some protection against errors, or enable you
to detect errors more easily. None of these things are essential to a program,
but by adopting such approaches you make your programs more secure,
easier to follow, and less prone to errors. This has to be good medicine,
since programming is still an inexact science, and we need all the help we
can get. All of the things we are talking about here could be grouped under
defensive programming. Let's review some of the most significant techniques.

Initializing Variables

You should initialize variables in their declarations wherever practicable. If
the majority of your variables have known values from the beginning, it
becomes less likely that you'll inadvertently use a variable that hasn't been
properly set. You should choose the values judiciously - scattering zeros
around is fine in general, but you can often choose an initial value that will
throw up an error if something doesn't get set properly. You should do this
whenever you can.

Naming Conventions

You should choose meaningful names for variables rather than using single
characters. Single character names can be tempting because they minimize
the amount of keying needed to enter your program. However, it's likely
that in most cases, two days hence you won't remember what they are.
There are some exceptions in specific contexts.

One exception perhaps is **for** loop counters, where variables such as **i**, **j**,
or **k** are frequently used. Another is for some parameters to mathematical
or geometric functions, where **x** is commonly used to represent an
independent variable, and **x** and **y** are normally understood to be point co-
ordinates. Where there is any possibility that a variable name might not be
clear, you should choose a suitable identifier to make it obvious what is
meant.

Adopting a convention for naming some types of variables can make your programs much more readily understood. You don't need to go as far as the full Hungarian notation but adopting a few conventions, such as beginning pointers with **p** and capitalizing identifiers specified in a **#define** directive, can be a tremendous help. As we saw when we first looked at variables, you shouldn't use names that begin with an underscore, and you should avoid names beginning with two underscores, just be on the safe side. This will avoid confusion with internal names defined in the standard header files.

Applying Constants

Constants should be constants. Where you define a constant such as:

```
char *pStr="Only the mediocre are always at their best";
```

there is nothing to prevent you changing the initializing string. However, the string is a constant and shouldn't be modified. By using the **const** modifier, you can make the string more secure:

```
const char *pStr="Only the mediocre are always at their best";
```

Your compiler now knows that the string pointed to by **pStr** is a constant. Your compiler will therefore give you an error message if you make any direct attempt to alter the string. The pointer has been defined as a pointer to a constant string, so although you're free to change the pointer to contain another address, it can't be used to alter the object it points to. Of course, this doesn't prevent you circumventing this in a variety of sneaky ways, but at least one wall is in place to protect the constant string. Don't forget that you can declare any kind of variable as const, so the opportunities to reduce errors in your program are legion.

Magic Numbers

You should avoid using 'magic numbers' in your program. A magic number is a number that appears out of thin air without any obvious indication of what it is, where it came from or what it represents. For example, in the code fragment:

```
for(i=0 ; i<50 : i++)
   sum+=a[i];
```

the value 50 controlling the loop is a magic number. Where did it come from? Presumably it represents the size of the array, in which case it should have been declared as:

```
#define ARRAYSIZE 50
...
double a[ARRAYSIZE];
```

and the loop should then be written as:

```
for(i=0 ; i< ARRAYSIZE: i++)
    sum+=a[i];
```

Now we know what is controlling the loop. As well as making the program easier to understand - this technique also gives you the flexibility to make global changes to array sizes, and have all the program code adjust automatically.

Parentheses in Expressions

If you know the precedence of all the operators in C then you'll know precisely where parentheses are necessary, and where they aren't. If you are at all in doubt, put the parentheses in, and you will always be correct.

One area where it's as well to use parentheses habitually is with expressions involving bitwise operators. This is for two reasons: firstly, because they're used relatively infrequently, and secondly, because they're a little weird and sometimes counter-intuitive, and therefore hard to remember. We can show this with a couple of examples. If you have an **if** statement such as:

```
if(a+b!=0)
    /* Do something */
```

it means what you expect it to mean. First, **a+b** is calculated, and if the result isn't equal to zero then the **if** condition is True. Contrast this with the statement:

```
if(a&b!=c)
    /* Do something */
```

Because the precedence of **&** (and the other bitwise operators) is lower than the operator **!=**, the expression **b!=0** is evaluated first, and the result is combined with **a** using the bitwise AND operator. Thus, to get them to work as you would typically want them to, bitwise expressions need to be parenthesized when appearing in a test expression. We can write:

```
if((a&b)!=0)
    /* Do something */
```

Now we'll AND **a** and **b** together, and then test whether the result is zero.

Pointers

Using pointers containing invalid addresses is likely to be a major contributor to bugs in your programs. Of course, initializing pointers to **NULL** when you declare them is an important defense mechanism, but you should also try to ensure that whenever the address contained in a pointer becomes invalid, then it's reset to **NULL**. This occurs most frequently when freeing memory you have allocated on the heap, and you can relieve yourself of the burden of having to remember to reset a pointer to **NULL** whenever you free some memory on the heap, by defining a macro as follows:

```
#define FREE(ptr) (free(ptr), ptr=NULL)
```

If you now use the macro **FREE()** instead of the function **free()**, you will automatically reset the pointer to **NULL** on each call. Of course, you still need to deal with other pointers that you may have set to the same address.

Pointers passed as arguments to a function are always a risk, because they provide a license to alter variables in the calling program. Where the intention is to provide access on a read only basis, you should use the **const** modifier in the function parameter definition. For example, a function to count the characters in a string could have the prototype:

```
int CountChars(const char *pStr);
```

This will ensure that there's no inadvertent alteration of the location pointed to by the passed pointer argument.

Using Functions

When implementing a function, it's a good idea to check that any argument passed to it falls within the range you're expecting. If a pointer is passed, check that it isn't **NULL**, and if a parameter is a person's height in inches, values less than 10 or greater than 100 are likely to be erroneous.

You should also take care to check the status return after calling a function, since error conditions are indicated this way. It's all too easy to assume that everything is correct, when in many circumstances, it won't be. This is particularly true of dynamic memory allocation, and operations on files.

Writing Macros

The most important thing to remember about macros is that they aren't functions. They're just a recipe for a blind substitution. There's no checking whatsoever by the pre-processor on the effect or the appropriateness of the substitutions made when a macro is used. You should always put parentheses around the parameters in the macro definition as well as the entire substitution string, to protect against errors caused by operator precedence. For example:

```
#define CUBE(x) ((x)*(x)*(x))
```

This ensures that statements such as:

```
Result = CUBE(iVal+jVal);
```

produce the answer you are looking for. You might think parentheses around the appearances of the parameter in the substitution string would be sufficient, but if you omit the parentheses around the whole thing, then the statement:

```
Result = Value/CUBE(iVal+jVal);
```

wouldn't produce the correct answer.

Diagnostics

Use the **assert()** macro liberally. It doesn't cost anything other than the time it takes to key in the statements - plus the time to get the typos out. You should also develop your own favorite message and fix up mechanism that you can switch on and off, which we discussed in the last chapter. In the early days of developing a new program, just having checks for such things as the array indexes being within bounds can save immense amounts of time. They will slow up your program, but as soon as you're reasonably sure that you're free of that particular kind of problem, you can switch them off.

You can leave statements using **assert()**, or other diagnostics controlled by identifiers appearing in **#define** directives, in your program permanently. They can be switched off for production versions of the code, and switched on when the need to make changes to the program arises. Naturally, you will need to document your own mechanism for diagnostics when you include them in a program. Otherwise, you will be working out what they all are once more, 6 months or a year later.

We have frequently omitted excessive error checking in examples in this book, due to pressures of space, and to avoid the examples involving more code than reasonably necessary to demonstrate the topic up for discussion. Practically, you should never do so. Always check error returns from all standard library functions that provide them. Errors crop up when you least expect them, and without the error checking in place, you'll waste an inordinate amount of time trying to find them.

Summary

To avoid unnecessary constraints to moving your programs between different machines, you need to adopt a few simple rules for code development:

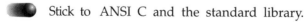 Stick to ANSI C and the standard library.

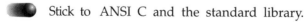 Use symbols defined in the standard library rather than explicit constants.

- Use the types defined in the standard library where necessary. These include **size_t** for values returned by the operator **sizeof**, **fpos_t** for positions in a file returned by the standard library function **fgetpos()**, and **ptrdiff_t** for the difference between two pointers.

- Avoid programming techniques that depend upon specific codes for characters.

- Assume only the minimum ranges of values for variable types.

- Always use the operator **sizeof** to obtain the memory space occupied by a variable.

You can make your programs easier to maintain and debug by adopting a clear and consistent programming style, and including comprehensive comments. By making sure that your program and header files are well structured and consistent, as well as including diagnostic code in your source, you will make tracing problems a lot easier, and the job of extending a program a simpler and thankfully more predictable task.

Chapter

Developing a Program in C

In this chapter we will write a program that is considerably larger than any of the other examples in this book, giving us an opportunity to see how some of the language features and techniques we have discussed, can be applied in a practical context.

The example has been chosen with several considerations in mind. First, it is compact enough to be worked through in a single chapter. This inevitably means some simplifying assumptions, but this in itself will provide a base for you to exercise your skills further in elaborating the example. Second, it needs to combine a reasonable spectrum of C capability, including file operations, and the way it has been implemented here is aimed at that. Third, it should be a simple application that doesn't involve a lot of technicality or complicated mathematics.

One application which fits these criteria is creating and maintaining a personal address file. I hope you enjoy it.

Defining the Problem

The starting point for any programming task lies in deciding what it is you are trying to do. Our program will provide a file containing basic information on acquaintances, friends, or even enemies. We will provide for the name, the address, and the telephone number of each individual, but the initial implementation of the program shouldn't inhibit expansion to include other details in the future.

The operations that the program will support are:

- Adding a record for a person.
- Deleting a record for a person.
- Listing the complete contents of the file in ascending alphabetical order, using the surname as the sort field.
- Searching the file for a particular entry.

This is a very simple application that is easy to understand, but as we shall see, it isn't completely trivial.

Structuring the Program

Even though the program is quite modest, it would be easier to manage as several files. We will need a standard header file into which we can put all the standard definitions. This will contain all the definitions specific to the program as well as the **include** files for the standard library functions that are used. Of course, this file would need to be included at the beginning of each of the source files that go to make up the program.

This will still leave quite a large source file which at this point doesn't seem to fall into particularly obvious functional groups, but it would be easier to manage if it were divided up in some way. One approach would be to group the lower-level service functions into one source file, and leave **main()** and the functions it calls directly, together in another.

However the source code is to be divided up, you need to remember to put an **include** statement for the program header at the beginning of each of the source files. You will also need to put **extern** declarations for any global variables that are used but not defined in a source file, as you can have only one definition for such a variable. If global variables are defined in the source file containing **main()**, which is the typical approach, then the source file containing the secondary functions will need to have an **extern** statement for each global variable that is used.

Managing the Application Data

We should decide from the outset that we will have a fixed-size data record. This will simplify operations with the file, and having a fixed record size, we will be able to program read and write operations on the file so that they won't need changing if the record size is subsequently altered.

The Name Structure

The name of a person can be tricky in a number of ways. We will assume that a person's name is split into two parts, a surname and a first name, and both of these will be alphabetic - this means no hyphenated names for instance. This isn't as flexible as you might like but if we package the name in a structure, it should be no problem to expand it later. We can define the structure as a type, as follows:

```
typedef struct name            /* Name structure type definition */
{
   char FirstName[NAMELEN];
   char Surname[NAMELEN];
}Name;
```

Since it's defined using **typedef**, we can declare objects of type **Name** without having to use the **struct** keyword. The length of each of the members of type **Name** are flexible, and assume this definition is preceded by a definition of the array length, such as:

```
#define NAMELEN    20          /* Maximum name length */
```

The **name** structure can easily be expanded later if you want. In order not to make the program overly long, we will limit ourselves to comparing surnames for sequencing file records, but you could easily extend this by providing a special function for comparing full names.

The Person Structure

We can define the structure to contain the complete data record on an individual, and we'll need to decide how we are going to relate these records. Since we want to search the 'person' file, a valid solution would be to maintain this file as an ordered linked list. We can also include backward pointers to allow for future operations, but we'll only use forward processing of the list from the beginning in our first attempt. We can define a record as:

```
typedef struct person          /* Person structure type definition */
{
   Name aName;                             /* Name structure */
   char Address[ADDRLINES][ADDRLEN];   /* Address up to five lines */
   char Phone[PHONELEN];                  /* Phone number as string */
   long Next;                   /* File position for next person */
   long Previous;               /* File position for previous person */
   int Deleted;                 /* Deleted record = 1, 0 otherwise */
}Person;
```

As with the case of the previous structure, we've used **typedef**, so we can use the type **Person** without the keyword **struct**. The members **Previous** and **Next** store the file pointers for the preceding and following records in the file. The **Deleted** member is a flag that will be set to 1 when a record is to be deleted. This will allow us to detect and overwrite deleted records when new ones are added, enabling us to use up unoccupied holes in the file, and avoid the need to clean it up or compress it.

The **Address[]** member is a two-dimensional array, where the dimensions will be defined by directives such as:

```
#define ADDRLINES  5      /* Maximum number of address lines */
#define ADDRLEN    40     /* Maximum address line length */
```

These would provide for 5 address lines, with up to 40 characters each.

The members the program will interact with are the **Name** member, the
Previous and **Next** members, and the **Deleted** flag. You could add other
members without affecting the program very much. The **Address[]** member
is just baggage.

The Person File

Each read or write operation on the file will transfer one **Person** object.
Since these objects will be linked in alphabetical name order using file
position pointers, we will process the file randomly. A typical structure for
the file is illustrated here:

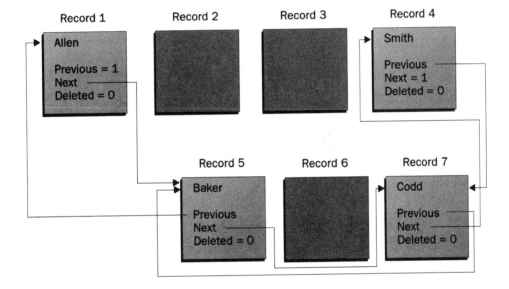

This shows a file containing seven records. The first record will always be
the first in the alphabetical sequence, but the following records can be
located anywhere. A record will be written in the next available space,
except when it's the first in sequence, in which case we will arrange to
move the previous first record to a vacant location somewhere else in the
file.

The **Next** member always points to the next record in sequence, or has the value -1 if there isn't a next record. We will define each pointer relative to the beginning of the file, so valid pointers are always greater than or equal to zero. The **Previous** member similarly points to the previous record, and the first record will have its **Previous** member set to -1.

Deleted records have the **Deleted** flag set to 1, while for a normal valid record the **Deleted** flag will be zero. The deleted records 2, 3, and 6 are shown greyed out in the diagram.

General Program Logic

We've defined a range of possible operations to be supported by the program. An easy way of implementing this is to provide a menu, like the one below, which prompts the user to enter a letter in order to select an option:

Enter a character to select an option:

```
        A    Add a person to the file
        D    Delete a person from the file
        L    List the file contents
        S    Search for data for a person
        Q    Quit - end the program
```

With the Quit option as part of the menu of choices, we can drive the program in an infinite loop from **main()**, with the character entered selecting a particular function to be called. A **switch** statement will do this very nicely. We could write the function **main()** incorporating this approach immediately:

```
int main(void)
{
  char *ch="Q";                /* Choice indicator */
  for(;;)
  {
      printf("\nEnter a character to select an option:\n"
             "\n\tA  Add a person to the file"
             "\n\tD  Delete a person from the file"
             "\n\tL  List the file contents"
             "\n\tS  Search for data for a person"
```

```
                "\n\tQ   Quit - end the program\n\n");

    scanf("%1s",ch);
    switch(*ch)
    {
        case 'A':case 'a':   /* Add a new person to the file */
            AddPerson();
            break;

        case 'D':case 'd':   /* Delete a new person from  the file */
            DeletePerson();
            break;

        case 'L':case 'l':   /* List the file */
            ListFile();
            break;

        case 'S':case 's':   /* Search for a person in the file */
            Search();
            break;

        case 'Q':case 'q':   /* Quit the application */
            return 0;

        default:
            printf("\nInvalid input - try again.");
    }
  }
}
```

This barely needs explaining. The input here uses **scanf()** with the format specifier **%1s** which will read the first non-blank character into 'ch'. Note that **ch** will point to a string of length 2. We could use **%c**, but this would rely on no blanks being entered before the character defining the selection from the range of options. Each option will work when either an upper or lower case letter is entered. The default case in the **switch** is there to catch incorrect entries. The function **main()** will cycle indefinitely until 'Q' or 'q' is entered to end the program, so that you can iterate round trying all sorts of combinations and sequences.

Each operation supported by the program is packaged into a separate function. To extend the program to support additional functionality, we just require additional options in the menu, correspondingly reflected by **case**s in the **switch** statement. To complete this version of the program all we need to do is add four functions, **AddPerson()**, **DeletePerson()**, **Search()**, and **ListFile()**.

Adding a Person to the File

We have no menu option to create a file, so the operation to add a person will need to create a file if it doesn't exist. We can specify the file name to be used in a global variable at the beginning of the source code, which will allow the file name to be changed by altering the initial value for the global variable. We would need a statement such as:

```
char *pFPersons="PERSONS";    /* Name for physical person file */
```

This defines the file name as **PERSONS**. If you are going to compile and run this example, you may want to change this to reflect the needs of your environment, perhaps with a full path specification.

We can see from the code for the function **main()** that the function **AddPerson()** is completely self-contained. It receives no arguments and returns nothing so its prototype is going to be:

```
void AddPerson(void);         /* Add a person to the file */
```

We should consider what the basic logic for adding a new person to the file is going to be. First of all, we must read in the data for a person and create a **Person** structure, and we could assume that we'll do this in a function **ReadPerson()**. We have a choice here: we could create the **Person** object dynamically and return a pointer to it, or we could have the calling program pass a pointer to an object and have the function fill in the data members with input values. In the interests of using the library function **malloc()**, let's go for the first option. We will need to remember that the calling program will need to release the memory for the **Person** object when it's no longer required. The prototype for **ReadPerson()** will be:

```
Person *ReadPerson(void);     /* Get input for a new person */
```

Having read the data and created a **Person** object, we'll need to open the file if it exists. If it doesn't exist, then we want to create it, so we need to open it in the first instance with a mode that will do this for us, either 'append' mode or 'write' mode. Once we have established whether the file exists, there are basically two possible courses of action, depending on the state of the file. We can write the record directly if the file is empty, but if it contains information, we will need to go into a record insert operation, which is likely to be a little complicated.

The general logic for the function **AddPerson()** is shown here:

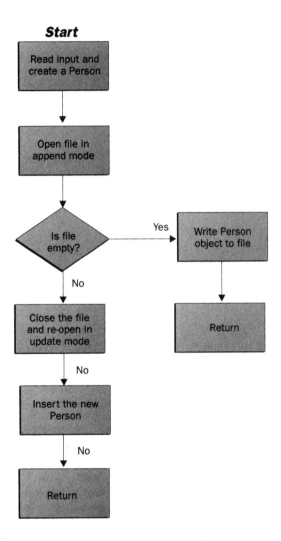

The first action is to call the function **ReadPerson()**, and the file is then opened in append mode, so that if it doesn't exist, then it will be created anyway. The choice of append mode rather than write mode is determined on the basis that write mode would allow the file to be overwritten, whereas append mode only allows the file to be added to, even if the mode **ab+** is specified.

If the file is empty then we need to write the **Person** object to the file, and since all our write operations will be identical, it would be a good idea to introduce a function to do this, which we will call **WriteFile()**. Then we can encapsulate error checking into the function, so we won't have to repeat it every time we write a record.

If the file isn't empty, we will insert the **Person** object at the appropriate point which will need another function we can call **Insert()**. We've now added two further functions to our program and can write their prototypes as:

```
void WriteFile(Person *pPerson);    /* Write a record to the file */
void Insert(Person *pPerson);       /* Insert a person in the file */
```

The function **WriteFile()** receives a pointer to the **Person** object to be written, and it will assume that the file is open and positioned at the place where the record is to be written. It has no return value. We will check for a write error in the function, but all we will do if it occurs, is to report it and bale out of the program.

Similarly, unless there is a catastrophic problem, like running out of disk capacity, we should always be able to insert a new record into the file, so the **Insert()** function has no return value. It has one argument which is a pointer to the **Person** object to be inserted. It will need to sort out where to write the record in the file and to make all the necessary connections to other records.

The Code for AddPerson()

Given these functions, we can put together the code for the function **AddPerson()**:

```
/**************************************************************************
 * Function to add a person to file.                                     *
 * A Person is read from stdin and inserted in the file in ascending     *
 * alphabetic sequence. If the file does not exist it will be created.   *
 **************************************************************************/

void AddPerson(void)
{
    Person *pPerson=NULL;      /* Pointer to a new Person object */
    long fPos=-1;              /* File position indicator */
```

```
    char *ch="n";                  /* Choice indicator on input */
    for(;;)
    {
       pPerson=ReadPerson();   /* Read input and construct a Person */
       if(pPerson==NULL)          /* NULL pointer means failure */
          return;
       if(!IsFile)                /* Check the global flag for no file */
       {                          /* Flag is not set so check for file */
          pFile=fopen(pFPersons,"ab+");/* Open to append, or create file*/
          if(pFile==NULL)
          {                       /* Cannot open file, so end */
             printf("\nUnable to open Persons file. Program ended.");
             exit(1);
          }
          IsFile=1;                      /* File is open so set flag */
          fseek(pFile, 0L, SEEK_END);    /* Make sure we are at the end */
          fPos=ftell(pFile);        /* Get the offset from file start */
          if(fPos==0L)             /* If it is 0, file is empty */
             WriteFile(pPerson); /* so write object */
          else
          {                                /* File is not empty */
             fclose(pFile);                /* So close it and */
             pFile=fopen(pFPersons,"rb+");  /* reopen it for update */
             if(pFile==NULL)
             {                          /* If we are here, open failed */
                printf("\nUnable to open Persons file. Program ended.");
                exit(1);
             }
             Insert(pPerson);        /* File is open so insert person */
          }
       }
       else
       {                          /* Flag is set so the file exists */
          pFile=fopen(pFPersons,"rb+");  /* Open it for update */
          if(pFile==NULL)
          {                              /* Open failed so drop out */
             printf("\nUnable to open Persons file. Program ended.");
             exit(1);
          }
          Insert(pPerson);        /* Insert the new Person object */
       }

       FREE(pPerson);             /* Write is done so release memory */
       fclose(pFile);             /* and close the file */

       printf("\nDo you want to add another person(y or n)? ");
       scanf("%1s",ch);
       if((*ch=='n')||(*ch=='N'))     /* Want to add another? */
          return;                      /* No, so return */
    }
}
```

375

The function implementation assumes a global variable **IsFile** which is set to 1 once it's established that the file exists. This will avoid checking for the file's existence every time we add a new **Person** record. The logic for checking **IsFile** wasn't shown in the general logic since it's not an essential element in the operation, just an added convenience.

The first time through the function the flag **IsFile** will be at its initial value 0, so we will check for the existence of the file by opening it in append mode:

```
pFile=fopen(pFPersons,"ab+");/* Open to append, or create file*/
```

Since this will either open the file or create it, **IsFile** is set to 1 and will remain so for as long as the program is running. Thus all subsequent add operations won't bother to check for the existence of the file.

Each attempt to open the file is verified by checking for a valid pointer returned from **fopen()**. It's most important to check that the open operation works because there are so many ways programming errors can cause failure, and trying to use an invalid pointer will surely crash the program.

The **AddPerson()** function is one big infinite **for** loop. This will allow you to add multiple records to the file without going back to the menu. Having to enter a new selection for each addition to the file can be a little bit tedious, especially when you're initially setting up the file.

When the record has been written, the heap memory is released, and the file is closed. To free the heap memory we use a macro **FREE()** which is defined as:

```
#define FREE(p)          (free(p),p=NULL)
```

By using this macro, we ensure that the pointer to the memory area is always set to **NULL** when the associated memory is deleted. This is a good safety precaution and will prevent us from accidentally accessing heap memory that has been freed, and may be allocated to something else.

After releasing the memory, there's then a local choice for the user as to whether another add operation is required. If not the program returns to the main menu in the function **main()**.

Creating a Person

The code for the function **ReadPerson()** is:

```
/*****************************************************************
 * Function to read in a person's details.                      *
 * A pointer to a Person structure on the heap is returned.     *
 *****************************************************************/
Person *ReadPerson(void)
{
    Person *pPerson=NULL;          /* Pointer to a Person object */
    char *ch="n";                  /* Choice indicator */
    int i=0;                       /* Loop counter */

    /* Get memory for a Person object */
    pPerson=(Person *)malloc(sizeof(Person));
    if(pPerson==NULL)
    {
        printf("\nMemory allocation failure. Program aborted.");
        exit(1);
    }

    /* Read the name of the person */
    while(!GetName(&pPerson->aName))
    {
        printf("\nInvalid name entered, do you want to try again?");
        scanf("%1s",ch);
        if(*ch=='n'||*ch=='N')
        {
            FREE(pPerson);          /* Release heap memory */
            return NULL;
        }
    }

    /* Read the address of the person */
    printf("\nEnter the address up to %d lines of %d characters.\n"
           "Enter an empty line after the last line"
           " if there are less than %d lines.\n",
           ADDRLINES, ADDRLEN, ADDRLINES);
    for(i=0;i<ADDRLINES;i++)
    {
```

```
        gets(pPerson->Address[i]);
        if(strlen(pPerson->Address[i])==0)  /* Empty line ends input */
           break;
     }
     printf("\nEnter the phone number for %s\n",pPerson->aName.FirstName);
     gets(pPerson->Phone);
     pPerson->Next=-1L;       /* Set file pointer to next and previous */
     pPerson->Previous=-1L;   /* person record to invalid values */
     pPerson->Deleted=0;      /* Set deleted flag for valid record */
     return pPerson;
  }
```

After using the standard library function **malloc()** to store a new **Person**
object in memory, the function **GetName()** is called to read the data into the
Name member of the **Person** object. The **GetName()** function will have the
prototype:

```
int GetName(Name *pName);          /* Read a name for a person */
```

The function will return 1 if a valid **Name** object has been created, or 0 if
otherwise. Having the **Name** object read by a separate function allows you to
make the name handling more sophisticated without affecting the rest of the
program.

Once the **ReadPerson()** function has obtained a valid **Name** object, up to
ADDRLINES address lines are read into the member **Address[]**. An empty
line being entered will terminate the process. Lastly the phone number is
read as a character string without checking, because, since all we do is
display it, we don't need to worry about its validity.

Reading a Name

The code for the function to read in the data for a **Name** object is:

```
/***************************************************************
 * Function to read in a name                                  *
 * Argument is a pointer to an array of length NAMELEN         *
 * 0 is returned if the surname contains an non-alphabetic     *
 *   character. The first name can be empty, and is set to     *
 *   empty if an non-alphabetic character is entered.          *
 * 1 is returned if a valid name is obtained.                  *
 ***************************************************************/
int GetName(Name *pName)
{
   printf("\nEnter a surname:");
   fflush(stdin);
```

```
    gets( pName->Surname);
    if(CheckName(pName->Surname)==0)    /* Check for invalid surname */
        return 0;                       /* If so abandon Name input */

    printf("\nEnter a first name:");
    gets(pName->FirstName);

    if(CheckName(pName->FirstName)==0) /* Check for invalid first name */
    {
        *pName->FirstName='\0';         /* Is so set to empty */
        return 1;
    }
}
```

This is quite straightforward. The only checking done is to ensure that the names are alphabetic, since spurious characters could upset the compare operations we will be carrying out later. The checking is done by the function **CheckName()** with code as follows:

```
/**********************************************
 * Function to verify a name is alphabetic *
 * Argument is a nul terminated name        *
 *   1 return indicates name is alphabetic  *
 *   0 return indicates it is not alphabetic*
 **********************************************/
int CheckName(char *pName)
{
    while((*pName)!='\0')
        if(!isalpha(*pName++))
            return 0;
    return 1;
}
```

This function simply checks that each character of a string passed to it is alphabetic. The check is made using the standard library function **isalpha()** declared in the header file **CTYPE.H**. If the name is valid, 1 is returned, 0 is returned if otherwise. This function could be expanded to accommodate hyphens, or allow names with embedded blanks such as Mary Lou Creighton-Featherstone, for example. The code to compare names we will get to later, but it would need to deal with whatever extended name was allowed if you modify the **CheckName()** function here.

Writing a Record

The code for the function **WriteFile()** to write a **Person** object to the file is as follows:

```
/*********************************************************
 * Function to write a record to the file               *
 * Argument is:                                         *
 *    pPerson: A pointer to the object to be written    *
 * The function assumes the file is open for update     *
 * and writes the object at the current position.       *
 *********************************************************/

void WriteFile(Person *pPerson)
{
   if(!fwrite(pPerson, sizeof(Person), 1, pFile))
   {                                      /* Write error so */
      perror("Write error.");            /* output message */
      fclose(pFile);                     /* close the file */
      exit(2);                           /* and exit */
   }
   return;
}
```

This uses the standard library function **fwrite()** to write the object to the file. If an error occurs with the operation, a message is displayed on **stderr**, the file is closed, and the program is exited.

Inserting a Person into the File

The **Insert()** function will be the most complex part of the operation to add a person to the file. The **Insert()** function is only called if there's at least one record in the file. There are three possible situations that we need to deal with in the function:

- Adding a **Person** record at the beginning of the file.
- Inserting a **Person** record between two existing records in the file.
- Adding a **Person** record to the end of the file.

We also need to take account of the possibility that all the file records have been deleted. This will be indicated if the first record has the **Deleted** flag set to 1. We can understand the general logic of the **Insert()** function using this block diagram:

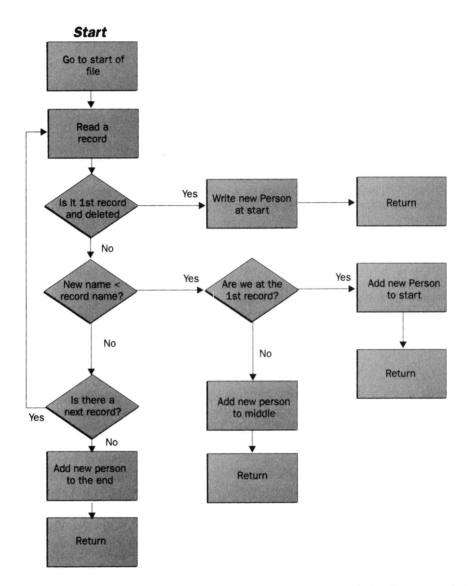

Start

Go to start of file

Read a record

Is it 1st record and deleted — **Yes** → Write new Person at start → Return

No

New name < record name? — **Yes** → Are we at the 1st record? — **Yes** → Add new Person to start → Return

No

Is there a next record? **Yes**

No

Add new person to the end

Return

Are we at the 1st record? **No** → Add new person to middle → Return

The function reads the file starting with the first record. If the first record has the **Deleted** flag set, then the file is empty, and the new **Person** becomes the first record. If the file isn't empty, then the **Name** for the new **Person** is compared to the.name of the first record read.

If the **Name** for the new **Person** is less than that of the current record, then we need to insert the new **Person** preceding that record. If the current record is the first, then we need to insert the new **Person** as the first record, which means that the current record must be moved somewhere else, and the following record needs to have its **Previous** pointer updated to reflect the new position of the current record.

If the current record isn't the first, then we must be inserting the new person between two existing records. This involves finding a place for the new **Person** in the file after setting its **Next** and **Previous** pointers, and updating the **Previous** pointer for the current record, and the **Next** pointer of its predecessor.

If the **Name** for the new **Person** isn't less than that of the current record, then we read the next record and repeat the process. If the current record is the last then we add the new **Person** to the end of the file.

Note that our version of the program will only consider surnames for sorting purposes, and will assume that there aren't any duplicates.

Using the logic from the previous diagram, we can write the code for the **Insert()** function:

```
/*****************************************************************
 * Function to insert a person in the file                      *
 * Argument is the pointer to the Person object to be inserted  *
 * The Person object will be inserted in alphabetic sequence    *
 * in the file                                                  *
 *****************************************************************/
void Insert(Person *pPerson)
{
    Person aPerson;            /* Place for a file record */
    long fPos=-1L;             /* Position in the file */
    long NewPos=-1L;           /* New position in the file */

    rewind(pFile);             /* Go to the start */
    fPos=ftell(pFile);         /* Record current position */

    for(;;)
    {

        if(Read(&aPerson)==-1L)              /* Read a file record */
        {
            printf("\nRead error. Ending program."); /* On error, output a */
            exit(1);                                  /* message and exit */
```

```
        }

        /* Check if the 1st record in the file has been deleted */
        if((fPos==0L)&&aPerson.Deleted)
        {                                   /* File exists but is empty */
            rewind(pFile);                  /* So go back to start */
            WriteFile(pPerson);             /* Now write the Person */
            return;                         /* and we are done */
        }

        /* Insert new person preceding any record with a greater surname */
        if(STRLT(pPerson->aName.Surname, aPerson.aName.Surname))
        {                                   /* New name is less than current */
            if(fPos==0L)                    /* Are we at the first record? */
            {
                AddFirst(pPerson, &aPerson);   /* Add new Person at start */
                return;
            }
            else                                     /* Otherwise we must be */
            {
                AddMiddle(pPerson,&aPerson, fPos);  /* adding in the middle */
                return;
            }
        }
        /* New person name is not less than current file record */
        if(aPerson.Next<0)                  /* If there is no next record */
        {                                   /* Add the new Person to the end */
            pPerson->Previous=fPos;         /* New Previous points to current */
            NewPos=Write(pPerson);          /* Write the new one somewhere */
            aPerson.Next=NewPos;            /* Save position in current Next */
            fseek(pFile, fPos, SEEK_SET);
            WriteFile(&aPerson);
            return;
        }
        /* There is a next one, so set the position for that */
        fPos=aPerson.Next;
        fseek(pFile, fPos, SEEK_SET);
    }
}
```

After setting the file position back to the start, all the work is done in the infinite **for** loop. When a record is read from the file we check whether it is the first record with the **Deleted** flag set. If so our problems are solved since the new **Person** object will be the first and only record in the file, so we just back up to the start and write it, and thus we're finished. Note that we don't read the file directly - we use the function **Read()** to do it for us. This allows us to check for and handle read errors within the function, so we don't need to worry about them externally.

If the first record isn't deleted, we compare the **Surname** member of the **Name** member of the new **Person** object with that for the record just read. The compare uses a macro which can be defined as:

```
#define STRLT(pS1,pS2)  (strcmp(pS1,pS2)<0)
```

This macro tests if the first string argument is less than the second, and returns True if it is. It's a question of personal preference as to whether you like to use the macro, or prefer to use the library function **strcmp()** directly.

Insertion Strategy

If the new surname is less, then we need to add the new person to the file with pointers set so that it precedes the record just read. If the record just read is the first record in the file, then we need to move it so that we can write the new **Person** as the first record, which is done by the function **AddFirst()**. If the current record isn't the first, then we must be adding the new **Person** object between the current record and its predecessor, and the function **AddMiddle()** achieves this.

If the surname for the new **Person** object isn't less than that of the current record, we need to check whether the current record is the last in the file, which will be indicated by a value of -1 for the **Next** pointer. In this case we need to add the new **Person** in an available space in the file (which may turn out to be the end), and update the **Next** pointer for the record we read from the file with the position of the new **Person** object. The function **Write()** searches for a vacant space for a new **Person** in the file, and if there's no embedded deleted record, then it will append the new record on the end.

If we're not at the last record in the file, then the file position is moved to where the next record in sequence is to be found. Its position is stored in the **Next** pointer of the current record. We then cycle through the loop again.

The code for adding a record at the start or in the middle of the file could have been included in the **Insert()** function, but it would have made the function rather long and somewhat difficult to follow.

Reading a Record

The code for the function to read a record from the file is as follows:

```
/*********************************************************
 * Function to read a person record from the file        *
 * Argument is a pointer to the record to be written.    *
 * The position in the file is returned, or -1 if        *
 * the end of file is reached                            *
 *********************************************************/
long Read(Person *pPerson)
{
    long fPos;                          /* Current file position */
    int ErrorCount=0;                   /* Count of file errors */

    fPos=ftell(pFile);                  /* Get current file position */
    for(;;)
    {
        fread(pPerson, sizeof(Person), 1, pFile);       /* Read a record */
        if(feof(pFile))                         /* Check for end of file */
        {
            clearerr(pFile);                    /* Clear EOF flag */
            return -1L;                         /* Return -1 */
        }

        /* Check for file read error */
        if(ferror(pFile))
        {
            perror("File read error");  /* Output error message */
            if(++ErrorCount==MAXERR)    /* If max error count reached */
            {
                fclose(pFile);          /* close the file */
                exit(1);                /* and exit */
            }
            clearerr(pFile);            /* Clear the error flag */
            fseek(pFile,fPos, SEEK_SET); /* Reset file position to re-read */
            continue;                   /* Go to next loop iteration */
        }
        else
            return fPos;                /* Return position record was written */
    }
}
```

The basic service performed here is to read a record into the structure pointed to by the function argument, and return its position in the file. The rest of the code is for error checking. The first check is for end of file, and if this is detected then -1 is returned. The second check is for a read error, and if this occurs a message is displayed on **stderr** by calling **perror()**, and the operation will be retried up to **MAXERR** times. If **MAXERR** successive read errors occur, then the program is terminated.

For most disk devices, a read error is a serious error, and you wouldn't typically try to read the record again, but simply end the program after an error message. If **MAXERR** is set to 1 then this is how the function will work. With other types of magnetic storage which are open to the air, a read error can be caused by dust on the medium, which is sometimes dislodged by backing up and trying the read operation again.

Adding a Record to the Start of the File

Adding a record to the start is a little messy because the first record in the file must always be the first in sequence. As a consequence it affects not only the first record, but the next in sequence, too. The effect on the existing file members is illustrated here:

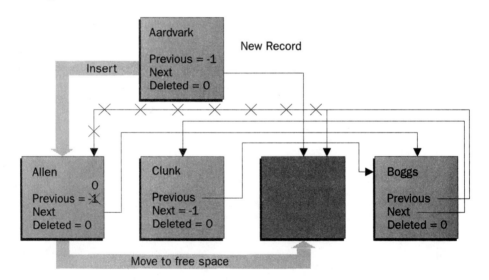

After setting the **Previous** pointer for the first record to 0, it's moved to the first free space in the file. The position is then recorded in the **Next** pointer of the new record. The record following the former first record is retrieved, and its **Previous** pointer altered to reflect the new position of the former first record. It can then be written back in the same place in the file.

Finally the new record can then be written as the first record in the file. The code for this is:

```
/*************************************************************
 * Function to add a Person to the beginning of the file    *
 * Arguments are:                                           *
 *    pPerson:  Pointer to Person to be inserted            *
 *    pHead:    Pointer to last record read, the head of     *
 *              the list in this case                        *
 * New Person will be added to the beginning of the file.   *
 * The previous first record, pHead, will be moved,          *
 * and the Previous pointer for the record following         *
 * pHead will be updated.                                    *
 *************************************************************/
void AddFirst(Person *pPerson, Person *pHead)
{
    long NewPos=-1L;        /* New file position for current */
    long fPos=-1L;          /* File position for follower */

    pHead->Previous=0L;     /* Set Previous for old head to 1st */
    NewPos=Write(pHead);    /* Find a new place for list head */
    pPerson->Next=NewPos;   /* Set Next for the new Person */

    if(pHead->Next>0L)      /* Check for follower to old head */
    {
        fseek(pFile, pHead->Next, SEEK_SET);        /* Go to it */
        if((fPos=Read(pHead))==-1L)                 /* and read it */
        {
            printf("\nRead error. Ending program.");   /* EOF Found */
            exit(1);
        }
        pHead->Previous=NewPos;                     /* Fix up Previous */
        fseek(pFile, fPos, SEEK_SET);               /* Back up */
        WriteFile(pHead);                           /* and write it back */
    }

    /* Get back to the start and write the new Person */
    fseek(pFile,0L,SEEK_SET);                       /* Reposition and */
    WriteFile(pPerson);                             /* write the file */
    return;                                         /* We are done */
}
```

Adding to the Middle of the File

Adding a record to the middle of the file is a lot simpler than adding to the beginning, insofar as we don't need to move any existing records. This diagram illustrates what we need to do:

387

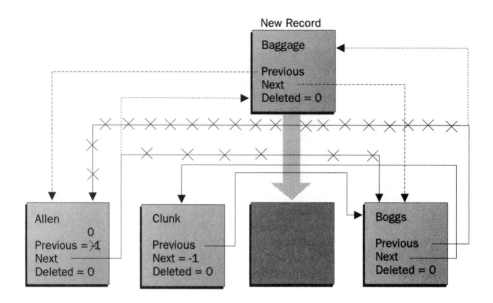

The old pointers that need to be changed are shown with crosses, and the new connections are shown with dashed lines. The links between the records for Allen and Boggs are broken, and reconnected so that Baggage sits in between them. The code to do this is as follows:

```
/******************************************************
 * Function to add a Person to the middle of the file   *
 * Arguments are:                                        *
 *   pPerson:  Pointer to Person to be inserted          *
 *   pCurrent: Pointer to last record read               *
 *   fPos:     File position for last record read        *
 * New Person will be inserted preceding last record read. *
 ******************************************************/
void AddMiddle(Person *pPerson, Person *pCurrent, long fPos)
{
    long NewPos=-1L;                /* New position for new Person */

    /* Set the pointers for the new Person and write it to the file */
    pPerson->Next=fPos;             /* Set new Person Next pointer */
    pPerson->Previous=pCurrent->Previous;    /* Set new person Previous */
    NewPos=Write(pPerson);          /* Write the new one to file */

    /* Update the current record, it will follow the new one */
    pCurrent->Previous=NewPos;      /* Set Previous to new position */

    /* Find position where we read the current record & rewrite in situ */
    fseek(pFile, fPos, SEEK_SET);
```

```
    WriteFile(pCurrent);

    /* Now update the record preceding the new one */
    fseek(pFile, pPerson->Previous, SEEK_SET);/* Find previous record and*/
    if(Read(pCurrent)==-1L)                /* read it into current */
    {
        printf("\nRead error. Ending program.");   /* EOF detected */
        exit(1);
    }
    pCurrent->Next=NewPos;                 /* Set Next to where the new one is */

    /* Now write the preceding record back in situ */
    fseek(pFile, pPerson->Previous, SEEK_SET);
    WriteFile(pCurrent);
    return;                                /* and we are done */
    }
```

Writing a Record to the File

We've used the function **Write()** to write a record to an available space in the file. The code for this function is:

```
/*****************************************************
 * Function to write a person record to the file *
 * Argument is a pointer to the person            *
 * If a deleted record exists, the new record     *
 * will overwrite it, otherwise the new record    *
 * will be written at the end of the file         *
 *****************************************************/
long Write(Person *pPerson)
{
    Person aPerson;           /* Space for a person */
    long fPos;                /* Current file position */
    int ErrorCount=0;         /* Count of file errors */

    rewind(pFile);            /* Start at the beginning */

    for(;;)
    {
        fPos=Read(&aPerson);    /* Read a record */

        /* Check for end of file, if so write it here */
        if(fPos==-1L)
        {
            /* Position at the end of the file and write the person */
            fseek(pFile,0L,SEEK_END);
            fPos=ftell(pFile);  /* Record the current position */
            WriteFile(pPerson);
            return fPos;        /* Return its position */
```

```
    }

    /* Check for a deleted record if so we can overwrite it */
    if(aPerson.Deleted)
    {
        fseek(pFile, fPos, SEEK_SET);    /* Set to record start */
        WriteFile(pPerson);
        return fPos;
    }
  }
}
```

The function accepts a pointer to the object to be written, and returns the position of the new record. The idea is to go through the file records in physical sequence looking for the first record that has its **Deleted** flag set. If one is found, then the file position is backed up to that point, the new record is written to replace it, and the position where the record was written is returned.

If no record in the file has been deleted then the new record is added to the end of the file. The last record is detected by checking the **Next** pointer of each record. The **Next** pointer in the last record will be -1.

Testing the Add Capability

There is enough here to allow us to test the program. We can create the file and add records to it. There are functions in **main()** that we haven't yet written, but we can replace each of them with a dummy function. For example:

```
void DeletePerson(void)
{
    printf("\n DeletePerson() function called.");
    return;
}
```

We can include a version of each of the functions we haven't yet produced which will just display a message. It would be judicious to include some **assert()** macro calls in the code we are testing, as well as some diagnostics of our own. A good general diagnostic for untested code is for each function to display a message when it is called, which you can surround with **#if-#endif**, controlled by a **#define** as we have seen previously. You can then compile and execute the program. Don't forget the header files that are needed for standard library functions. You must also remember to include a prototype for each function.

Deleting a Record

The **DeletePerson()** function will delete a record from the file, and the process has a lot in common with the insert mechanism we've just looked at. The essential logic is very simple. We read the name for the record to be deleted, we search the file for the record, and if we find it, we delete it. If it isn't there then we display a message. The complications arise with the actual process of deleting a particular record.

The code for the **DeletePerson()** function is:

```
/**********************************************
 * Function to delete a person from the file  *
 **********************************************/
void DeletePerson(void)
{
   Person aPerson;                       /* Record to be deleted */
   Name aName;
   long fPos=-1L;
   char *ch="n";

   pFile=fopen(pFPersons,"rb+");         /* Open file for update */
   if(pFile==NULL)
   {
      printf("\nUnable to open Persons file. Program ended.");
      exit(1);
   }
   for(;;)
   {
      if(!GetName(&aName))
      {
         printf("\nInvalid name entered. Delete aborted.");
         fclose(pFile);                  /* So close the file */
         return;
      }
      if((fPos=FindEntry(&aName, &aPerson))==-1L)
      {
         printf("\nDo you want to delete another?");
         scanf("%1s",ch);
         if((*ch=='n')||(*ch=='N'))
         {
            fclose(pFile);
            return;
         }
         else
            continue;
      }
```

```
      printf("\nThe person to be deleted is:");
      Display(&aPerson);
      printf("\nConfirm delete (Y or N)?");
      scanf("%1s",ch);
      if((*ch=='y')||(*ch=='Y'))
      {
         /* Mark record as deleted and write back */
         aPerson.Deleted=1;            /* Set deleted flag */
         fseek(pFile,fPos,SEEK_SET);
         WriteFile(&aPerson);

         if(aPerson.Previous<0L)       /* Check for previous record */
            DeleteFirst(&aPerson);     /* None - we are deleting the first */

         else if(aPerson.Next<0L)      /* See if its the last record */
            DeleteLast(aPerson.Previous);     /* It is - so delete it */

         else                          /* Its not the first or the last so */
            DeleteMiddle(&aPerson);    /* we are deleting from the middle */
      }
      printf("\nDo you want to delete another?");
      scanf("%1s",ch);
      if((*ch=='n')||(*ch=='N'))       /* Chance for another go */
      {
         fclose(pFile);                /* No - so close the file */
         return;                       /* and return */
      }
   }
}
```

After opening the file for update, all the action takes place within an infinite **for** loop to allow for an arbitrary number of successive delete operations to be requested. A name is read using the **GetName()** function we saw earlier, and the **FindEntry()** function is called to search the file for the record containing the name. The **FindEntry()** function has the prototype:

```
long FindEntry(Name *pName, Person *pPerson);
```

The first argument is the name to be found, and the record corresponding to the name will be restored in the structure pointed to by the second argument. The position in the file of the record found is returned from the function, or it will return -1 if no record containing the name passed as the first argument exists.

If a record is found, then it is checked to see whether it's the first or last record in the file. The first record always has the **Previous** pointer set to

-1, and the last record has its **Next** pointer set to -1. If it's neither of these then it must be in the middle - a separate function deals with each case.

Once a search has been processed, or if a name wasn't found, then the user is prompted for another delete operation. If the response to this is negative then the function returns.

Finding a Record

The **FindEntry()** function that we used to find a record to be deleted, will also be used in the search operation to display a particular record. Finding a record corresponding to a particular name is quite straightforward. We read the file from the beginning in alphabetical sequence by following the **Next** pointers. As each record is read, the **Name** member is checked to see if it's the one that we're looking for. If it is then we return its position.

If the name we are looking for isn't in the file, then the process ends when a record is read with a name greater than the one sought, or we reach the last record in the file. The code to do this is as follows:

```
/**********************************************************
 * Function to find the file record for a given name *
 * Arguments are:                                     *
 *   pName: Pointer to name for entry sought          *
 *   pPerson: Pointer to struct to store entry found  *
 * Return value is position in the file of entry, or  *
 * -1 if name is not found.                           *
 **********************************************************/
long FindEntry(Name *pName, Person *pPerson)
{
   Person aPerson;
   long fPos=-1L;

   /* Search the file for the name entered */
   rewind(pFile);                      /* Get to the start of the file */
   for(;;)
   {
      fPos=Read(&aPerson);             /* Read a person record */
      if(fPos==-1L)                    /* Check for end of file */
      {
         printf("\nEnd of file. Name not found.");
         return -1L;
      }

      if((fPos==0L)&&aPerson.Deleted)
      {
```

```
            printf("\nFile is empty, search failed.");
            return -1L;
     }

     /* Look for the name */
     if(STREQ(pName->Surname,aPerson.aName.Surname))/*Have we found it?*/
     {
         *pPerson=aPerson;                        /* Yes, so copy record */
         return fPos;
     }

     /* Check if the current name from the file is less than last read */
     if(STRLT(pName->Surname, aPerson.aName.Surname))
         {                                   /* If so the target is not there */
             printf("\nName not found.");
             return -1L;
         }

     fPos=aPerson.Next;
     if(fPos)                                /* Next pointer must be positive */
     {
         fseek(pFile, fPos, SEEK_SET);
         continue;
     }
     printf("\nName not found.");      /* Otherwise we are at the end */
     return -1L;                        /* so return to caller */
  }
}
```

After getting to the beginning of the file, records are read by following the
Next pointers. The first check is for the end of file being read, which is to
deal with the possibility that someone is attempting to search a file that
exists, but has never had any records written to it. The next check that it is
essential for us to make is for an initial record with the **Deleted** flag set.
This is to cover for the possibility of a file having had all its members
deleted, and if we don't check this then we could end up wandering
around deleted records in a file. If the first record is valid, then we will
only be looking at valid records since we sever the links to deleted records.

We then start looking for a name match in the current record. This uses a
macro to test for strings being equal, and can be defined as:

```
#define STREQ(pS1,pS2)  (strcmp(pS1,pS2)==0)
```

As with the macro **STRLT()** which we saw earlier, it makes it a little more
obvious what we are doing.

If we find the name, we copy the **Person** object from the record to the calling memory pointed to by the parameter **pPerson**, and return the file position. This is a very simplistic approach - it doesn't check the first name and doesn't allow for multiple file records with the same surname. This is an extension you might like to have a go at yourself.

If we don't find an equal surname, then we check for the possibility that the surname we're looking for is less than the surname in the current file record. If it is, then there is no point in looking at the rest of the file since all subsequent records will be greater as the file is in ascending alphabetical sequence. We return a value of -1 to signal that the name wasn't found.

If the current record name isn't greater than the name we're looking for, we pick up the file position of the next record from the **Next** pointer, and assuming that we're not at the last record, we cycle through the loop again.

Deleting the First Record

There's a lot of work to delete the first record because there must always be one unless all the records have been deleted. The original record already has the deleted flag set in the function **DeletePerson()**, so here we have to fix up the other records that may be affected. The code to execute this is as follows:

```
/**************************************************************
 * Function to delete the first record in the file           *
 * The argument is a pointer to a Person object which         *
 * has just been deleted from the file.This function moves    *
 * the second record to the first position, if it exists.     *
 * It also modifies the Previous pointer of the third         *
 * record if it exists.                                       *
 **************************************************************/
void DeleteFirst(Person *pPerson)
{
   Person bPerson;
   long fPos=-1L;
   if(pPerson->Next<0L)
      return;                              /* No next one */

   /* But there is a next one */
   fseek(pFile, pPerson->Next, SEEK_SET);
   Read(&bPerson);                         /* Read next record */
   bPerson.Previous=-1L;                   /* Set previous to none */
```

```
    /* Now rewrite the next record at the beginning */
    rewind(pFile);
    WriteFile(&bPerson);

    /* Delete previous copy of next record */
    bPerson.Deleted=1;                           /* Set the deleted flag */
    fseek(pFile, pPerson->Next, SEEK_SET);       /* Get to where it is */
    WriteFile(&bPerson);                         /* and rewrite it */

    /* Now fix the Previous pointer for the following record */
    if(bPerson.Next>0L)
    {
        fseek(pFile, bPerson.Next, SEEK_SET);    /* Got to the next */
        fPos=Read(&bPerson);                     /* and read it */
        bPerson.Previous=0L;                     /* Set to first record */
        fseek(pFile, fPos, SEEK_SET);            /* Get to where it is */
        WriteFile(&bPerson);                     /* and rewrite it */
    }
}
```

If the first record is the only one in the file, then it's easy. We just set the deleted flag and write the record back. If there's more than one record in the file, then we need to read the second record, and copy it to the position occupied by the first after setting its **Previous** member to -1. Following this, we need to delete the original copy of the second record by setting its deleted flag, and writing it back to where it was. We then need to see if there was a third record. If there was, its **Next** pointer contains the wrong file position for what was the second record and has now been promoted to first. So we read the third record, set its **Next** pointer to 0, the position for the first record, and write it back in place.

Deleting from the Middle

The record being deleted has already been fixed by the calling function **DeletePerson()**, so again we're going to fix other records that are affected. It is quite clear in this case. We need to modify the records either side of the one we have deleted. The code to do this is as follows:

```
/***********************************************************
 * Function to delete a record from the middle of the file *
 * The argument is a pointer to a Person object which      *
 * has just been deleted from the file.This function fixes *
 * the predecessor and the successor to that deleted.      *
 ***********************************************************/
void DeleteMiddle(Person *pPerson)
{
```

```
    Person bPerson;
    long fPos=-1L;
    /* Fix the Next pointer for previous record */
    fseek(pFile, pPerson->Previous, SEEK_SET);       /* Go to the previous */
    fPos=Read(&bPerson);                              /* and read it */
    bPerson.Next=pPerson->Next;                       /* Bypass the deleted */
    fseek(pFile, fPos, SEEK_SET);                     /* Reposition */
    WriteFile(&bPerson);                              /* and write it back */


    /* Fix the previous pointer for the following record */
    fseek(pFile, pPerson->Next, SEEK_SET);
    fPos=Read(&bPerson);                              /* Read next record */
    bPerson.Previous=pPerson->Previous;               /* Bypass deleted */
    fseek(pFile, pPerson->Next, SEEK_SET);            /* Reposition */
    WriteFile(&bPerson);                              /* and write it back */
    return;                                           /* We are done */
}
```

This works out quite easily. We read the preceding record and fix the **Next** pointer to point to the following record. We then read the following record and change the **Previous** pointer to point to the preceding record - and that's it.

Deleting the Last Record

This is the simplest case of all. The only record to be affected is the second to last, which now becomes the last. It must exist if this function is called, because if it didn't, we would be deleting the first which is already taken care of. The code for this function is:

```
/**************************************************************
 * Function to delete the last record in the file            *
 * The argument is the file position of the record preceding  *
 * the last record which has been deleted so that it now      *
 * becomes the last.                                          *
 **************************************************************/
void DeleteLast(long fPos)
{
    Person aPerson;
    fseek(pFile, fPos, SEEK_SET);                     /* Position to 2nd to last */
    Read(&aPerson);                                   /* and read it */
    aPerson.Next=-1L;                                 /* There is now no next */
    fseek(pFile, fPos, SEEK_SET);                     /* Reposition */
    WriteFile(&aPerson);                              /* and write it back */
    return;
}
```

397

This just reads the second to last record, sets the **Next** pointer to -1 so that it becomes the last record, and writes it back.

Searching for a Record

We have done most of the work to search for a record with the previous function, **FindEntry()**. All we need in addition to this is the ability to display a record once we have found it. The code for the function **Search()** will be:

```
/*********************************************
 * Function to search for data on a person *
 * The function will search for as many     *
 * entries as required. The first equal     *
 * name is the entry displayed. An invalid  *
 * name will discontinue the search.        *
 *********************************************/
void Search(void)
{
   Name aName;                              /* Name to be found */
   Person aPerson;                          /* Person record from the file */
   long fPos=-1L;                           /* Current file position */
   char *ch="n";                            /* Continue indicator */

   /* Open the file to read it */
   pFile=fopen(pFPersons,"rb");
   if(pFile==NULL)                          /* Check we got a good file pointer */
   {
      printf("\nUnable to open the file. Exiting program.");
      exit(1);
   }

   /* Now search for as many entries as required */
   for(;;)
   {
      if(!GetName(&aName))
      {
         printf("\nInvalid name entered. Search aborted.");
         fclose(pFile);                     /* So close the file */
         return;
      }

      /* Search the file for the name entered */
      fPos=FindEntry(&aName, &aPerson);      /* Find the entry */
      if(fPos!=-1L)                  /* If EOF not returned, name was found */
      {
```

```
        Display(&aPerson);                          /* so show details */
    }
    printf("\nDo you want to search for another?");
    scanf("%1s",ch);
    if((*ch=='n')||(*ch=='N'))          /* Check response for negative */
    {                                   /* No more searches needed */
        fclose(pFile);                  /* So close the file */
        return;                         /* and return to caller */
    }
  }
}
```

After opening the file and making sure that we have a valid name to search
for, the search process itself is very simple. We call the function
FindEntry() to get hold of the record corresponding to the name entered,
and we call the function **Display()** to display it. The operation takes place
in a **for** loop to permit several successive searches to be made without
necessitating going back to the set of choices in **main()**.

Displaying a Record

The function to display a record just writes the personal information
contained in the **Person** object to **stdout**:

```
/*****************************************
 * Function to display a Person record   *
 * Argument is a pointer to the Person.   *
 * There is no return value.              *
 *****************************************/
void Display(Person *pPerson)
{
    int i=0;                                    /* Loop counter */
    printf("\n\nName:\t%s %s\nPhone:\t%s\nAddress:",
        pPerson->aName.Surname, pPerson->aName.FirstName, pPerson->Phone);
    for(i=0; i<ADDRLINES;i++)
    {
        if(strlen(pPerson->Address[i])==0)      /* Check for empty line */
            return;                             /* If so we are done */
        printf("\n\t%s", pPerson->Address[i]);
    }
    return;              /* After ADDRLINES output we are done anyway */
}
```

The address is displayed by the **for** loop, which ends the function when
the first empty address line is found. If the address contains the full set of
ADDRLINES lines, the **return** following the loop is executed.

399

Listing the File

The last operation we support in the program is that of listing the entire contents of the file. This again is a simple process. We need to read the file from the beginning, displaying each record as we go. The code to do this is as follows:

```
/************************************************
 * List the contents of the file                *
 * Records are read in alphabetical sequence *
 * from the beginning, and displayed on         *
 * stdout.                                       *
 ************************************************/
void ListFile(void)
{
   Person aPerson;                    /* Store a record here */
   long fPos=-1;                      /* File position for the current record */

   pFile=fopen(pFPersons,"rb"); /* Open the file to read it */
   if(pFile==NULL)
   {
      printf("\nUnable to open Persons file. Program ended.");
      exit(1);
   }
   for(;;)
   {
      fPos=Read(&aPerson);            /* Read a record */
      if((fPos==0)&&aPerson.Deleted)/* Check for a deleted first record */
      {
         printf("\nFile empty.");    /* If it is, the file is empty */
         return;
      }
      Display(&aPerson);             /* Display the record */
      fPos=aPerson.Next;             /* Get the position of the next */

      if(fPos<0L)                    /* Check for no next record */
      {
         fclose(pFile);              /* If so we close the file */
         return;                     /* and we are done */
      }
      fseek(pFile, fPos, SEEK_SET); /* Move the file position to next */
   }
}
```

There's nothing new here. We read the file in the **for** loop to accommodate an arbitrary number of records. We then check that the first record isn't deleted. Each record is displayed using the function **Display()**, and the file position for the next record is obtained from the **Next** pointer of the current record. The process stops when we find a **Next** value of -1, indication that there is no next record.

The Program Header File

We have discussed all the program code, so now we should come back to how it should be divided up between files. There's always a good case for a program header file, and sometimes several are appropriate if the program is large, or if it contains groups of functions which may not be needed by all the source files. Header files shouldn't contain anything that generates object code, but should accommodate all definitions required by the program. With our program one header file should suffice, and is listed in Appendix D.

The **include** file contains all the definitions specific to the program as well as the **include** files for the standard library functions that are used. Of course, this file would need to be included at the beginning of all the source files making up the program.

In case you have trouble gathering together all the bits that make up the program, a complete listing is provided in Appendix D. This listing is in three files, two source files, and a header file. It should compile and run as it is if you manage to type it all in correctly.

Summary

This wasn't a particularly complicated application, but nevertheless it led to a requirement for nineteen functions. This should have provided you with a little insight into how managing the source code for an application is a very important part of program development. If you have worked through the code step by step, you may well have introduced a few typos which will also demonstrate the value of diagnostic code in your program.

The program is by no means fully developed. There is a lot of scope here for you to extend it, and to improve the code we have gone through. The whole process of dealing with names is very primitive, both in terms of what you might realistically want to allow as a valid name, and in terms of the comparison mechanism. There are quite a few holes in the way interactions with the user are handled. In particular, only testing for `n` or `N`, and assuming that `Y` is otherwise entered isn't a very secure basis for input. You could also experiment with other strategies for storing the data, and searching the file. If there were a lot of records, a sequential search mechanism is going to be rather slow.

If you've worked diligently through all the examples in the book, you have a good knowledge of C and should be reasonably competent at applying it. All you need to polish your skills is practice, and the more the better. Enjoy your programming.

Exercises

1 Try to develop this personal address book system into a much more sophisticated application by implementing some of the following additions:

- Extend the search mechanism to allow a first name to be given as a search criterion in addition to the surname.

- Extend the search mechanism to allow any field to be used as a search criterion.

- Extend the search mechanism to retrieve multiple records for a given search criterion.

- Extend the list operation to provide a partial list capability, such as 'list the entries with surnames beginning with B or D'.

- Extend the Person structure to include additional fields, such as age or date of birth. Modify the search and list operations to incorporate any additional fields.

- Add a function to find, display and edit a record.

- Extend the delete function to enable the deletion of multiple records at once, based on single or multiple criterion.

2 Create an application that will accept a text string from the keyboard and output an answer to simulate the response of human trapped inside your computer. You will need a variety of responses to anticipate what a user will ask. The output should simply be conversation based, like this (with user input in italics):

> Hello, my names Bob and I'm stuck inside your computer.
> *Why?*
> Because my parents named me after Robert Hope.
> *Ha ha.*
> You like my jokes - hey we'll get along just fine.
> What's your name?

This type of dialogue could continue indefinitely, or at least until the user types *'Goodbye'*, *'Get lost'* or something similar.

Of course having responses ready for everything a user can type isn't very practical, but if you guide the user by asking questions and changing the subject then you can simulate a conversation with another human being. And remember, they don't have to be trapped inside your computer, you could produce responses for different scenarios.

Prizes for the Best Conversation Simulator

If you feel particularly happy with your conversation simulator and you feel that you would like to share it with us, then please send them in. We always welcome feedback, especially productive exercises that you've slaved over from our book. There are free books on offer to the best three we receive.

Where Do We Go From Here?

You may or may not have had opinions on or ideas about the C language before you read this book, but we are sure that you've found this tour an enlightening, informative and eye-opening experience. Not only have we tried to remove the excess stuffy baggage that traditionally drags programming guides down, but we've also attempted to pack everything you need to know into a compact, cost-effective reference guide.

There is no doubting the popularity of the C language - it has consistently been at the forefront of the programming revolution for the last 20 years. The vast back catalog of existing software and the number of new spin-off languages shows that your choice in learning C was a very wise one. Why don't you try some of our other titles such as *Revolutionary OOP Using C++*, a natural progression from Instant C, or perhaps *Revolutionary Visual C++* if you would like to delve into Windows programming. Whatever path you choose to take, we are sure that this introduction to C has proved worthwhile.

Now that you've had a taste of our refreshing style, would you like to know more about Wrox Press and our other publications? If you do then why don't you ask for our latest catalog, or check out our Web page. And remember when you're down at your local bookstore, look out for our distinctive red binding - your guarantee of Wrox value.

Are you interested in writing or reviewing any of our future books? We warmly welcome any willing contributors that can help Wrox to publish *even* better books. If you're interested then contact us right away - see the details at the back of this book.

You can contact Wrox via the reply card also at the back of this book, or you can correspond with us by any of the following means:

Snail mail	Wrox Press Ltd, Unit 16, 20 James Road, Birmingham, B11 2BA, United Kingdom.
Electronic mail (e-mail)	johnf@wrox.demon.co.uk
World Wide Web	http://www.wrox.com
CompuServe	100063,2152
Telephone	(44121) 706 6826
Facsimile	(44121) 706 2967

Formatted Input/Output Summary

Formatted Input

Reading data from the standard input stream **stdin**, usually the keyboard, is provided by the standard library function **scanf()**, which has the prototype:

```
int scanf(const char *pFormat,...);
```

The first parameter is a format string determining how data is to be read, and the subsequent arguments are pointers to variables which are to receive the input values. It is a common error to accidentally specify an argument that isn't a pointer, which usually leads to a program crash, since whatever is passed as an argument will be interpreted as a pointer. The integer value returned is the number of values read, or **EOF** if an error occurred.

Conversion Specifiers

Conversion specifiers determine the way in which input data is interpreted. Each pointer argument must correspond to a conversion specifier. The format specifiers must also be consistent with the type of variable being used to store the data. The function **scanf()** has no way to verify that this is the case, or that the number of format specifiers is equal to the number of pointer arguments. The conversion specifiers are all of the form:

```
%[*][width][h or 1 or L] conversion_character
```

The optional components of the conversion specifier are enclosed within square brackets to emphasise that you must always have the **%** character and a **conversion_character**. If the ***** is present, then this indicates that the input data isn't to be stored in a variable, but should be skipped and the next input value read.

The **width**, if present, is an integer specifying the maximum number of characters in the input field.

The **h**, **1**, specifies that the integer value is to be converted as **short** or **long** respectively. The **L** applies to the conversion of floating point values to type **long double**.

Conversion Characters

Possible **conversion_character** values and their corresponding meanings are shown here:

For Reading Integer Values:

d	Decimal value of type **int**.
i	A value of type **int** that may be decimal, octal (with a leading **0**), or hexadecimal (with a leading **0x** or **0X**).
u	A decimal value of type **unsigned int**.
x	A hexadecimal value to be stored as type **int** (the **0x** or **0X** can be omitted).
o	An octal value to be stored as type **int** (the **0** can be omitted).
n	Stores the count of the number of input characters read up to this point as a value of type **int**.

For Reading Floating Point Values:

e, f, or g	A value of type **float** where a leading sign, a decimal point, and an exponent are all optional. The exponent may be written with a leading **e** or **E**, or a sign, or both.

For Reading Characters:

c	The characters specified by the **width** field, including whitespace characters, are stored as type **char** with no terminating **'\0'**.
s	A string of non-whitespace characters stored as type **char** - **%1s** will read the first character that isn't whitespace.
%	Specifies a **%** sign. Nothing is stored.
[search_set]	Successive characters are stored as a string of type **char**, as long as they belong to the characters specified by **search_set**. For example, **%[abc]** will read a string consisting of only **a**, **b**, or **c**. The first character not in **search_set** stops the process.
[^search_set]	Successive characters are stored in a string of type **char** as long as they are not included in **search_set**.

For Reading Pointer Values:

p	A pointer value is stored as type **void** *. The form of the input is implementation dependent.

The scanf() Function

The function **scanf()** will ignore blanks or tabs in the format string, but a sequence of characters other than **%** included in the format string, and not part of a format specification, indicates that the input should be matched to the specified characters.

A generalized version of the **scanf()** function is available in the standard library, which has the prototype:

```
int fscanf(FILE *pFile, const char *pFormat,...);
```

The first argument is a pointer to a file stream.

The function **fscanf()** operates in the same way with the same format specifiers as the **scanf()** function, and the **scanf()** function is equivalent to the **fscanf()** applied to **stdout**.

Formatted Input from Memory

The standard library also provides a function to convert data stored in memory. Its prototype is:

```
int sscanf(char *pStr, const char *pFormat, ...);
```

This also operates identically to **scanf()** except that the input data is obtained from the string pointed to by **pStr**.

Formatted Output

The standard library function for general formatted output has the prototype:

```
int fprintf(FILE *pFile, const char *pFormat, ...);
```

This will write formatted data to the file stream defined by the pointer **pFile**. The formatting of the output is controlled by the format string pointed to by **pFormat**. A variable number of arguments can follow the format string argument, and they are matched in sequence with the format specifiers appearing in the format string. The number and type of the variables to be written must correspond with the format specifiers appearing in the format string.

The function **printf()** is equivalent to the function **fprintf()** applied to **stdin**.

The general format of a format specifier for output is:

```
%[flags][width][.precision][h, or l, or L]
conversion_character
```

The elements shown between square brackets here are optional.

Conversion Characters

The conversion character specifies the type of the value to be output and how it is to be converted. The possible conversion characters are shown here:

For Outputting Integer Values:

d or **i**   Output of a number of type **int** as a **signed** decimal value.

o   Output of a number of type **int** as an **unsigned** octal value.

x or **X**   Output of a number of type **int** as an **unsigned** hexadecimal value. If **x** is used then **a** through **f** are used as digits, and if **X** is used then **A** through **F** are used as digits.

u   Output of a number of type **int** as an **unsigned** decimal value.

n   The characters output up to this point are *stored* in the corresponding argument, which must be of type **int** *.

For Outputting Floating Point Values:

e or **E**   Output of a number of type **float** as a **signed** floating point value with an exponent. If **e** is used then the exponent is preceded by **e**, and if **E** is used then the exponent is preceded by **E**.

f   Output of a number of type **float** as a decimal value without an exponent.

g or **G**   Output of a number of type **float** in **e** or **f** form depending on the value. If **G** is specified and an exponent is necessary then it will be in **E** form.

For Outputting Characters:

c   Output of a single character of type **int** after conversion to type **unsigned char**.

s   Output of a sequence of characters specified by an argument of type **char** *. Output stops when a '\0' character is found, or until the number of characters specified by precision have been output.

%   Outputs a % sign - no corresponding variable is required.

For Outputting a Pointer:

p   Outputs a pointer of type void * in an implementation
                     dependent form.

Flags

The flags in the format specifier are optional, but if they are present, they
affect how the output is presented. If more than one flag is specified then
they can be in any order. They are as follows:

+   Causes the output to be presented with a leading **+** or -
                     sign.
-                    Causes the output to be presented left justified in its
                     field. Right justified output is the default.
space   Causes the output to be presented with a leading space
                     if there's no leading sign.
0   Causes the output for integer values to be presented
                     with leading zeros.
The effect of this flag depends on the conversion
                     character. For **o** conversion the value will be preceded
                     by **0**. For **x** or **X** conversion the output will be preceded
                     by **0x** or **0X**. For floating point conversions the output
                     will always contain a decimal point. By default, no
                     decimal point appears if the digits following it are zero.

Width Modifier

The width element in the conversion specifier is optional, and determines a
minimum field width for output. It can be specified either as an integer
value defining the minimum number of character positions, or it can be an
asterisk, specifying that the next argument in the function call represents a
field width value. The value must be of type **int**.

If the output requires more characters than that defined by a width modifier, then the field is expanded to accommodate the output value. If the width is specified with a leading zero, then the output is padded with leading zeros to the left of the number. If a - flag is also used, the number is left justified and blanks are used instead.

Precision Specification

If a precision specification is present, it always begins with a period which acts as a separator between the width and precision specification. As in the case of a width value, it can be an integer value determining the number of digits of precision, or it can be specified as * indicating that the next argument in the function call specifies a value for the precision. The argument must be of type **int**.

If the output needs more characters than specified by the precision, it may be truncated or rounded to fit the number of positions specified.

Size Modifier

The optional size modifiers **h**, or **l**, or **L**, affect how the type of the arguments are interpreted.

The modifier **h** only applies to conversion characters **d**, **i**, **o**, **x**, **X**, or **u**, and specifies that the argument is of type **short int**.

The modifier **l** can be applied to conversion characters **d**, **i**, **o**, **x**, **X**, or **u**, and when present specifies that the argument is of type **long**, or it can be applied to conversion characters of type **e**, **E**, **f**, **g**, or **G**, where it specifies that the argument is of type **double**. The modifier **L** only applies to conversion characters of type **e**, **E**, **f**, **g**, or **G**, where it specifies that the argument is of type **long double**.

Formatted Output to Memory

Analogous to the **sscanf()** function, the standard library provides a function to output formatted data to a user defined buffer in memory. Its prototype is:

```
int sprintf(char *pStr, const char *pFormat, ...);
```

Apart from the fact that output is to the memory area pointed to by the first parameter, **pStr**, this function operates identically to the **fprintf()** function. The output generated is terminated by '**\0**'. The count of output characters returned, doesn't include the terminating '**\0**'.

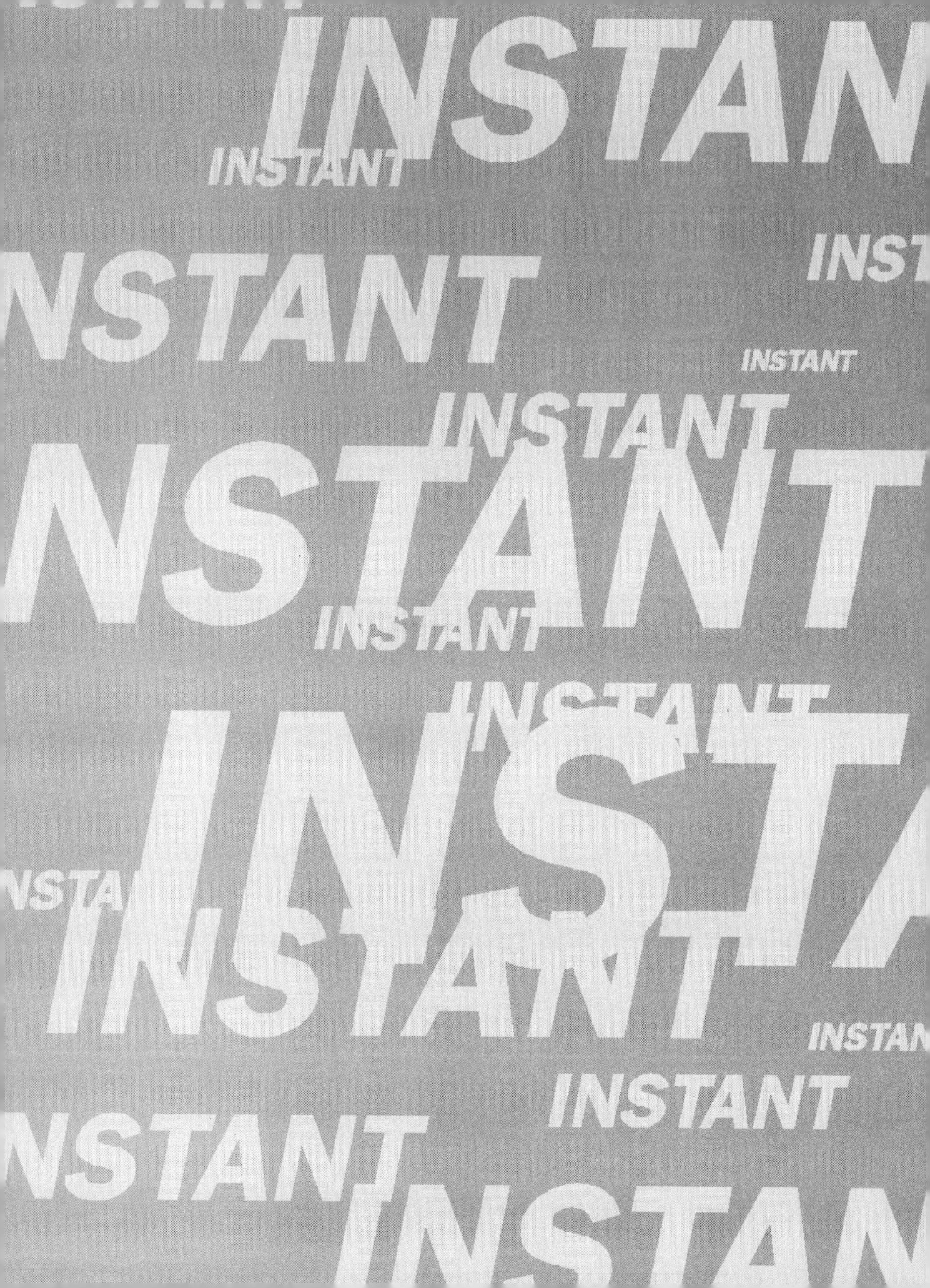
INSTANT
INSTANT
INSTANT
INSTANT
INSTANT
INSTANT
INSTANT

Appendix

The ASCII Table

The American Standard Code for Information Interchange or ASCII assigns values between 0 and 255 for upper and lower case letters, numeric digits, punctuation marks and other symbols. ASCII characters can be split into the following sections:

0 - 31   Control functions

32 - 127   Standard, implementation-independent characters

128 - 255   Special symbols, international character sets - generally,
            non-standard characters.

Since the latter 128 characters are implementation-dependent and have no fixed entry in the ASCII table, we shall only cover the first two groups in the following table:

ASCII Characters 0 - 31

Decimal	Hexadecimal	Character	Control
000	00	null	NUL
001	01	✪	SOH
002	02	●	STX
003	03	♥	ETX
004	04	♦	EOT
005	05	♣	ENQ
006	06	♠	ACK
007	07	●	BEL (Audible bell)
008	08		Backspace
009	09		HT
010	0A		LF (Line feed)
011	0B		VT (Vertical feed)
012	0C		FF (Form feed)
013	0D		CR (Carriage return)
014	0E		SO
015	0F	¤	SI
016	10		DLE
017	11		DC1
018	12		DC2
019	13		DC3
020	14		DC4
021	15		NAK
022	16		SYN
023	17		ETB
024	18		CAN
025	19		EM
026	1A	➡	SUB
027	1B	♦	ESC (Escape)
028	1C	L	FS
029	1D		GS
030	1E		RS
031	1F		US

ASCII Characters 32 - 127

Decimal	Hexadecimal	Character	Decimal	Hexadecimal	Character
032	20	space	064	40	@
033	21	!	065	41	A
034	22	"	066	42	B
035	23	#	067	43	C
036	24	$	068	44	D
037	25	%	069	45	E
038	26	&	070	46	F
039	27	'	071	47	G
040	28	(	072	48	H
041	29	)	073	49	I
042	2A	*	074	4A	J
043	2B	+	075	4B	K
044	2C	,	076	4C	L
045	2D	-	077	4D	M
046	2E	.	078	4E	N
047	2F	/	079	4F	O
048	30	0	080	50	P
049	31	1	081	51	Q
050	32	2	082	52	R
051	33	3	083	53	S
052	34	4	085	55	U
053	35	5	086	56	V
054	36	6	087	57	W
055	37	7	088	58	X
056	38	8	089	59	Y
057	39	9	090	5A	Z
058	3A	:	091	5B	[
059	3B	;	092	5C	\
060	3C	<	093	5D	]
061	3D	=	094	5E	^
062	3E	>	095	5F	_
063	3F	?	096	60	`

Continued

Decimal	Hexadecimal	Character	Decimal	Hexadecimal	Character
097	61	a	113	71	q
098	62	b	114	72	r
099	63	c	115	73	s
100	64	d	116	74	t
101	65	e	117	75	u
102	66	f	118	76	v
103	67	g	119	77	w
104	68	h	120	78	x
105	69	i	121	79	y
106	6A	j	122	7A	z
107	6B	k	123	7B	{
108	6C	l	124	7C	|
109	6D	m	125	7D	}
110	6E	n	126	7E	~
111	6F	o	127	7F	delete
112	70	p			

ASCII Characters 128 - 255

The ASCII characters between 128 and 255 are system-dependent, so we can't print them here. What we can do though is give you a program which will print out the all the codes between 32 and 255 on your machine:

```
/* A program to output the ASCII character set */
#include <stdio.h>
void main()
{
   unsigned char i=0, j=0;            /* Index values */

   /* Print table heading */
   printf("                    ASCII TABLE");

   /* Print the column headings for the table */
   printf("\n     ");
   for(i=0; i<= 0xF ; i++ )
      printf(" %01X  ", i);           /* Hex digit for each column */
   printf("\n");
   for(i=0; i<= 0xF ; i++ )
   {
      printf("\n %01X   ", i);        /* Display the row heading */
```

```
for( j = 0; j <= 0xF ; j++ )  /* Display the row characters */
switch((i<<4)|j)              /* Sort out non-printing characters */
{
case 0X0:                              /* NUL1 character */
   printf(" NUL");
   break;

case 0X1:
   printf(" SOH");
   break;

case 0X2:
   printf(" STX");
   break;

case 0X3:
   printf(" ETX");
   break;

case 0X4:
   printf(" EOT");
   break;

case 0X5:
   printf(" ENQ");
   break;

case 0X6:
   printf(" ACK");
   break;

case 0X7:                              /* Audible bell */
   printf(" BEL");
   break;

case 0X8:                              /* Backspace */
   printf(" BS ");
   break;

case 0X9:
   printf(" tab");                     /* Horizontal tab */
   break;

case 0XA:                              /* Newline */
   printf(" \\n ");
   break;

case 0XB:                              /* Vertical Tab */
   printf(" VT ");
   break;
```

```
        case 0XC:                       /* Form feed */
           printf(" FF ");
           break;

        case 0XD:                       /* Carriage return */
           printf(" CR ");
           break;

        case 0XE:
           printf(" SO ");
           break;

        case 0XF:
           printf(" SI ");
           break;

        case 0X10:
           printf(" DLE");
           break;

        case 0X11:
           printf(" DC1");
           break;

        case 0X12:
           printf(" DC2");
           break;

        case 0X13:
           printf(" DC3");
           break;

        case 0X14:
           printf(" DC4");
           break;

        case 0X15:
           printf(" NAK");
           break;

        case 0X16:
           printf(" SYN");
           break;

        case 0X17:
           printf(" ETB");
           break;

        case 0X18:
           printf(" CAN");
           break;
```

```
    case 0X19:
        printf(" EM ");
        break;

    case 0X1A:
        printf(" SUB");
        break;

    case 0X1B:
        printf(" ESC");
        break;

    case 0X1C:
        printf(" FS ");
        break;

    case 0X1D:
        printf(" GS ");
        break;

    case 0X1E:
        printf(" RS ");
        break;

    case 0X1F:
        printf(" US ");
        break;

    case 0X7F:                          /* Delete */
        printf(" del");
        break;

    default:                            /* Most of the rest should display */
        printf(" %c  ", (i<<4)|j);
    }
  }
  printf("\n\n Select the row for the first hexadecimal digit,\n"
    "     and the column for the second hexadecimal digit.\n"
    " Some characters above 0X7F may not print on your system");
  return;
}
```

423

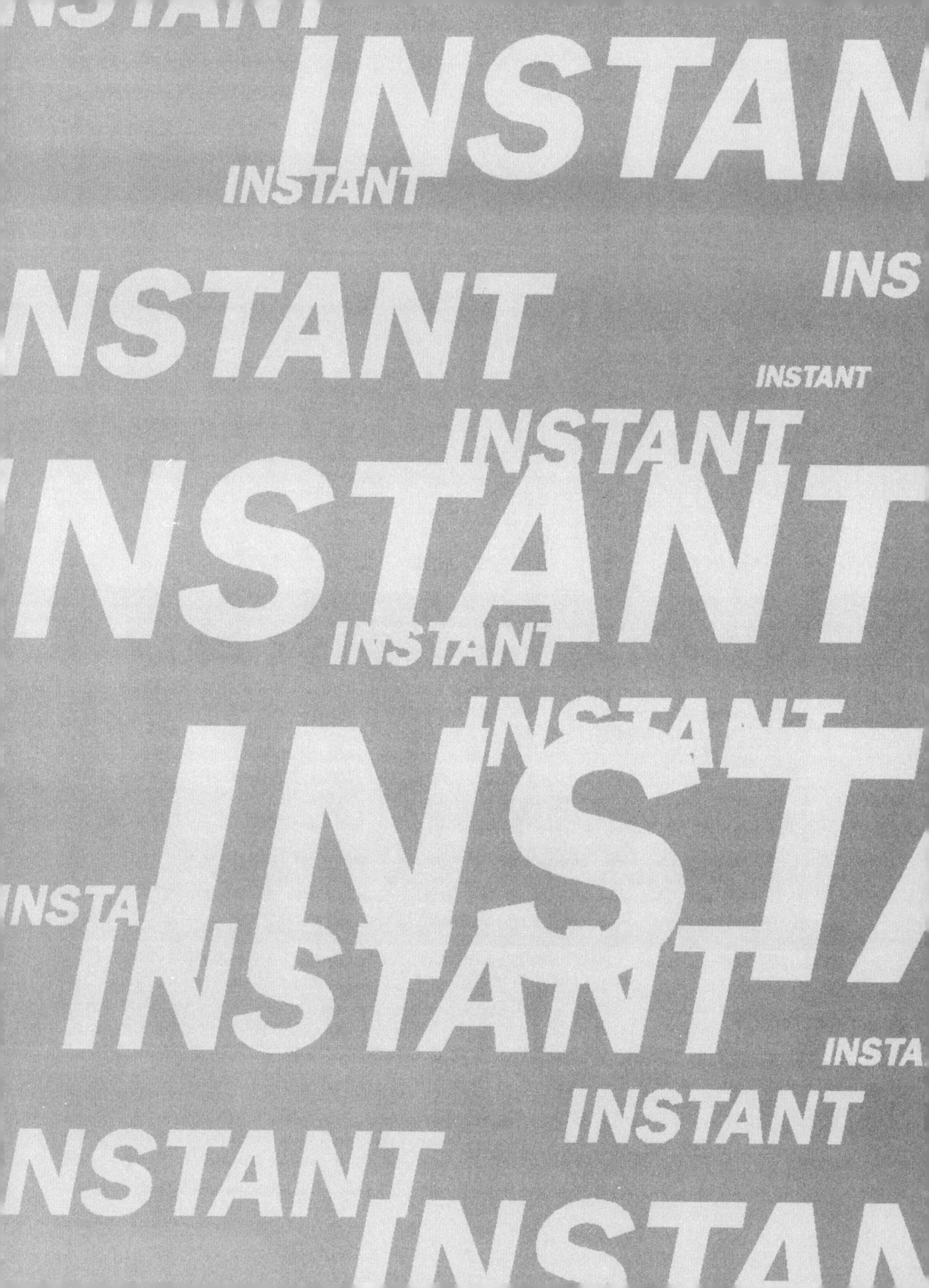
INSTANT
INSTANT
INSTANT
INSTANT
INSTANT
INSTANT

Appendix

Keywords in C

Keywords are reserved words that you can't use as identifiers. ANSI standard C has 32 keywords defined:

auto	int
break	long
case	register
char	return
const	short
continue	signed
default	sizeof
do	static
double	struct
else	switch
enum	typedef
extern	union
float	unsigned
for	void
goto	volatile
if	while

The significance of the case of these keywords is important. For example, the identifiers **WHILE**, **EXTernal** and **unSIGNed** will not be recognized as keywords.

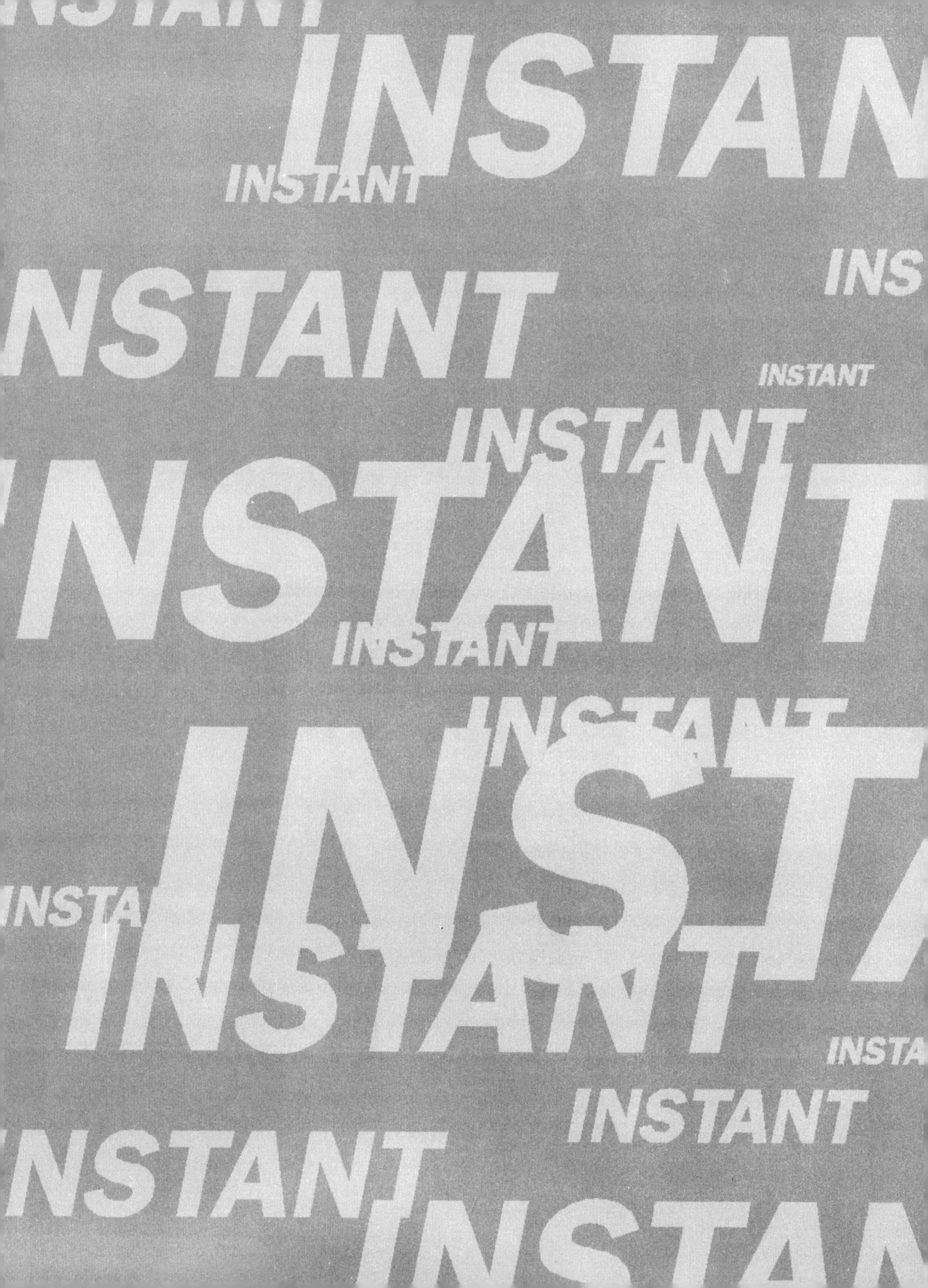
INSTANT
INSTANT
INSTANT
INSTANT
INSTANT
INSTANT
INSTANT

Appendix

The Address Book Source Code

In Chapter 11 we developed the address book program consisting of three files:

- The header file **MYHEADER.H**
- The source file **EX11-01.C**
- The source file **FNCTNS.C**

MYHEADER.H

```
/*   MYHEADER.H Include file for address book application */
#include <stdio.h>
#include <stdlib.h>
#include <string.h>
#include <ctype.h>


#define NAMELEN    20              /* Maximum name length */
#define ADDRLINES  5              /* Maximum number of address lines */
#define ADDRLEN    40              /* Maximum address line length */
#define PHONELEN   20              /* Maximum phone number length */
#define MAXERR      5              /* Maximum file read retries */


/* Macro definitions */
#define StrEQ(pS1,pS2)   (strcmp(pS1,pS2)==0)
#define StrLT(pS1,pS2)   (strcmp(pS1,pS2)<0)
#define Free(p)          (free(p),p=NULL)


/* Structure definitions */
typedef struct name               /* Name structure type definition */
{
   char FirstName[NAMELEN];
   char SurName[NAMELEN];
}Name;

typedef struct person             /* Person structure type definition */
{
   Name aName;                             /* Name structure */
   char Address[ADDRLINES][ADDRLEN];       /* Address up to five lines */
   char Phone[PHONELEN];                   /* Phone number as string */
   long Next;                       /* File position for next person */
   long Previous;                   /* File position for previous person */
   int Deleted;                     /* Deleted record = 1, 0 otherwise */
}Person;


/* Function prototypes */
Person *ReadPerson(void);          /* Get input for a new person */
int GetName(Name *pName);          /* Read a name for a person */
void AddPerson(void);              /* Add a person to the file */
void DeletePerson(void);           /* Delete a person from the file */
long FindEntry(Name *pName, Person *pPerson);  /* Find a file record */
void Search(void);                 /* Find data on a person in the file */
void Insert(Person *pPerson);      /* Insert a person in the file */
void AddFirst(Person *pPerson,Person *pCurrent); /* Add Person to start */
```

```
void AddMiddle(Person *pPerson, Person *pCurrent, long fPos); /*& middle*/
long Write(Person *pPerson);            /* Write a person record to the file */
long Read(Person *pPerson);             /* Read a person record */
int CheckName(char *pName);             /* Verify a name is alphabetic */
void Display(Person *pPerson);          /* Display data for a person */
void ListFile(void);                    /* List the contents of the file */
void WriteFile(Person *pPerson,size_t Size);/* Write a record to file */
void DeleteMiddle(Person *aPerson); /*Delete a record from file middle */
void DeleteLast(long fPos);             /* Delete the last file record */
void DeleteFirst(Person *aPerson);  /* Delete the first file record */
```

EX11-01.C

```
/*  EX11-01.C A Program to create and maintain a name and address file */
#include "MYHEADER.H"

/* Global variables */
char *pFPersons="PERSONS";              /* Name for physical person file */
FILE *pFile;                            /* File pointer to person file */
int IsFile=0;                           /* File presence indicator */


int main(void)
{
   char *ch="Q";                        /* Choice indicator */
   for(;;)
   {
     printf("\nEnter a character to select an option:\n"
            "\n\tA  Add a person to the file"
            "\n\tD  Delete a person from the file"
            "\n\tL  List the file contents"
            "\n\tS  Search for data for a person"
            "\n\tQ  Quit - end the program\n\n");

     scanf("%1s",ch);
     switch(*ch)
     {
         case 'A':case 'a':       /* Add a new person to the file */
            AddPerson();
            break;

         case 'D':case 'd':       /* Delete a new person from  the file */
            DeletePerson();
            break;

         case 'L':case 'l':       /* List the file */
            ListFile();
            break;
```

```
      case 'S':case 's':          /* Search for a person in the file */
          Search();
          break;

      case 'Q':case 'q':          /* Quit the application */
          return 0;

      default:
          printf("\nInvalid input - try again.");
    }
  }
}


/***********************************************************************
 * Function to add a person to file.                                   *
 * A Person is read from stdin and inserted in the file in ascending   *
 * alphabetic sequence. If the file does not exist it will be created. *
 ***********************************************************************/
void AddPerson(void)
{
  Person *pPerson=NULL;             /* Pointer to a new Person object */
  long fPos=-1;                     /* File position indicator */
  char *ch="n";                     /* Choice indicator on input */
  for(;;)
  {
    pPerson=ReadPerson();           /* Read input and construct a Person */
    if(pPerson==NULL)               /* NULL pointer means failure */
      return;
    if(!IsFile)                     /* Check the global flag for no file */
    {                               /* Flag is not set so check for file */
      pFile=fopen(pFPersons,"ab+");/* Open to append, or create file*/
      if(pFile==NULL)
      {                                 /* Cannot open file, so end */
        printf("\nUnable to open Persons file. Program ended.");
        exit(1);
      }
      IsFile=1;                     /* File is open so set flag */
      fseek(pFile, 0L, SEEK_END);   /* Make sure we are at the end */
      fPos=ftell(pFile);            /* Get the offset from file start */
      if(fPos==0L)                  /* If it is 0, file is empty */
        WriteFile(pPerson,sizeof(Person));    /* so write object */
      else
      {                                 /* File is not empty */
        fclose(pFile);                  /* So close it and */
        pFile=fopen(pFPersons,"rb+");   /* reopen it for update */
        if(pFile==NULL)
        {                                 /* If we are here, open failed */
          printf("\nUnable to open Persons file. Program ended.");
          exit(1);
        }
```

```
        Insert(pPerson);               /* File is open so insert person */
        }
     }
     else
     {                                  /* Flag is set so the file exists */
       pFile=fopen(pFPersons,"rb+");/* Open it for update */
       if(pFile==NULL)
       {                                /* Open failed so drop out */
         printf("\nUnable to open Persons file. Program ended.");
         exit(1);
       }
       Insert(pPerson);               /* Insert the new Person object */
      }

    Free(pPerson);                     /* Write is done so release memory */
    fclose(pFile);                     /* and close the file */

    printf("\nDo you want to add another person(y or n)? ");
    scanf("%1s",ch);
    if((*ch=='n')||(*ch=='N'))         /* Want to add another? */
       return;                         /* No, so return */
  }
}


/**********************************************
 * Function to delete a person from the file *
 **********************************************/
void DeletePerson(void)
{
   Person aPerson;                                /* Record to be deleted */
   Name aName;
   long fPos=-1L;
   char *ch="n";

   pFile=fopen(pFPersons,"rb+");                  /* Open file for update */
   if(pFile==NULL)
   {
     printf("\nUnable to open Persons file. Program ended.");
     exit(1);
   }
   for(;;)
   {
     if(!GetName(&aName))
     {
       printf("\nInvalid name entered. Delete aborted.");
       fclose(pFile);                             /* So close the file */
       return;
     }
     if((fPos=FindEntry(&aName, &aPerson))==-1L)
     {
```

431

```
            printf("\nDo you want to delete another?");
            scanf("%1s",ch);
            if((*ch=='n')||(*ch=='N'))
            {
                fclose(pFile);
                return;
            }
            else
                continue;
        }
        printf("\nThe person to be deleted is:");
        Display(&aPerson);
        printf("\nConfirm delete (Y or N)?");
        scanf("%1s",ch);
        if((*ch=='y')||(*ch=='Y'))
        {
            /* Mark record as deleted and write back */
            aPerson.Deleted=1;                       /* Set deleted flag */
            fseek(pFile,fPos,SEEK_SET);
            WriteFile(&aPerson,sizeof(Person));

            if(aPerson.Previous<0L)      /* Check for previous record      */
                DeleteFirst(&aPerson);   /*None - we are deleting the first */

            else if(aPerson.Next<0L)     /* See if its the last record     */
                DeleteLast(aPerson.Previous); /* It is - so delete it      */

            else                         /* Its not the first or the last so*/
                DeleteMiddle(&aPerson);  /* we are deleting from the middle */
        }
        printf("\nDo you want to delete another?");
        scanf("%1s",ch);
        if((*ch=='n')||(*ch=='N'))       /* Chance for another go          */
        {
            fclose(pFile);               /* No - so close the file         */
            return;                      /* and return                     */
        }
    }
}


/*******************************************
 * Function to search for data on a person *
 * The function will search for as many    *
 * entries as required. The first equal    *
 * name is the entry displayed. An invalid *
 * name will discontinue the search.       *
 *******************************************/
void Search(void)
{
    Name aName;                          /* Name to be found */
```

```
    Person aPerson;                         /* Person record from the file */
    long fPos=-1L;                          /* Current file position */
    char *ch="n";                           /* Continue indicator */

    /* Open the file to read it */
    pFile=fopen(pFPersons,"rb");
    if(pFile==NULL)                     /* Check we got a good file pointer */
    {
        printf("\nUnable to open the file. Exiting program.");
        exit(1);
    }

    /* Now search for as many entries as required */
    for(;;)
    {
        if(!GetName(&aName))
        {
          printf("\nInvalid name entered. Search aborted.");
          fclose(pFile);                            /* So close the file */
          return;
        }

        /* Search the file for the name entered */
        fPos=FindEntry(&aName, &aPerson);           /* Find the entry */
        if(fPos!=-1L)               /* If EOF not returned, name was found */
        {
            Display(&aPerson);                      /* so show details */
        }
        printf("\nDo you want to search for another?");
        scanf("%1s",ch);
        if((*ch=='n')||(*ch=='N'))      /* Check response for negative */
        {                               /* No more searches needed */
            fclose(pFile);              /* So close the file */
            return;                     /* and return to caller */
        }
    }
}


/*********************************************
 * List the contents of the file            *
 * Records are read in alphabetical sequence *
 * from the beginning, and displayed on      *
 * stdout.                                   *
 *********************************************/
void ListFile(void)
{
    Person aPerson;             /* Store a record here */
    long fPos=-1;               /* File position for the current record */

    pFile=fopen(pFPersons,"rb"); /* Open the file to read it */
```

433

```
    if(pFile==NULL)
    {
        printf("\nUnable to open Persons file. Program ended.");
        exit(1);
    }
    for(;;)
    {
        fPos=Read(&aPerson);              /* Read a record */
        if((fPos==0)&&aPerson.Deleted)/* Check for a deleted first record */
        {
            printf("\nFile empty.");    /* If it is, the file is empty */
            return;
        }
        Display(&aPerson);               /* Display the record */
        fPos=aPerson.Next;               /* Get the position of the next */

        if(fPos<0L)                      /* Check for no next record */
        {
            fclose(pFile);               /* If so we close the file */
            return;                      /* and we are done */
        }
        fseek(pFile, fPos, SEEK_SET);    /* Move the file position to next */
    }
}
```

FNCTNS.C

```
/* FNCTNS.C  Creating and maintaining a name and address file */
#include "MYHEADER.H"

extern FILE *pFile;                        /* File pointer to person file */


/*****************************************************************
 * Function to read in a person's details.                     *
 * A pointer to a Person structure on the heap is returned.    *
 *****************************************************************/
Person *ReadPerson(void)
{
    Person *pPerson=NULL;                  /* Pointer to a Person object */
    char *ch="n";                          /* Choice indicator */
    int i=0;                               /* Loop counter */

    /* Get memory for a Person object */
    pPerson=(Person *)malloc(sizeof(Person));
    if(pPerson==NULL)
    {
```

```
      printf("\nMemory allocation failure. Program aborted.");
      exit(1);
   }

   /* Read the name of the person */
   while(!GetName(&pPerson->aName))
   {
      printf("\nInvalid name entered, do you want to try again?");
      scanf("%1s",ch);
      if(*ch=='n'||*ch=='N')
      {
         Free(pPerson);                       /* Release heap memory */
         return NULL;
      }
   }

   /* Read the address of the person */
   printf("\nEnter the address up to %d lines of %d characters.\n"
          "Enter an empty line after the last line"
          " if there are less than %d lines.\n",
           ADDRLINES, ADDRLEN, ADDRLINES);
   for(i=0;i<ADDRLINES;i++)
   {
      gets(pPerson->Address[i]);
      if(strlen(pPerson->Address[i])==0)    /* Empty line ends input */
         break;
   }
   printf("\nEnter the phone number for %s\n",pPerson->aName.FirstName);
   gets(pPerson->Phone);
   pPerson->Next=-1L;              /* Set file pointer to next and previous */
   pPerson->Previous=-1L;         /* person record to invalid values */
   pPerson->Deleted=0;            /* Set deleted flag for valid record */
   return pPerson;
}


/************************************************************
 * Function to read in a name                             *
 * Argument is a pointer to an array of length NAMELEN     *
 * 0 is returned if the surname contains an non-alphabetic *
 *   character. The first name can be empty, and is set to *
 *   empty if an non-alphabetic character is entered.      *
 * 1 is returned if a valid name is obtained.             *
 ************************************************************/
int GetName(Name *pName)
{
   printf("\nEnter a surname:");
   fflush(stdin);
   gets( pName->SurName);
   if(CheckName(pName->SurName)==0)          /* Check for invalid surname */
      return 0;                              /* If so abandon Name input */
```

```
   printf("\nEnter a first name:");
   gets(pName->FirstName);

   if(CheckName(pName->FirstName)==0)    /* Check for invalid first name */
   {
      *pName->FirstName='\0';            /* Is so set to empty */
      return 1;
   }
}


/*******************************************
 * Function to verify a name is alphabetic *
 * Argument is a nul terminated name       *
 *  1 return indicates name is alphabetic  *
 *  0 return indicates it is not alphabetic*
 *******************************************/
int CheckName(char *pName)
{
   while((*pName)!='\0')
      if(!isalpha(*pName++))
         return 0;
   return 1;
}


/*************************************************************
 * Function to write a record to the file                   *
 * Arguments are:                                           *
 *     pPerson: A pointer to the object to be written       *
 *     Size:    Size of the object to be written            *
 * The function assumes the file is open for update         *
 * and writes the object at the current position.           *
 *************************************************************/

void WriteFile(Person *pPerson,size_t Size)
{
   if(!fwrite(pPerson, Size, 1, pFile))
   {                                         /* Write error so */
      perror("Write error.");                /* output message */
      fclose(pFile);                         /* close the file */
      exit(2);                               /* and exit */
   }
   return;
}

/**************************************************************
 * Function to delete the first record in the file           *
 * The argument is a pointer to a Person object which        *
 * has just been deleted from the file.This function moves   *
```

```
 * the second record to the first position, if it exists.  *
 * It also modifies the Previous pointer of the third      *
 * record if it exists.                                    *
 **********************************************************/
void DeleteFirst(Person *pPerson)
{
   Person bPerson;
   long fPos=-1L;
   if(pPerson->Next<0L)
      return;                                       /* No next one */

   /* But there is a next one */
   fseek(pFile, pPerson->Next, SEEK_SET);
   Read(&bPerson);                          /* Read next record */
   bPerson.Previous=-1L;                    /* Set previous to none */

   /* Now rewrite the next record at the beginning */
   rewind(pFile);
   WriteFile(&bPerson,sizeof(Person));

   /* Delete previous copy of next record */
   bPerson.Deleted=1;                       /* Set the deleted flag */
   fseek(pFile, pPerson->Next, SEEK_SET);   /* Get to where it is */
   WriteFile(&bPerson,sizeof(Person));      /* and rewrite it */

   /* Now fix the Previous pointer for the following record */
   if(bPerson.Next>0L)
   {
      fseek(pFile, bPerson.Next, SEEK_SET);   /* Got to the next */
      fPos=Read(&bPerson);                    /* and read it */
      bPerson.Previous=0L;                    /* Set to first record */
      fseek(pFile, fPos, SEEK_SET);           /* Get to where it is */
      WriteFile(&bPerson,sizeof(Person));     /* and rewrite it */
   }
}


/***********************************************************
 * Function to delete the last record in the file          *
 * The argument is the file position of the record preceding *
 * the last record which has been deleted so that it now    *
 * becomes the last.                                        *
 **********************************************************/
void DeleteLast(long fPos)
{
   Person aPerson;
   fseek(pFile, fPos, SEEK_SET);            /* Position to 2nd to last */
   Read(&aPerson);                          /* and read it */
   aPerson.Next=-1L;                        /* There is now no next */
   fseek(pFile, fPos, SEEK_SET);            /* Reposition */
   WriteFile(&aPerson,sizeof(Person));      /* and write it back */
```

```
      return;
}


/***********************************************************
 * Function to delete a record from the middle of the file *
 * The argument is a pointer to a Person object which      *
 * has just been deleted from the file.This function fixes *
 * the predecessor and the successor to that deleted.      *
 ***********************************************************/
void DeleteMiddle(Person *pPerson)
{
   Person bPerson;
   long fPos=-1L;
   /* Fix the Next pointer for previous record */
   fseek(pFile, pPerson->Previous, SEEK_SET);      /* Go to the previous */
   fPos=Read(&bPerson);                            /* and read it */
   bPerson.Next=pPerson->Next;                     /* Bypass the deleted */
   fseek(pFile, fPos, SEEK_SET);                   /* Reposition */
   WriteFile(&bPerson,sizeof(Person));             /* and write it back  */


   /* Fix the previous pointer for the following record */
   fseek(pFile, pPerson->Next, SEEK_SET);
   fPos=Read(&bPerson);                            /* Read next record */
   bPerson.Previous=pPerson->Previous;             /* Bypass deleted */
   fseek(pFile, pPerson->Next, SEEK_SET);          /* Reposition */
   WriteFile(&bPerson,sizeof(Person));             /* and write it back */
   return;                                         /* We are done */
}


/*********************************************************
 * Function to find the file record for a given name *
 * Arguments are:                                    *
 *   pName: Pointer to name for entry sought          *
 *   pPerson: Pointer to struct to store entry found  *
 * Return value is position in the file of entry, or  *
 * -1 if name is not found.                           *
 *********************************************************/
long FindEntry(Name *pName, Person *pPerson)
{
   Person aPerson;
   long fPos=-1L;

   /* Search the file for the name entered */
   rewind(pFile);                          /* Get to the start of the file */
   for(;;)
   {
      fPos=Read(&aPerson);                 /* Read a person record */
      if(fPos==-1L)                        /* Check for end of file */
```

```
     {
        printf("\nEnd of file. Name not found.");
        return -1L;
     }
     if((fPos==0L)&&aPerson.Deleted)
     {
        printf("\nFile is empty, search failed.");
        return -1L;
     }

     /* Look for the name */
     if(StrEQ(pName->SurName,aPerson.aName.SurName))/*Have we found it?*/
     {
        *pPerson=aPerson;                    /* Yes, so copy record */
        return fPos;
     }

     /* Check if the current name from the file is less than last read */
     if(StrLT(pName->SurName, aPerson.aName.SurName))
        {                                    /* If so the target is not there */
        printf("\nName not found.");
        return -1L;
     }
     fPos=aPerson.Next;
     if(fPos)                         /* Next pointer must be positive */
     {
        fseek(pFile, fPos, SEEK_SET);
        continue;
     }
     printf("\nName not found.");  /* Otherwise we are at the end */
     return -1L;                   /* so return to caller */
   }
}


/*****************************************************************
 * Function to insert a person in the file                      *
 * Argument is the pointer to the Person object to be inserted *
 * The Person object will be inserted in alphabetic sequence   *
 * in the file                                                  *
 *****************************************************************/
void Insert(Person *pPerson)
{
   Person aPerson;                          /* Place for a file record */
   long fPos=-1L;                           /* Position in the file */
   long NewPos=-1L;                         /* New position in the file */

   rewind(pFile);                           /* Go to the start */
   fPos=ftell(pFile);                       /* Record current position */

   for(;;)
```

```
{
    if(Read(&aPerson)==-1L)                          /* Read a file record */
    {
        printf("\nRead error. Ending program.");/* On error, output a */
        exit(1);                                     /* message and exit */
    }

    /* Check if the 1st record in the file has been deleted */
    if((fPos==0L)&&aPerson.Deleted)
    {                                                /* File exists but is empty */
        rewind(pFile);                               /* So go back to start */
        WriteFile(pPerson,sizeof(Person)); /* Now write the Person */
        return;                                      /* and we are done */
    }

    /* Insert new person preceding any record with a greater surname */
    if(StrLT(pPerson->aName.SurName, aPerson.aName.SurName))
    {                                                /* New name is less than current */
        if(fPos==0L)                                 /* Are at the first record? */
        {
            AddFirst(pPerson, &aPerson);/* Add new Person at start */
            return;
        }
        else                                         /* Otherwise we must be */
        {
            AddMiddle(pPerson,&aPerson, fPos); /* adding in the middle */
            return;
        }
    }
    /* New person name is not less than current file record */
    if(aPerson.Next<0)                               /* If there is no next record */
    {                                                /* Add the new Person to the end */
        pPerson->Previous=fPos;                      /* New Previous points to current*/
        NewPos=Write(pPerson);                       /* Write the new one somewhere */
        aPerson.Next=NewPos;                         /* Save position in current Next */
        fseek(pFile, fPos, SEEK_SET);
        WriteFile(&aPerson,sizeof(Person));
        return;
    }
    /* There is a next one, so set the position for that */
    fPos=aPerson.Next;
    fseek(pFile, fPos, SEEK_SET);
    }
}


/***********************************************************
 * Function to add a Person to the beginning of the file   *
 * Arguments are:                                          *
 *   pPerson:  Pointer to Person to be inserted            *
```

```
 *    pCurrent: Pointer to last record read              *
 * New Person will be added to the beginning of the file. *
 * The previous first record, pCurrent, will be moved,    *
 * and Previous pointer for the record following pCurrent *
 * will be updated.                                       *
 ********************************************************/
void AddFirst(Person *pPerson,Person *pCurrent)
{
   long NewPos=-1L;                       /* New file position for current */
   long fPos=-1L;                         /* File position for follower */

   pCurrent->Previous=0L;                 /* Yes-so current Previous to 1st*/
   NewPos=Write(pCurrent);                /* Find a new place for current */
   pPerson->Next=NewPos;                  /* Set Next for the new Person */

   if(pCurrent->Next>0L)                  /* Check for follower to current */
   {
      fseek(pFile, pCurrent->Next, SEEK_SET);        /* Go to it */
      if((fPos=Read(pCurrent))==-1L)                 /* and read it */
      {
         printf("\nRead error. Ending program.");    /* EOF Found */
         exit(1);
      }
      pCurrent->Previous=NewPos;                     /* Fix up Previous */
      fseek(pFile, fPos, SEEK_SET);                  /* Back up */
      WriteFile(pCurrent,sizeof(Person));            /* and write it back */
   }

   /* Get back to the start and write the new Person */
   fseek(pFile,0L,SEEK_SET);                         /* Reposition and */
   WriteFile(pPerson,sizeof(Person));                /* write the file */
   return;                                           /* We are done */
}

/*************************************************************
 * Function to add a Person to the middle of the file      *
 * Arguments are:                                          *
 *   pPerson:  Pointer to Person to be inserted            *
 *   pCurrent: Pointer to last record read                 *
 *   fPos:     File position for last record read          *
 * New Person will be inserted preceding last record read. *
 ********************************************************/
void AddMiddle(Person *pPerson, Person *pCurrent, long fPos)
{
   long NewPos=-1L;                        /* New position for new Person*/

   /* Set the pointers for the new Person and write it to the file */
   pPerson->Next=fPos;                     /* Set new Person Next pointer*/
   pPerson->Previous=pCurrent->Previous;   /* Set new person Previous */
   NewPos=Write(pPerson);                  /* Write the new one to file */
```

441

```
   /* Update the current record, it will follow the new one */
   pCurrent->Previous=NewPos;             /* Set Previous to new position */

   /* Find position where we read the current record and rewrite in situ */
   fseek(pFile, fPos, SEEK_SET);
   WriteFile(pCurrent,sizeof(Person));

   /* Now update the record preceding the new one */
   fseek(pFile, pPerson->Previous, SEEK_SET);/* Find previous record and*/
   if(Read(pCurrent)==-1L)                   /* read it into current */
   {
      printf("\nRead error. Ending program.");        /* EOF detected */
      exit(1);
   }
   pCurrent->Next=NewPos;            /* Set Next to where the new one is */

   /* Now write the preceding record back in situ */
   fseek(pFile, pPerson->Previous, SEEK_SET);
   WriteFile(pCurrent,sizeof(Person));
   return;                                    /* and we are done */

}


/*************************************************
 * Function to write a person record to the file *
 * Argument is a pointer to the person           *
 * If a deleted record exists, the new record    *
 * will overwrite it, otherwise the new record   *
 * will be written at the end of the file        *
 *************************************************/
long Write(Person *pPerson)
{
   Person aPerson;                         /* Space for a person */
   long fPos;                              /* Current file position */
   int ErrorCount=0;                       /* Count of file errors */

   rewind(pFile);                          /* Start at the beginning */

   for(;;)
   {
      fPos=Read(&aPerson);                          /* Read a record */

      /* Check for end of file, if so write it here */
      if(fPos==-1L)
      {
         /* Position at the end of the file and write the person */
         fseek(pFile,0L,SEEK_END);
         fPos=ftell(pFile);                 /* Record the current postion */
         WriteFile(pPerson,sizeof(Person));
         return fPos;                       /* Return its position */
```

```
      }

      /* Check for a deleted record if so we can overwrite it */
      if(aPerson.Deleted)
      {
         fseek(pFile, fPos, SEEK_SET);                  /* Set to record start */
         WriteFile(pPerson,sizeof(Person));
         return fPos;
      }

   }
}


/**********************************************************
 * Function to read a person record from the file        *
 * Argument is a pointer to the record to be written.     *
 * The position in the file is returned, or -1 if         *
 * the end of file is reached                             *
 **********************************************************/
long Read(Person *pPerson)
{
   long fPos;                                /* Current file position */
   int ErrorCount=0;                         /* Count of file errors */

   fPos=ftell(pFile);                        /* Get current file position */
   for(;;)
   {
      fread(pPerson, sizeof(Person), 1, pFile);/* Read a record */
      if(feof(pFile))                         /* Check for end of file */
      {
         clearerr(pFile);                     /* Clear EOF flag */
         return -1L;                          /*  Return -1 */
      }

      /* Check for file read error */
      if(ferror(pFile))
      {
         perror("File read error");  /* Output error message */
         if(++ErrorCount==MAXERR)    /* If max error count reached */
         {
            fclose(pFile);                              /* close the file */
            exit(1);                                    /* and exit */
         }
         clearerr(pFile);            /* Clear the error flag */
         fseek(pFile,fPos, SEEK_SET);/* Reset file position to re-read */
         continue;                   /* Go to next loop iteration */
      }
      else
         return fPos;                /* Return position record was written */
   }
```

443

```
}

/****************************************
 * Function to display a Person record  *
 * Argument is a pointer to the Person. *
 * There is no return value.            *
 ****************************************/
void Display(Person *pPerson)
{
   int i=0;                                     /* Loop counter */
   printf("\n\nName:\t%s %s\nPhone:\t%s\nAddress:",
       pPerson->aName.SurName, pPerson->aName.FirstName, pPerson->Phone);
   for(i=0; i<ADDRLINES;i++)
   {
      if(strlen(pPerson->Address[i])==0)        /* Check for empty line */
         return;                                /* If so we are  done */
      printf("\n\t%s", pPerson->Address[i]);
   }
   return;                /* After ADDRLINES output we are done anyway */
}
```

Index

D

Notes

Notes

INSTANT DELPHI PROGRAMMING

This book provides a fast guide to the essentials of Borland's new development tool. Borland have put together fast executable Pascal code with a truly intuitive event-driven environment. The result is a powerful, yet easy to use program, and this book caters for programmers who want to master its fundamental advantages. Taking developers through the strengths of the innovative Object Pascal code, its access to a database engine, as well as advanced features such as using VBX controls, this book will help programmers from many different backgrounds move successfully into Borland's strong new package.

ISBN: 1-874416-57-5   PRICE: $24.95 C$34.95 £22.99   AUTHOR: Dave Jewell

INSTANT UNIX

Written by experienced UNIX and PC developers, Instant UNIX encompasses the whole UNIX spectrum from simple user commands and logging in, to complex administration and configuration issues - all in just one volume. Every important UNIX aspect is covered including e-mail, security and file systems. You also get invaluable information on X Windows, PC to UNIX connectivity and how to access the Internet from UNIX. The book also covers Linux - the free implementation of UNIX - and tackles such issues as where to obtain it, how to install it and how to configure it to your system. With so much information, this book is an invaluable reference guide.

ISBN: 1-874416-65-6   PRICE: $24.95 C$34.95 £22.99
AUTHORS: Andrew Evans, Neil Matthew and Richard Stones

THE BEGINNER'S GUIDE TO OOP USING C++

Learn object-oriented programming using C++ the easy way. This book will take you as a C programmer through the differences between C and C++, providing you with all the knowledge you need to write object-oriented programs. Easy to understand explanations and plenty of example code will ease your transition into the world of OOP. From page one you will be shown how to use objects, and with an easy to follow tutorial, your confidence with objects will grow, until you have complete proficiency in writing programs incorporating objects.

ISBN: 1-874416-27-3   PRICE: $29.95 C$41.95 £27.99
AUTHORS: Laureen Romanovskaya, Tatyana Shapetko and Sergei Svitkovsky

Wrox Press present
their new *bestselling* author:

WIN FREE BOOKS

TELL US WHAT YOU THINK!

Complete and return the bounce back card and you will:

- Help us create the books you want.
- Receive an update on all Wrox titles.
- Enter the draw for 5 Wrox titles of your choice.

FILL THIS OUT to enter the draw for free Wrox titles

Name _____

Address _____

_____

_____

_____ Postcode/Zip _____

Occupation _____

How did you hear about this book?

☐ Book review (name) _____

☐ Advertisement (name) _____

☐ Recommendation

☐ Catalogue

☐ Other _____

Where did you buy this book?

☐ Bookstore (name) _____

☐ Computer Store (name) _____

☐ Mail Order

☐ Other _____

I would be interested in receiving information about Wrox Press titles by email in future. My email/Internet address is:

_____

What influenced you in the purchase of this book?

☐ Cover Design

☐ Contents

☐ Other (please specify) _____

How did you rate the overall contents of this book?

☐ Excellent   ☐ Good

☐ Average   ☐ Poor

What did you find most useful about this book? _____

What did you find least useful about this book? _____

Please add any additional comments. _____

What other subjects will you buy a computer book on soon? _____

What is the best computer book you have used this year? _____

Note: This information will only be used to keep you updated about new Wrox Press titles and will not be used for any other purpose or passed to any other third party.

WROX PRESS INC.

Wrox writes books for you. Any suggestions, or
ideas about how you want information given in
your ideal book will be studied by our team.
Your comments are always valued at WROX.

Free phone in USA 800 814 4527
Fax (312) 465 4063

Compuserve 100063,2152.
UK Tel. (44121) 706 6826   Fax   (44121) 706 2967

Computer Book Publishers

NB. If you post the bounce back card below in the UK, please send it to:
Wrox Press Ltd. Unit 16, Sapcote Industrial Estate, 20 James Road, Birmingham, B11 2BA